THE GERMAN
PREDICAMENT

THE GERMAN PREDICAMENT

MEMORY AND POWER
IN THE NEW EUROPE

ANDREI S. MARKOVITS
and
SIMON REICH

CORNELL UNIVERSITY PRESS

ITHACA AND LONDON

First published 1997 by Cornell University Press

Library of Congress Cataloging-in-Publication Data

Markovits, Andrei S.
   The German predicament : memory and power in the new Europe / by
Andrei S. Markovits and Simon Reich.
     p.   cm.
   Includes index.
   ISBN 0-8014-2802-5 (alk. paper).
   1. Germany—Politics and government—1990– 2. Germany—Relations—
Europe. 3. Europe—Relations—Germany. 4. Political culture—
Germany.   I. Reich, Simon, 1959– . II. Title.
DD290.29.M37   1997
320.943—dc20   96-42943

Printed in the United States of America

This book is printed on Lyons Falls Turin Book, a paper that is totally chlorine-free and acid-free.

Cloth printing   10 9 8 7 6 5 4 3 2 1

To Irina and Linda
and
to the memory of our parents
with thanks

"The past will not release us"

–Klaus Kinkel, German foreign minister,
addressing the Bundestag, February 1996

CONTENTS

PREFACE

What is the future role for the Germans in Europe? One answer sees the Germans as resurrected and tamed in the aftermath of Auschwitz and the formation of the Federal Republic. The new Berlin Republic is, it believes, constrained by domestic institutions; rid of the conservative coalitions that fostered National Socialism; socialized by educational policies that have explored the causes of the onset of Germany's uniquely heinous brand of fascism; and enmeshed in a web of international commitments. German power in this view has been either blunted or saddled to good effect in the context of the European Union. The country now is trustworthy, firmly embedded in the camp of stable, capitalist, liberal-democratic, Western nations. Germans themselves are "peaceful and green." In public opinion polls, Germans consistently emphasize these values, which are espoused by Germany's political and economic elites. The predatory behavior of the past is finished. This is the Germany of the Bundesrepublik; the country has been "Europeanized."

A second answer focuses on the less recent past. The same proclivities that fostered Auschwitz have, in this view, been suppressed rather than obliterated. Germany's stability is more fragile than its proponents recognize. Germany's liberal democracy was imposed from without by the allied victors; shorn of the Cold War's structures, it will fray, if not disintegrate, under conservative impulses. With unification will therefore come a return to the predatory expansion of the past. Proponents of this view point out that adverse developments occur around the Germans—the disintegration of Yugoslavia, economic recession in Europe—and they attribute such events to malign German intent. This is the Germany of Deutschland; the fear is that Europe will be "Germanized."

How can these answers be reconciled? If Germany has no interest in expansion, no pretense to regional domination, why is it that skeptics find corroborating evidence, however superficial, for their views?

In this book, we argue that both views of Germany are partially correct. Germans have indeed internalized liberal and pacifist principles. The result has been a German "ideology of reticence," a desire to see themselves (and for others to see them) as simply a larger Austria or Switzerland. Germans are not interested in projecting power in the traditional, *Realpolitik* sense.

This ideology constrains the projection of German power and is complemented by a second limitation—the rejection of German cultural values abroad. Hegemony, the nightmare of those who fear the "Germanization of Europe," is not simply the product of economic or military power. It also depends on the effectiveness of cultural policy. Germany's neighbors are now more willing than ever to tolerate and even trust the Germans, but they are not eager to accept Germany's cultural values. As a result Germany will not assume the mantle of a regional hegemon even if its preponderant domestic ideology should change.

So why do problems arise around the Germans? Where does fault lie? The answer, we believe, is to be found in the enormous disparity between Germany's structural power, particularly its economic power, and its domestic ideology. Germany's present position is historically comparable to America's interwar ability but unwillingness to accept a position of leadership in underwriting the international trading system. The result was Depression. Like the Americans then, so the Germans now deny their own power, even refuse to talk about the subject, as if denial renders it nonexistent.

Power ignored is not power dissolved; it is power used irresponsibly. Germany cannot, must not seek to expand its power. But it must recognize and harness its power if the "good guys" are to work to good effect. The prescription is not necessarily a greater German global role, but it may be in a more central role in Europe—underwriting currency stability, adopting a less declaratory diplomatic policy, showing a greater willingness to commit forces abroad. Adversity develops now because the Germans have so much influence and latitude but fear the consequences of responsible leadership. The issue of troop deployment shows recent, limited moves away from isolation, but no broader trend toward leadership and engagement is yet apparent.

The substantive focus of this book also allows us to offer an answer to a second, conceptual question: What is the relationship among history, ideology, and foreign policy? What links these elements together? Much of the recent literature on values, norms, and ideology has relied heavily on historical interpretation but often focuses on elite analyses of liberal democratic systems, as if the people these elites represent have little bearing on their decisions. The link between history and ideology is often imprecise, blurred by unstated relationships between what masses think and what elites do.

Scholars have focused on the influence of mass public opinion on foreign policy, but they largely overlook historical dimensions, how ideologies cohere or elites influence the thrust or form of policy. Public opinion surveys seek to perfect the measurement of attitudes, but the link between mass opinion and ideology has also remained imprecise.

We attempt to bridge these differences by employing the concept of collective memory. Collective memory is the lens through which the past is viewed and helps both masses and elites interpret the present and decide on policy. Accessible through both mass survey data and elite discourse, collective memories are the foundation stones for contemporary ideologies. Though often incoherent themselves, these collective memories form the *Weltanschauung* upon which more coherent ideologies are built.

These two questions—one substantive, the other conceptual—are linked in this book through the study of Germany's relationship with its neighbors. Here we examine the dominant cluster of collective memories: how they are reflected in public opinion surveys and in elite debates; how they congeal to form an ideology of reluctance; and, ultimately, how this symbiotic process influences German policy.

The future of Europe and the projection of German power are not solely dependent on German choices. They also depend on how Germany's friends and neighbors feel about the Germans. Relying on the same recipe of mass public opinion and elite discourse, we also examine the attitudes of the United States, Israel, members of the European Union, and several eastern European countries toward a newly unified Germany.

These peoples are more accepting and, indeed, trusting of the Germans than ever before. This trust creates conditions for the expansion of German influence. Yet Germans themselves provide the main (though not the only) impediment to their country's assuming a greater leadership role. This German reticence, we conclude, will change when the preponderant collective memory of the Holocaust begins to fade—when the leaders headed by Helmut Kohl are replaced by a younger generation whose political culture and understanding of history have been shaped in the era of the Bundesrepublik. The risk is that a new generation might forgo the present option, responsible and cautious leadership, in favor of one of two comparable evils—isolation from Europe, or domination of Europe.

In a nutshell, Germany has emerged as Europe's most powerful country. Despite this position of pre-eminence Germany has not become a hegemon, nor is it likely to develop into one in the near future. The reasons are its internal culture of restraint and reticence on the one hand, and the absence of its cultural acceptance and attractiveness to its European neighbors on the other. Both of these developments hail in good part from Germany's recent history and the collective memory that defines political discourse and public behavior in Germany (as well as Europe) to this day. This ambivalence has fostered problems of two different kinds: it has led Germany to flee its responsibilities and avoid involvement where such was needed; it has also furnished an exercise of power which on occasion appeared careless, perhaps even callous. How the new German regime of the

Berlin Republic will balance these two extremes is unknown at this time. The only certainty is that however Germany solves this puzzle, it will be sure to influence Europe's future.

Books get written for different reasons. Both of us have been keenly interested in Germany for much of our adult lives, and this book began its journey as a conference paper undertaken as an expression of our friendship and our common interest. In the ensuing five years, we not only produced an array of papers and articles that served as intellectual building blocks to the present book. Much more significantly, we solidified our profound respect and affection for each other in the process of our collaboration. Indeed, this furnishes the only aspect of our final product which fills us with unmitigated pride and undiminished satisfaction.

Friends, relatives, and colleagues helped us along the way. Three people in particular provided invaluable help: Gerard Braunthal, Peter Katzenstein, and Andrew Moravcsik. Each took a very different perspective on the work; each disagreed with major aspects of it; and each enriched the final product immeasurably.

Then there were people whose contribution lay in the research and writing of the book. The efforts of Manik Hinchey, Frank Westermann, and Carolyn Höfig are hardly reflected in the fact that they are credited as co-authors of individual chapters. Manik's contributions beyond her individual chapter are especially noteworthy. Furthermore, we would be remiss not to mention the research assistance provided by Andrew Bell–Fialkoff, Viktoria Murphy, Steven Brener, and Yoshiko Koda. Andrei Markovits gratefully acknowledges the Program for the Study of Germany at the Center for European Studies at Harvard University and the Center for German and European Studies at the University of California, Berkeley, for their support for parts of the research for this book. Simon Reich also thanks the Council on Foreign Relations, which supported his work on this book while he was an International Affairs Fellow.

Both of us have worked with many editors; none has been finer than Roger Haydon. He shepherded us, as usual, through the labyrinth of the production process. But, in an act of great generosity, Roger also agreed to render our prose intelligible—for which we are truly grateful.

On a personal note, Andrei Markovits owes everything to the warmth, love, and unfailing support that Irina Friedmann and Dovi offered him throughout this lengthy process. Andy will always cherish their comforting presence with awe and affection. The fact that nature was not to permit Ludwig Markovits, Andy's biggest fan, to read this work with his usual enthusiasm and critical generosity remains an acute source of sadness in Andy's life.

Simon Reich thanks Linda Myers Reich for her unfailing stamina and inexplicable patience with him, and Jamie, Melissa, and Amanda for being the three greatest distractions that any parent could ever have. Jamie, this is your father's "footprint." Finally, two people failed to complete the journey with Simon; both his mother, Elisabeth Reich, and brother, Dennis Reich, left the rest of us along the way. They depart leaving a hole that will never be filled.

ANDREI S. MARKOVITS
SIMON REICH

Cambridge, Massachusetts
Pittsburgh, Pennsylvania

Introduction:

The Latest Stage of the German Question

Immigrants seem to be flooding into Germany nowadays; I don't know why, because history suggests that if they wait around long enough, Germany will come to them.

—Jay Leno, Tonight Show

In one brief comment, Jay Leno captures the ambivalence that Europeans feel toward Germany. They have often wanted to emulate the Germans, to share in their achievements, but not to be possessed by them. Leno thus describes the essence of the German Question.

That question, in more formal terms, focuses on how its neighbors can contain Germany's nationalist—and in recent times, destructive—impulses. The concern dates from the first successful efforts at Prussian expansion in the 1860s.[1] Europe's largest economy, located in the geographic center of the continent, is poorly endowed with natural resources and has pursued expansionist military and economic policies for much of its existence.

Germany has baffled social scientists, and the German Question has taken many forms. Why economic industrialization without political modernization? Why start World Wars I and II? Why the breakdown of democracy and the rise of fascism in 1933? Why Auschwitz? Why was the Federal Republic an economic giant but a political dwarf in the first four decades of the postwar period?

To be a contemporary German is to acknowledge these questions, to recognize that the answers are fundamentally linked to the way that Germans perceive their country's role in the world. And to be a German entails a response that is curiously counterintuitive—as we will explore in this book.

The latest stage of the German Question differs markedly from its historical predecessors. The historical Answer to prior versions has involved various security arrangements designed to contain Germany. These arrangements have sometimes meant formal cooperation, whether the Triple Entente between Britain, France, and Russia or NATO. At other times they have developed more informally, fear of the Germans making strange bedfellows; for instance, the joint efforts of Stalin, Churchill, and FDR. Each set of arrangements has ultimately succeeded in containing German expansion, although never have the banks of European resistance come as close to breaking as between 1939 and 1945.

No comparable arrangement exists in the 1990s. Russian troops have pulled out of eastern Germany, and the United States, despite its military involvement

1

in Bosnia, will gradually be retrenching. Some commentators claim that the European Union and NATO still curtail Germany. But we believe that the greatest inhibitor of German ambition is not external but internal: the dominant beliefs of its citizenry and the politics of collective memory. It is collective memory that links history to ideology, defining the area in which foreign policy operates, and the collective memory that now dominates in Germany strongly mitigates the exercise of German power.

Russian self-absorption, American focus on the Pacific, West European impotence, and East European naiveté have combined to enlarge German autonomy in a way not manifest for a half-century. The potential sphere of German influence—economic, diplomatic, cultural, even military—is enormous. Yet dominated by a deeply ingrained, perhaps obsessive, collective memory of past power-seeking, the German response is characterized by caution and confusion rather than opportunism and predatory behavior.

In all its prior guises, the question has always assumed an unswerving German pursuit of power. Germany has historically pursued *more*—land, natural resources, even food. German theorists played a notable role in proclaiming and justifying the notion of the expansionist German nation-state.[2] Power, according to their view, is the product of purposive action—the objective product of their subjective intent. To be powerful, Germany must strive toward expansion.[3]

In this book, we contend that the latest stage of the German Question is unique in German history. We are faced with an unprecedented notion: Germany now exercises as much power as it ever has, despite its desire *not* to do so. Germany has options in the exercise of power, ones that it largely seeks to avoid.

Current German power does not take the form of tanks and guns. It is not power borne of purposive intent; nor is it simply the capacity to get others to do what the Germans want them to do. The structural power that we emphasize involves the capacity to set agendas and limit the alternatives among which Germany's neighbors choose. As Steven Lukes observes, "the most effective and insidious use of power is to prevent . . . conflict from arising in the first place."[4]

Germany's structural power emanates from the size and strength of its economy and resulting patterns of commerce. It is also evident in Germany's diplomatic influence in multilateral organizations, and the German capacity to act independently. In the past fifty years, however, Germany has chosen not to act unilaterally but to be a consummate team player—the ultimate European.

It has chosen this course out of self-interest, and because of the constraints as well as structures of collective memory domestically and among its neighbors. Germany surrendered its interest only in the brief period between the end of the war and the formation of the Federal Republic in 1949, when no German state existed. The Bonn Republic's policies, strategies, and actions were guided just like any other state's by efforts to optimize its interests. The objective changes in German power and position of the past few years do not imply powerlessness on the part of the Bonn Republic, but Germany now has an enormous and increasing structural power that demands recognition by its government.

Dominated by an ideology of smallness, Germany has to recognize that when it sneezes, others catch a cold, perhaps even pneumonia. Driven by the normative idea that Germany is not and should not seek to become a great power, Germany's citizens and governments seek to abstain from international responsibilities.[5] Although the Bundestag voted in December 1995 to send German peacekeeping troops to Bosnia, the intense opposition which that decision generated, particularly on the country's vocal and vibrant Left, indicates that many Germans are still not comfortable with Germany's new role.[6]

The German situation in contemporary Europe is thus analogous to the global position of the United States in the interwar period, possessing the capacity to underwrite the rules of the international system but unwilling to do so. Britain then was unable but willing to be the lender of last resort. American structural power was not consistent with its reticent ideology; Britain's aggrandizing ideology lacked the capabilities to implement appropriate policies. The result was a world plunged into depression.[7]

Is Germany now replaying the U.S. role of the interwar years? The United States now is viewed as either a declining power or as a superpower in an era when being a superpower has declined in significance.[8] In the European context, despite its interventions in Northern Ireland and Bosnia, the United States certainly appears to be a declining power. More generally, it is caught between a declining structural position that leaves it unable to respond effectively in an increasing number of situations, and a powerful ideological predisposition to consider itself responsible for global stability even when U.S. national interest is not directly evident. In the Gulf War, for instance, Germany and Japan relied on Gulf oil, and so had a clear national interest in maintaining regional stability, yet it was the United States that sent troops.

A long-standing debate rages, of course, over such behavior. American policy has been characterized as myopic and self-interested, benevolent and positive-sum. Our purpose is simply to note that an ideological predisposition exists in the United States to assume that the United States bears primary (though not sole) responsibility for stabilizing the prevailing balance. Like Britain before it, the United States may be playing out the frustrating fate of a hegemon in decline.[9]

Germany is the reverse: its ideological predisposition toward smallness lags behind its increasing structural power. We believe that Germany may never have the political/cultural, military or economic base to become the Britain or America of the twenty-first century. But Germany—at least in Europe—is now assuming the position of what Nicos Kotzias calls a hegesy: a potentially rising hegemon, but one ultimately lacking both the broad political base and the cultural or "soft" dimensions of power necessary to assume a hegemonic position.[10]

Realist theory assumes that all states aspire to the mantle of hegemon.[11] We believe that Germany may differ from the Realist stereotype view of an aspiring hegemon. In the German case, the disjuncture between ideology and structural position is one of imperial *under*reach, manifest as a refusal to accept responsibility for its actions. It is clear that, in contrast to Realist views of international relations, domestic German ideology—shaped by the collective memory of Germany and its neighbors—rather than Realism's tangible structural factors decide German foreign policy.

André Malraux famously suggested that he liked Germany so much that he wanted two of them. The current view of Germany by its neighbors is overwhelmingly positive, despite inconclusive evidence about the benefits of German behavior.[12] Indeed, we observe a reversal of attitude between Germany and many of its neighbors. While Germany seeks limited forms of engagement at very limited costs (although the German commitment to send troops to Bosnia may signal that this attitude is slowly changing), Germany's neighbors seek greater German integration and invite broader German participation.

There is an apparent clash between the current interests of these countries and their collective memory. Their current interest is to have Germany share the military burden in a way commensurate with Germany's economic might; their prevailing collective memories instruct them to remain suspicious of any display of German power.

Germany's prevailing ideology of limited aspirations may appear at first glance prudent and self-effacing. Its prudence is dictated by a potent, collective memory that guides Germany's actions as well as its neighbors' apprehensions. Yet such prudence ignores the growth of real power. Power is not simply defined by its purposive exercise. It is exercised, whether intentionally or not.

We do not advocate the recent prescriptions boldly articulated by the German Right, which seeks to encourage greater German intervention.[13] No doubt the fluidity of the current situation, the decline of American power in Europe and Germany's normalization, has revived the desire of many Germans to render their country's power "normal." More concretely, this view holds that German reluctance to project power died with unification. Perhaps the most significant qualitative difference between the old Bonn and the new Berlin Republic, between the Bundesrepublik and Deutschland, is the need for the latter to shed the former's inhibitions. Centered on the unrestrained exercise of power, this shedding of inhibitions will also occur in the realm of acceptable political discourse, in socially condoned behavior, and in general public culture. In short, the Bundesrepublik's threshold of shame is to be lowered, slowly but surely, in the new Deutschland.

This normalcy argument has also been advocated by a few members of the "national Left." Most prominent has been Brigitte Seebacher-Brandt, who quit the Social Democratic party in good part over substantial disagreements on this very issue.

We reject this view unequivocally as dangerous and undesirable for Europe and for Germany. Ours is not a justification for German aggression or its im-position of preferred policies. We do not suggest that Germany should seize power as an appropriate response. Rather, we believe that Germany has to become sensitive to the broader implications of its actions. When the Bundesbank acts, for example, it cannot justify its activities solely in terms of domestic monetary discipline. It has to recognize that it is, functionally, the European bank of last resort and that the Deutsche Mark serves as a benchmark currency.[14] Oscillations in the mark's value have significant regional (if not global) repercussions, and so on occasions broader stability may preclude particular policy choices. The German Right seeks to use the country's resources to guide Europe according to German principles. Such a strategy is not accepting responsibility, and with it the internalization of costs; it is seizing power as a means of externalizing costs—a perverse definition of the idea of internationalization. We reject such a position.

While we agree empirically that the Berlin Republic's power is becoming normal, meaning that it will be much more substantial than that of the Bonn Republic, we do not share the desire that this power be deployed in a normal fashion. We concur in this analysis with the German Left (SPD and Greens), but we reject their wishful thinking that through various, mostly unspecified, mechanisms Germany somehow can be Austrianized—meaning that by quitting NATO, becoming neutral, and developing an ethos of pacifism, Germany somehow can become an innocuous waif in the middle of Europe. Even a completely demilitarized, well-meaning, reticent Germany ruled by the pacifist Left would be a powerful country whose actions, for better or worse, would have enormous consequences for its neighbors.

Power is an inevitable product of Germany's size, geography, and economic capacity, whether Germany pursues it or not. The decision, then, is whether to make others adjust to German requisites, as the Right would like, or to make Germany adapt. Historically, Germany has externalized costs through imperial expansion and the ideology of *Weltpolitik*.[15] The current situation differs in that the solution of mainstream Germans is to seek minimal or zero involvement. Germany now wants not to externalize costs so much as to ignore them. The contemporary German ideology of smallness is deeply selfish, for it is oblivious to the costs and benefits for others. There is an inherent contradiction between an ideology of smallness and the claim that Germany—its values, political institutions, and economy—has become internationalized in a broader Europe. The contradictions will only grow more tense as Germany moves from being a key regional to a central global actor.

Germany is now in an unprecedented situation. Historically, it has been a country governed by great-power pretensions, constrained by its neighbors and its limited natural resources. Now, it is a country with access to more natural resources through open trade and peaceful political arrangements, a country whose neighbors accord it greater respect and responsibilities than ever before. But it is governed by an ideology that, though internationalist in character, is reluctant to recognize German centrality to the new global order.

The result is a reluctant power that is nevertheless exercised: This reluctant exercise of power is fraught with significant dangers for Germany's neighbors. The danger is no longer from German Panzers but from the insistent effort to abstain from the exercise of power. This anomaly is the current form of German exceptionalism. It is the latest stage of the German Question—a diffident exercise of power which results from a unique configuration of German identity and memory.

The consequences of the unwilling (and often unwitting) exercise of German power are manifest in two recent developments. First, self-absorbed German anti-inflation policy threw Europe's economies into financial turmoil and ruined the immediate prospects for a successful and equitable Economic and Monetary Union. Some nations were thrown into recession, yet German bankers denied responsibility: they were "merely" responding to a combination of systemic and domestic pressures unleashed by unification.[16]

Second, Yugoslavia's dissolution and civil war was precipitated in no small part by the rushed, bipartisan consensus between government (CDU/CSU/FDP) and opposition (SPD and Greens) to recognize Croatia and Slovenia.[17] Germany's solo act had, if anything, more to do with the country's liberal and Wilsonian impulses than it did with the German Right's traditional sympathies for Croatia and that country's hostility toward Serbia.[18]

These examples obviously are not comparable in scope to the national policies that precipitated two world wars. But their effects have been grave. The German attempt to think small, to conceive of itself as merely a large Austria or Switzerland, is ideologically irresponsible and may threaten the welfare of Europe even as it attempts to reassure Europeans about Germany's benign intent. Paradoxes abound.

That European fear of German expansionism is ill-founded may be objectively true; most of the time Germany and its neighbors do indeed enjoy a mutually beneficial relationship. But it remains the case that policies consciously designed to avoid what many Germans see as aggressive engagement have had malign (if unintended) effects. The historic German propensity to think big was a problem for Europeans; now, the propensity to think small threatens Europe's future in a different way.[19]

There are several possible responses to Germany's changed circumstances. One, already mentioned, is to suggest that Germany should seize power and guide Europe toward a glorious future—a view fraught with the anxieties of the past and oblivious to the constraining power of collective memory. Another is to agree with our assessment of the potentially malign effects of German policies, but to suggest that these policies are governed by a self-interested propensity toward aggrandizement. This book, and the evidence it uses, explicitly responds to this argument. It does so by analyzing what masses and elites, both in Germany and abroad, feel about German unification and the postunification relationship between Germany and its neighbors.

In sum, we argue that a more self-interested Germany can find more effective ways to express its power. In a way, Germany is once again in an unenviable predicament. It is damned if it acts in a way commensurate with its structural power, and it is damned if it stays aloof and acts small. Germany is caught between the Scylla of collective memory which will not permit it to exercise power in a normal manner, and the Charybdis of contemporary exigencies, which demand German acceptance of its responsibilities in Europe and maybe even the world.

To use the vocabulary made famous by Albert O. Hirschman, we come to the following conclusion: the German Left and many liberal elements want Germany to exit from the world of power while remaining loyal to and continuing to have voice in the world of collective memory. The German Right and the conservative Lager want exactly the opposite: exit from the world of collective memory (exactly what the term *Schlussstrich*, drawing the line, connotes) while increasing Germany's voice in and loyalty to the world of power.

The same vocabulary clarifies the conflicts and tensions among Germany's neighbors. On the one hand they are terrified by the prospect of German exit. Indeed, the Maastricht Treaty is an institutional attempt, by the French and their late president François Mitterrand, to deny Germany all possible exit options from Europe. This fear is predicated on the still immensely powerful collective memory of the pernicious results of Germany's unique pattern of development, better known as the *Sonderweg*. Europe and the United States want Germany to remain inside the institutional networks of the postwar era, which to a considerable degree were constructed to keep Germany loyal to the West. Yet most members of Europe's political classes—as well as a considerable number of America's—are wary, not to say suspicious and hostile, of Germany's attaining too much voice in the new world order. They would prefer a Germany loyal to the structures of the Bonn Republic's world. Many in Germany share this wish. Alas, we argue, the loyalty option will become increasingly difficult for Germany to maintain. Between growing pressure for a voice in the international arena and the concomitant desire to exit, loyalty will become a difficult, frustrating, and at times costly balancing act for the Germans.

This constitutes the argument of our book. We begin with a discussion of the notion of collective memory, its relationship to history and ideology, and the conflicting collective memories that ultimately condition Germany's current exercise of power.

The Contemporary Power of Collective Memory

Is the new Germany different from all the other Germanies since 1871? We are reminded of what Chou En Lai reportedly said when asked what he thought of the French Revolution: "It's too soon to tell."

If 1989 meant anything to the social sciences, it should have been a call for more modesty and a modicum of humility instead of the hubris and swagger that seem to dominate. It is still too early to assess that year's complexities. Here, we challenge conventional interpretations of politics which see the pursuit of interest as manifested in state power as the principal motor of political action. Realists rely on the centrality of interest and its maximization as the most convincing explanation of political behavior. Actors do certain things and behave in certain ways because it is in their interest (as defined by power) to do so. Nation states behave *a fortiori* in just such a way. For Realists—and Marxists and Weberians—interest is closely linked to power as measured by the adage "A has power over B to the extent that A can get B to do something that B would not otherwise do."[20]

Postwar Germany and Japan are the two countries that have not exercised political power nor developed military capabilities commensurate with their economic might. They challenge Realist assumptions about how states should (and actually do) act. But until 1989 Germany, by virtue of its division along the front lines of the Cold War, was in no way normal. The Bonn Republic was an ideal-typical manifestation of neoliberalism, demanding an emphasis on institutional analysis and the primacy of structural interests.

We do not mean to say that the Bundesrepublik was powerless, that it failed to realize its interests and was subject to the whims of others. Far from it. Germany was a potent political force from the moment when Konrad Adenauer recognized the advantage of membership in the European Coal and Steel Community, which served as a vehicle for the articulation of national interest and for a new type of governance in the international system. This arrangement did not tame German power. Rather, it offered a new institutional context wherein Germany, always in coalition with others, frequently France but also Italy and the Benelux countries, actively pursued a political union in which Germany would get pride of place.

The same pertains to the North Atlantic Treaty Organization, the most salient political and military framework in the reordering of postwar western Europe. Here, too, there is plenty of evidence that the old Bundesrepublik was a key political player which saw that its interests were represented.

Will the Berlin Republic act as the Bonn Republic did? The institutions have largely remained the same.[21] Still, there are important changes. Shifts in values and priorities, especially among members of the political class, are more important in understanding a country's choices than is the continuity of institutions. The articulation of hitherto prohibited topics and the rethinking of hitherto unacceptable options bespeak a qualitative change. Briefly, we think that a noticeable shift in the quality and quantity of "the acceptable" in German discourse concerning the country's projection of power renders the new Berlin Republic substantially different from its Bonn predecessor.

The basic question is simple: Will this new country continue to be tied down by its collective memory? If yes, then the Realists and the neoliberals will have a significant deviant case to explain and will have to adjust. If no, then the explanatory power of their theory will prove a good deal more powerful than some of us would have anticipated.

We will look at history's shadow over Germany's activities and policy options, particularly in the area of foreign policy. We differentiate between history and collective memory, and show that it is mainly the latter—in its multiplicity, its murkiness, its malleability—that is a formidable influence on the ideology of reluctance that shapes German foreign policy.

The politics of collective memory—impossible to quantify, hard to measure with the methods of survey research, yet still very real—is a major ingredient of the political arena, the public discourse, and the policy setting in every country. It circumscribes the acceptable. It defines such key ingredients as pride, shame, fear, revenge, and comfort for a large number of a country's citizens. It is central to an understanding of the forces of nationalism. In few areas of public life is the politics of collective memory more charged than in foreign policy, yet precisely in this domain has it been least studied.

We do not pretend to fill this lacuna, but we discuss the importance of collective memory in Germany, and identify cases where collective memory has influenced policy in a profound manner. In the chapter that follows, we map the multiplicity of collective memories currently competing in Germany's lively pluralist polity. Specifically, we look at key junctures that created new collective memories and values. One can almost speak of competing generations of collective memories, which are not linear and progressive but circular, repetitious, and profoundly unpredictable.

Collective Memory and Germany

Realism is not simply a theory of international relations. It is a *Weltanschauung* or world view, that consists not only of a theory of causal relations but also of a substructure of assumptions regarding who the actors are, what motivates them, and what dominant forms of relationship define their world. This construct forms the basis of theories. At the hard core of Realist theory lie assumptions about the dominance of self-interest defined as power, about states as the appropriate unit of analysis, about unitary actors in a hierarchically ordered domestic system in which policy is (for all practical purposes) perfectly implemented. Force acts as the dominant form of power.[22]

As Realism has evolved since its initial comprehensive formulation under Thucydides (and not evidently for the better), it has paid decreasing attention to domestic aspects of the nation state and increasing—and in some variants exclusive—attention to the systemic aspects of interstate relations.[23]

The domestic "taming" of the German state under the Bonn Republic was therefore irrelevant to Realists. What made Germany abnormal were its external relations, a spider's web whose four founding corners were beyond the sovereign authority of the German government: *Osthandel* and *Ostpolitik* vis-à-vis the East, the EU and NATO vis-à-vis the West.[24] These structures may have enhanced the Federal Republic's security by reducing the threat of war, but they absolved German politicians of responsibility for many decisions over military and economic security.

Paradoxically, the huge West German army, the largest in Western Europe, was not inconsistent with the Bonn Republic's development as a *Handelsstaat*, a trading state, which requires enlightened, multinational, and interdependent foreign and security policy. Realists, however, never perceived the tremendous success of German economic development as an imbalance in the delicate intra-European power arrangements. Rather, Germany's strength was merely fortuitous in forming a front-line bulwark against communism. The immediate European context always remained subordinate to the larger global one, which seemed the only legitimate arena for the exercise of real political power.[25]

Germany's domestic institutional reforms were thus ignored, and its external relations, like Japan's, were outside the bounds of Realist theory. If Germany did exercise power, it was not through the state as a unitary, hierarchical actor but through private and quasi-public institutions. Its power was manifest not through military means but through trade or its diplomatic capacities to bridge East and West.[26]

Realists, striving for generalizability, therefore discounted Germany as a representative case. The country's external features rendered it outside the purview of normal cases. In contradictory fashion, it could be ignored as a test of Realist theories while remaining central to Realist analysis of East-West relations.

What, though, of the new Federal Republic—the Berlin variant? John Mearsheimer, in a singularly influential article published in the aftermath of unification, suggested that Germany had become once more a normal country. One consequence, he suggested, was that nuclear weapons should be proliferated under German sovereignty, as a means of maintaining the peace.[27]

Mearsheimer, consistent with Realist assumptions, did not dwell on the possibility that the leaders of the Berlin Republic would reject sovereignty over nuclear missiles, nor that their closest allies would panic at such a move. Power defined as interest, in which military force is the final arbiter, would result in Germany's leaders assuming responsibility for weapons of mass destruction.

Yet is the Berlin Republic normal—at least in the sense used by Realists? Helmut Kohl's catch phrase, "A good German is a good European," remains the dominant adage. If the Bonn Republic is not yet normal, however, it can be argued that the Berlin Republic provides evidence that Germany has started on the road toward normalcy, at least in terms of growing sovereignty and autonomy. As Klaus Kinkel said, "Making Germany a partner capable of assuming a full range of duties . . . is a priority task aimed at providing for the future. Our citizens understand that the time when we were in an exceptional situation is over.

. . . We have no need to demonstrate our ability for normality both at home and abroad if we do not want to sustain severe political damage."[28]

The debate over the foreign deployment of German troops, with the final decision to expand such commitments confirmed by legislative and judicial actions in 1993, 1994, and 1995, indicates both a tendency toward normalcy and the relative malleability of Germany's supposedly tamed institutions. So does the controversy surrounding Joschka Fischer's letter dated August 2, 1995, in which this savvy politician exhorted his Green Party comrades to qualify their dogmatic pacifism in light of special cases such as genocide in Bosnia. The acerbity of the resulting debate shows how sensitive the issue of normalcy remains. The whole passionate controversy was conducted in the context of collective memory and its continued relevance to all aspects of German life. What, after all, did Auschwitz teach the Germans? Never to engage in *any* military activities under *any* circumstances, no matter how urgent the case and noble the effort? Or never to tolerate genocide and the humiliation of the weak? No such passion and vehemence were provoked in any other NATO country whose troops were to be deployed: not in Britain, France, Italy, or the United States. The difference lay in one crucial variable: that of collective memory.

If Germany is becoming more normal, then surely German leaders should behave in a manner more consistent with Realist assumptions. But we suggest that this is not the case. The definition of security is, for Germans, inconsistent with even the weakest form of the Realist argument. Furthermore, the historical context adds weight to the problem that Germany presents. As the dominant economy in the heart of Europe, Germany has exhibited a historical orientation toward the ideologies of *Weltpolitik* and *Lebensraum* which has often approximated the Realist prescription. Among the major powers of Europe, Germany has perhaps most closely approximated in historical terms the behavior characteristic of states in the Realist paradigm—a power seeker whose behavior is dictated by self-interest, often defined as territorial expansion, military aggrandizement, and economic domination.

Yet Germany is also an opposing case for those interested in the influence of collective memory and how contrasting collective memories contest to influence foreign policy. In no other contemporary great power (except perhaps Japan, though to a different degree) are history, memory, and foreign policy so intertwined.[29] The historical orientation of Germany's ideology and foreign policy is consistent with Realism, yet its modern ideology and foreign policy contradict it.

A severe challenge to Realism on this issue has come from scholars who focus on cognitive processes of decision making. Their unit of analysis has always been the nonrational behavior of the individual, although a few scholars have stressed the net effects of "groupthink."[30] There has been a missing link in the literature on values between those who focus on individuals and those who stress highly aggregated numbers (as in the discussion of norms or ideology). Collective memory provides one means to link these two formulations. It emphasizes cognitive processes in a way that aggregates individual preferences—what Richard Ned Lebow has referred to as "generational learning."[31] Collective memories are the vessel through which pass individual, scattered, fragmented, and populist attitudes, on the one hand, and elite, coherent worldviews on the other. They are the bridges linking history (as fact) to ideology (as myth).

To demonstrate such linkages, we examine how the clusters of collective memories characterized in Chapter 2 of this book competed in the Bonn Republic, and how a dominant, consensual view emerged to define Germany as a *Handelsstaat*, never a great power.[32] Thus, as we chronicle, both Germany's citizenry and its contemporary government look to abstain from international governance and from the responsibilities that Germany must confront. Germany exercises power through the huge size of its economy and its capacity to set agendas but does not seek aggrandizement of its military security.

Germany now stands on the threshold of assuming the position of a great power internationally and that of a dominant power regionally. Will it aspire to the position of a regional hegemon, or will it favor what we have characterized as hegesy—a country structurally capable of dominance but ideologically reluctant to engage in expansionist behavior?[33] Is contemporary Germany comparable to the United States in the interwar period, able but unwilling to assume leadership? And will the consequences of refusal be as dramatic?

If the new Berlin Republic is to reject the Realist option and deliberately stay a "small" country, it will do much to repudiate the Realist paradigm. Sustained rejection of power will do much to reinforce the view that ideology is increasingly important in explaining German behavior—and, correspondingly, that Realism has little to recommend it in the study of German foreign policy. As Stanley Hoffmann, reflecting on the German question in the aftermath of unification, concludes:

> It would take an extraordinary amount of mischief to turn the new German state into a modern version of the dangerous and unsettling Germany of the past. Neither Germany's partners, nor even its adversaries in the East, are in any way eager to antagonize or provoke it; and German elites have no desire to return to that past.[34]

Realism, of course, is not the only way to understand international relations; its arguments are increasingly contested by neoliberalism, which combines use of the state as an actor with rational assumptions about behavior. The greatest area of disagreement concerns the effects of the principles and norms of international (or supranational) institutions in determining state policies.[35] Yet both groups of analysts reject or minimize the importance of domestic influences, particularly of ideology, on decisions and policy making.

Our work thus contests the basic presuppositions and conclusions of the neoliberal as well as the Realist agenda. The implication of our work is clear: the determinants of German foreign policy are far from rational (and in that sense value-maximizing). Collective memory, rather, is the ideological foundation that leads to policy, which is determined by rather different criteria.

The Realist and neoliberal projects both focus on rationality and self-interest (whether in power or institutional terms) as determinants of decision making. We stress nonrational, ideological factors. Why is this important? Because our critique notes the limits and the substance of German aspirations in Europe—not to build a power base through institutions or cruder forms of influence peddling, but through a genuinely felt reluctance. Germany does not seek hegemony in a Realist sense or maximize power and minimize transaction costs in a liberal sense. Often it foregoes opportunities because of the limits imposed on its freedom to maneuver by collective memory.

Such terms as ideology, norms, and culture are often used interchangeably, but what is the origin of ideologies? The answer is historical experience; Japanese technonationalism is a prime example.[36] To say that history shapes ideology is, however, both true and meaningless, for it underspecifies the relationship between them. A better way to understand the relationship between the two is to think about the concept of collective memory; how ideological frameworks are contested and subsequently constructed. The concept is a sociological building bloc for understanding why countries do what they do—either as governments through policies, or in broader societal terms.

In many ways, Germany is an easy case, a case where collective understandings have been so contested in the twentieth century, yet where a majority has reached a shared opinion about Germany's role in the world. Furthermore, it is an easy case because Germany's conception of its foreign policy decides how Germany acts, and in turn Germany's actions are central to European developments. Germany's collective memory and its "memory map" are significant factors in the future construction of what Mikhail Gorbachev called the "common European home."

Rational, structural forms of understanding that focus on states as unitary actors cannot accomodate the notion that choices are nonrational. They assume that states seek to maximize self-interest, either through the use of power or through the use of supranational institutional structures (i.e., regimes). By focusing on ideology, we seek to explain patterns of behavior which are inconsistent with rational explanations. One key puzzle is why the Germans sometimes chose not to exercise power when they might have gained, in a tangible sense, from doing so. We also seek to explain why adverse consequences—for example, EMU, the post-Yugoslav crisis—were partly the product not of German intent but of Germany's reluctance to comprehend its power. Rational arguments can often account for consequences only as intended, by inferring them from outcomes.

We attempt to locate the form, roots, and influence of this ideology for the future of German foreign policy. We suggest that among the Bonn Republic's accomplishments were a resistance to military engagement and expansionist foreign policy, and a correspondingly greater acceptance and trust of Germany among its traditional adversaries. These developments created a greater potential "space" for German decision makers to exploit, should they adapt a Realist orientation. Yet despite the occasional misgivings expressed about Helmut Kohl, evidence suggests that such a shift is less likely than ever.[37] The clusters of collective memories in Germany and its regional partners have transformed the way that the parties conduct foreign policy. Will Germany's postwar foreign policy be sustained under the Berlin Republic, or will it revert to the impulses of earlier, darker periods in German history? The initial indications are that some incremental changes may be in process, but we do not know where they will take Germany.

What we *can* now recount is a fascinating German debate on Germany's collective memory, a debate that has captured the country's elites and political class and which has helped develop a new ideology. Begun in the latter years of the Bundesrepublik (with Ronald Reagan's visit to the Bitburg cemetery and the historians' debate of the mid-to-late 1980s), it took on a completely new political salience with the momentous events of 1989–90. We believe that the nature—as well as the very existence—of this debate matters profoundly in the construction of Germany's foreign policy.

Collective Memory and the Construction of Foreign Policy

In what remains one of the most influential works on collective memory, Maurice Halbwachs differentiates astutely between historical memory and collective memory.[38] History is an externalized and objectified process, anchored in the task of preserving the past. It is factual, impartial, unitary, and universalistic in its endeavor to preserve the past in a cognitively accountable manner. History records events of the past; it is about knowing and understanding it.

Collective memory, in contrast, is not a record of events but a locus of tradition. If history is universalistic, collective memory is particularistic. If history is timeless, collective memory is time-bound. Above all, collective memory is always plural. Each group—just like each epoch—has its collective memory. (It might be more appropriate, though perhaps stylistically awkward, to use the plural "collective memories." One might speak of one history, but one could never speak of one collective memory.) If history is about cognition and knowledge, collective memory is about experience and feeling. If history is a matter of the past, collective memory is a phenomenon of the present. Indeed, one could interpret collective memory as a contemporary experiencing, a constant reinterpretation, of the historic past. Collective memory is always present. It is in constant flux, subject to relatively sudden changes. Many different memories can—and do—coexist in every society, sometimes in harmony, at other times in competition. They overlap freely, and obvious contradictions among them do not diminish their potency and experienced reality. Akin to myth, only tangentially related to empirical truth, collective memory plays a key role in the symbolic discourse of politics, in the legitimation of political structures and action, and in the justification of collective behavior.

Several useful insights about collective memory as a major ingredient of modern politics can be inventoried here[39]:

There is a clear relationship between collective memory and modernity. Closely tied to two of the pillars of modern politics—the individual and nationalism—collective memory in politics is either an artifact of modernity or at the very least heavily fostered by it. At a minimum, modern means are absolutely necessary to politicize, mobilize, revive, sustain, subdue, and perhaps delete collective memories.

Collective memory has much more to do with the present than it does with the past. Indeed, collective memory constitutes the past for present and contemporary purposes. As such, it is clearly functionalized and is, in fact, utilitarian for the here-and-now. Collective memory is the selective use of the past to legitimate present conditions of power.

Functionalization occurs both structurally and through an active instrumentalization on the part of actual people. The purposes of actual people are manifold, but one definite factor entails the use of collective memory for purposes of legitimation. Crudely put, the ruling collective memories in any given society at any given time are the collective memories of the ruling class. (One could easily substitute the concept of elites or power holders if one is uncomfortable with the Marxian notion of the "ruling class.") Collective memory has much to do with contemporary power, which harnesses the past for its own present purposes.

Collective memory has a skewed and orthogonal relationship to history, but a relationship nonetheless exists. Many of the allegedly primordial hatreds that have fueled the vengeful collective memories of certain peoples in the Balkans are far from ancient. Indeed, they are of recent historical origin, and their current acerbity has much more to do with contemporary power struggles than with actual history. The genocidal tragedy of the former Yugoslavia is a consequence of elite politics, particularly the mutually reinforcing megalomanias of Slobodan Milosevic and Franjo Tudjman. The destructive dimensions of these collective memories were clearly fanned from above.[40] Still, collective memories are not wholly random: Hungarians do not invoke the Swiss in their collective memory of victimhood, and Poles are far less anti-Turkish than are Greeks. Collective memory is anchored in some of the real-life events—the real history—of the collective. Hatreds have to be contextualized in memory, which is based in some sort of believability. Thus collective memory is deeply influenced—though not exclusively determined—by geography and time.

The following rule of thumb applies: the greater the temporal and spatial distance to an event, the less likely will be its appearance and acuteness as an ingredient of collective memory. Serbs still rally around the collective memory of the Battle of Kosovo-Polye, in which their armies were defeated by the Ottoman Turks in 1389; Jews bemoan the destruction of the Second Temple in Jerusalem at the hands of Titus and his legions in 70 C.E.; and William III's victory over the Catholic armies at the Battle of the Boyne in 1690 still leads to annual tensions and disturbances between Catholics and Protestants in Ulster.

It is, of course, not the original events that rile these communities; instead, it is the constant use of these icons, their contemporary and repeated enactment on an annual basis, which renders them so real. Their reality is reinforced by their symbolic representation of more recent and genuinely experienced hardships: Jasenovac in the case of Serbs, centuries of persecution and antisemitism in the case of Jews, discrimination and subjugation in the case of Irish Catholics. Collective memory is continuously enlivened for contemporary purposes. However many thousands of times the citizens of Quebec see their provincial license plates, adorned with "Je me souviens," none actually remembers the defeat of General Montcalm on the Plains of Abraham in early September 1759. It is not history which is invoked on Quebec license plates but collective memory, which in the case of Francophone citizens of La Belle Province, speaks to centuries of subjugation at the hands of the English. Without Charles De Gaulle's epoch-setting "Vive le Québec libre" speech in June 1967, the symbolic meaning of 1759 would be far less acute in contemporary Quebecois politics. Put bluntly, history is confined to libraries; collective memory finds its way onto the license plates of citizens' cars.

Actual experience does not reach back further than a century, the life span of human beings who experienced events either as active participants or as contemporaries. (The German word *Zeitzeuge*, time witness, captures this concept superbly.) With the physical disappearance of *Zeitzeugen*, collective memory enters the realm of myth. Collective memory is what links ideology to historical interpretation, and it is profoundly tied to generations, a point to which we will return.

Collective memory is a key ingredient of what Emile Durkheim labeled "conscience collective."[41] Comprising both collective conscience and collective consciousness, *conscience collective* is a difficult-to-describe social bond among people whose shared experiences and contemporary interpretations of the past form a crucial foundation of their community. Such bonds aggregate experiences and are key to the formulation of national ideologies.

Collective memory on a national level loves to dwell on negative experiences. Victim, victimhood, and victimization play crucial roles in the collective memory of virtually every country. Intensity may vary according to time and space, but every country seems to have had at least one trauma that continues to haunt its collective memory. "Coming to terms with the past" is by no means confined to Germany: it is ubiquitous. Clearly one driving force is the desire for justice, an overwhelming human need to right wrongs that contributes to the positive side of the salience of victimhood and victimization. The negative aspect manifests itself in the human trait of *ressentiment*. Both positive and negative aspects are constantly present in a nation's collective memory, but their articulation and manifestation vary, both synchronically and diachronically. Interestingly, in both guilt cultures and shame cultures, victimhood offers a powerful filtering of the past which affects assessments of present and future.[42]

Like generals who always fight the last war, countries fight their last trauma, the event in which they were somehow wronged and victimized. Regardless of the actual perpetrators or instigators, collective memory eventually succeeds in clustering around the axis of victimization and victimhood. U.S. collective memory sees Americans as victims of the Vietnam War even though the argument can certainly be made that it was the United States which destroyed Vietnam. But on all counts—the POWs/MIAs, the 58,000 dead and many more wounded, the absence of final victory—the power of the "Vietnam experience" lies precisely in the fact that we Americans regard ourselves as (at least partial) victims of this awful war.

Collective memory is a source of power as well as identity, and above all a construct that fosters social solidarity. Tragedies and defeats are particularly potent and lasting repositories of collective memory for virtually every country: the Vichy experience in France, the Holocaust in Israel, the "Dirty War" in Argentina, Hiroshima in Japan.[43]

As we show in later chapters on public opinion, most Europeans continue to share considerable reservations about German power because in their collective memories they have been victimized by Germany. Tony Judt has shown in a brilliantly argued paper that this notion of having been victimized by the Germans became an indispensable staple of the collective memories of most postwar European peoples, even those who had in fact benefited from Germany's power during the Nazi era.[44] Thus arose the collective myth of resistance against the Nazis, which Judt believes was essential in legitimating a "feel-good" Europe in which victimization by the Germans became a part of the "foundation myth."

Of course the Nazis victimized millions of Europeans. But even those whom they did not mistreat developed a myth of victimization which—on the whole—served them well in the legitimation of their postwar policies. Austrians managed to be declared Nazi Germany's first victims (and so the country was official exonerated in the Moscow Declaration of 1943), and the French maintained a fifty-year myth of having been a nation of resistance fighters. Every country derived considerable postwar mileage from having been victimized by the Germans.[45]

Among this number are, of course, the Germans, for they too defined themselves as victims of the Nazis. The Germans constructed further instances of victimization for their collective memory: the forced displacement of millions of Germans from eastern Europe and the Soviet Union immediately after the war; the occupation of Germany by the Allies; and Germany's division. In short, there are very few countries (perhaps some very small and very rich ones, such as San Marino and Liechtenstein, though certainly not now Kuwait) in whose collective memories some sort of slight or wrong does not play a significant myth-making and legitimating role. Why human collectivities dwell so persistently on bad things is not clear to us, but that they do so is very clear.

The study of collective memory is virtually unknown to the discipline of political science.[46] The topic seems to have remained outside of political scientists' interest in good part because of its perceived "mushiness." In a discipline in which measurement is reified as explanation, where numbers and calculations are the only valid expressions of conceptual rigor, collective memory can hardly be viewed as an analytic category worth serious study.[47] We regret this scientistic attitude, for we believe that collective memory is a crucial ingredient in every country's policymaking and perhaps nowhere more important than in foreign policy.[48]

On a national level, collective memory is the view of the past articulated by national leaders and the political class. This is collective memory in two senses. First, it is memory about a collectivity, the nation state, about its domestic developments and its foreign involvements. Second, it is, in an extended sense, memory of a collectivity. National leaders, representatives of the polity as a whole, articulate memories in the name of the nation state. Citizens of a particular state—even members of the political elite—will rarely agree on a particular account of the past. Memories articulated by national leaders can, however, be considered collective memories in much the same way that their external actions constitute a single, national foreign policy.

The collective memories articulated by leaders have three related dimensions: narrative, evaluative, and prescriptive. The narrative dimension is obvious: leaders tend to select disparate elements from national experience and juxtapose them in a meaningful way. Narratives relate seminal events, such as a nation state's founding and its revolutions, wars, and economic depressions. They can privilege events in the recent or the distant past, in internal politics or external relations. The evaluative dimension is embedded within the narrative: in rendering the past, national leaders simultaneously assess it, using literal and figurative qualifiers and the selection and juxtaposition of events. Finally, collective memory not only renders and evaluates the past, it also serves to prescribe action for the present and future. Evocation of the past often serves to place current actions as continuous with previous successes or discontinuous with previous failures.

The memories expressed by national leaders are not simply the result of individual reflection on the past and its implications for the present. They have broader national and international sources. At the national level, leaders draw on memories articulated by political, social, and cultural elites. Those memories are embedded in the authoritative texts, rituals, and commemorations of key institutions: government bureaucracies, political parties, interest groups, media, and academia. At the international level, national elites increasingly interact with their counterparts in other states. As a result memories can be influenced by participation in international networks.

Political constraints, too, shape these collective memories, for leaders are politicians as well as problem solvers. Their efforts to win and maintain office can shape their articulation of historical memories. Because leaders depend on the support of a shifting coalition of parties and societal groups, they are likely to espouse views of the national past that resonate within these memories.

Ultimately, however, there are two senses in which reflection at the individual level remains important. First, there is a moment of autonomy in the articulation of particular memories. The memories expressed by leaders cannot be reduced to broad international and national pressures. Second, those memories, once articulated, congeal into points of principle. These principles become foundations for ideology—an obvious example is collective memory's linkage between the Great Depression and the importance of sustaining free trade for every American president since FDR. These ideological principles have significant effects on policy, which in turn shapes new events, which eventually will be the source for new collective memories.

In sum, at the individual level, memories of the past can serve to orient national leaders confronted with international ambiguity. At the national level, those memories help to legitimate policy choices in the domestic political sphere. Finally, at the international level, they can serve to communicate policies to other governments. The greater the ambiguity of the policy context, the greater is the difficulty in calculating costs and benefits and relying on set rules and norms. Here ideological principles become increasingly important and thus collective memory grows more salient.[49]

We thus assert that in the formulation, conceptualization, and implementation of virtually every country's foreign policy, that country's collective memories will play a significant role. The country's eventual course of action will not be diametrically opposed to its earlier missteps and mistakes, of course, nor will it be a replica of earlier policies. But collective memory, and its constant construction and reconstruction, are a key ingredient in the political behavior of every country. One cannot understand recent American foreign policy and its search for a new world order without recognizing the significance of the Vietnam syndrome and the collective memory of the Cold War; the French, without Algeria and Dien Bien Phu on the one hand, and a showing-it-to-the-Americans panache on the other; the British, without the retreat from Suez and the "special relationship" with the United States. Israel's foreign policy remains anchored in the collective memory of the Holocaust[50]; Japan's in the Meiji Restoration and World War II; and Russia's in a web of admiration for and fear of the West, coupled with the powerful presence of the Great Patriotic War and the Cold War.

The Latest Stage of the German Question

Here we make explicit some of our assumptions, because articulating them dictates certain tasks for this book. First, we have to define what characteristics this latest version of the German Question shares with its predecessors, and why it is distinct. Second, we have to demonstrate the ideological positions of the Germans, their European neighbors, and their transatlantic partners. Third, we must describe the consequences of the exercise of reluctant power.

In the next chapter we define the contours of the German Question and chronicle its historical variants, before linking this history to collective memories and then to national ideology. We then examine two positions regarding future directions, those of the optimists and those of the pessimists.

The second section of the book entails an empirical examination of the linkage between collective memory and public opinion—both mass and elite. We consider the response to German unification, and the concerns it has raised, in the minds of Israeli, American, and various European publics.

The third section examines the dimensions of German power. We analyze the debate over military deployment before turning attention to the heart of German power—the regional economic prowess of Germany's firms in eastern and western Europe. The section concludes by examining what Germans consider the third pillar of German foreign policy, cultural policy. This, we argue, has in many ways been the weakest link in German foreign policy. Certainly it would be Germany's Achilles heel should German public opinion change and begin to favor a more hegemonic role in Europe.

The book concludes with a brief chapter that considers Germany's political landscape after the Kohl era. We are not convinced that his departure bodes well for any project seeking to sustain the Europeanization of Germany.

Part One

HISTORY AND ANALYSIS

CHAPTER ONE

Europe and the German Question

I'm sure that you have heard that Germany has re-united. The only question now, I guess, is when will it go on tour again.

—Jay Leno, *Tonight Show*

Leave it to the comedians to get to the essence. The vernacular of popular culture often captures sensitive matters that politicians are too hypocritical to articulate, intellectuals too cautious to disseminate, scholars too slow to investigate. Comics, like court jesters of old, are essential to any democratic polity precisely because they tackle taboos.

The German Question has played a crucial role in modern European history.[1] It continues unabated after the events of November 9, 1989 and October 3, 1990. In the new Berlin Republic it has attained a hitherto unseen character, a novel manifestation. What will this Germany be like? Wasn't the band already on tour, with the stage name Bundesrepublik and its members less numerous? What kind of tour will it be? a popular one, cheered by fans all over Europe and welcomed by local promoters? or will an enlarged band, with a different repertoire and new choreography, make its former fans uneasy, fearful, perhaps even angry?

Such questions have preoccupied Europeans, and opinions, views, hopes, and analyses abound. All revolve around an idea of normalcy which is deeply colored by memory and history. Never was this more obvious than in 1995, the "super-year" of anniversaries: the fiftieth anniversary of the liberation of Auschwitz; fiftieth anniversary of the bombing of Dresden; the fiftieth anniversary of VE-Day, a day of liberation (or was it occupation?) for Germans, and of the founding of the United Nations, and of the dropping of the atomic bombs at Hiroshima and Nagasaki. These anniversaries infuse the debate surrounding history and collective memory in contemporary Germany.[2] They are all about German identity and a still-elusive German normalcy. What *is* "normal" for Germans? Forty years of a prosperous but politically innocuous Bundesrepublik and a repressive, gray German Democratic Republic? Weimar? The Third Reich? Or the new Deutschland, whose prognosis as a liberal democracy is good but which has yet to be tested?

Ultimately, the question is all about how Germany will construct its new political identity, coordinating power on the one hand and democracy on the other. Until 1949, the synthesis had produced only disasters. Power and democracy seemed entangled in a brutal zero-sum game in which democracy was the loser. All this changed with the Bundesrepublik, which became a model democ-

23

racy. But the skeptics worry that the jury is still out: the Bundesrepublik could afford to be democratic because it was not a major power. As the new Germany becomes normal, the power question has reemerged. How will it affect the German polity? What will its implications be for German democracy? Above all, how will it change Germany's role in Europe and the world?

The old Bundesrepublik is surely dead. The demise of the GDR and the geographic and demographic expansion of the Federal Republic entail more than a change in mere quantity. The new Deutschland is also qualitatively different, and its changed status has already been seen in every aspect of German and European politics.

Two important features defined the Bundesrepublik and now provoke major discussion throughout Europe. The first was the absence of an independent German foreign policy; and the second centered on the Federal Republic's subordinate role as a military power. Both were manifestations of the Federal Republic's incomplete sovereignty, and its concomitant dependence on the political leadership of the United States in the global arena and France in Europe. This structural arrangement formed the core of the quintessential bundesrepublican trait: "Economic giant, political dwarf." With Deutschland, on October 3, 1990, came full sovereignty. How will Germany's metamorphosis into a political adult change things? Will this person necessarily become a giant? a gentle giant or a bully? Does it have to become a giant, even against its will, or can it develop into a regular, "normal" person? Germany's troubled history makes normalization potentially horrendous.

The eventual results of this interaction between power and democracy are far from certain, but we can discern three developments. On an institutional, legal, and formal level the continuity between the Bundesrepublik and Deutschland is remarkable. With the exceptions of the enlarged Bundestag and, more important, the enhanced Bundesrat, in which five new Laender can be heard, very few institutions have changed in any substantial way since the fall of the Berlin Wall. In institutions such as parties, interest groups, and government agencies, the Bundesrepublik continues more or less unabated. Unification amounted to little more than a takeover of the GDR by the Bundesrepublik.

Curiously, this seamless continuity on the institutional level seems a bit frayed at the level of policy. Whether in immigration and asylum or the extension of social benefits to increasingly marginalized members of a crisis-ridden society, the new Deutschland has proved to be a little harsher than the old Bundesrepublik. Equally, one can discern policy changes in the new Germany's foreign affairs which bespeak a new power that the country wants to project. Whether in Germany's disastrous foray into the Yugoslav tragedy or its difficulties in maintaining the formerly vaunted Franco-German alliance (in which the Bundesrepublik clearly played a subordinate role, at least at the level of political leadership), the new Deutschland's policies are increasingly subject to the logics of power and sovereignty rather than cooperation and coexistence.

It is on the ephemeral yet tangible level of atmosphere and political culture that one can discern the most noticeable change. For fairness' sake we note that harbingers of this atmospheric shift had already appeared in the 1980s. The Bitburg incident in the spring of 1985 and the *Historikerstreit* (historians' debate about the Holocaust) beginning in the summer of 1986 were instances in which the very essence of the Bundesrepublik was subject to acrimonious controversies. Still, the new Deutschland is a different place from the old Bundesrepublik. The editorial pages of Germany's paper of record, the *Frankfurter Allgemeine Zeitung*, bear witness to this change. What was once a centrist newspaper with a deeply conservative streak has become a Rightist paper with a nationalist bent.

This change from Bundesrepublik to Deutschland has been—to nobody's surprise—particularly marked on the right of the political spectrum. The radical or fringe Right has newly won political and thematic, if not numerical, prominence. More alarming is the established and *salonfähig* (socially acceptable) Right's precipitous movement away from its bundesrepublican tradition, from a catch-all constitutional conservatism into the nationalist camp. It is best captured by the generational shift in the CDU from men like Helmut Kohl, who anchored their conservatism in a deeply felt commitment to a supranational Europe and NATO, to men like Wolfgang Schäuble, who do not even bother to conceal their primary allegiance to German nationalism pure and simple.

We begin with the recognition that for two centuries Germany has constantly defied the expectations of scholars and commentators. The institutionalization of such concepts as *die Wende* (literally the big change), *der Sonderweg* (which emphasized the uniqueness of German development in comparison to the supposed Western norm), and the *German Question* itself has given the unpredictable a semblance of the expected. The accepted truth is that the only thing predictable about Germany is its unpredictability. Germany consistently confounds us, rendering incontrovertible theories irrelevant on a regular basis.

German history divides into neat periods (Bismarckian, Wilhelmine, Weimar, Nazi, Bundesrepublik), but German historians have, since the nineteenth century, traditionally encompassed great historical sweeps in an effort to find coherence where little exists.[3] They have come to rely on the German Question as a term to capture the uneven, quixotic disjunctures of German history. *Der Sonderweg* and *die Wende* signify the end of one episode and the beginning of another—distinguishing watersheds of change from periods of continuity.

These notions are tacked together by the amorphous German Question, which has now endured for over a century. The Question has changed in substance, but it is the stitching that holds together the quilt of German history.[4] Yet its forms tempt us to adopt an exaggerated reliance on inappropriate, simplifying generalizations. We describe the context to identify both the similarities and the distinct features of the present situation, and we focus on three issues in the remainder of this chapter. First, we sketch the German Question's symbolic representation to Germany and its neighbors; second, we turn to its successive manifestations over the course of the century; and last, we map the memories of the Federal Republic to illustrate how the various permutations of the German Question—different expressions of German identity—coexist in the collective consciousness of today's Deutschland.

The Symbolic Importance of the German Question

When the Danes voted on the Maastricht referendum, a twofold trauma affected their decision; the German occupation of Denmark in 1940, and the memory of 1864, when Prussians and Austrians (in the name of the German Federation) stripped Denmark of the duchies of Schleswig, Holstein and Lauenburg. Only on the second vote did the Danes choose to overcome the significance of the past and vote, as one Dane suggested, with their brains and not their hearts.[5] This case illustrates both the importance of symbolism and collective memory as determinants of current policy, and the ultimate limits of that symbolism for policy.

Both brains (interest) and hearts (collective memory) are essential components in the formulation of any policy. For most Europeans both components have a very high valence in their relations with Germany. Germany matters to them, in areas pertaining to interest, much more than any other country in Europe, arguably in the world. Yet overwhelmingly influenced by the horrors of World War II, the Europeans' collective memories are more pronounced about the Germans than about virtually anybody else. Germany's actions therefore have a particular immediacy for most Europeans. Marked by a tension between collective memory and interest (another Dane characterized the choice as between "hearts and wallets"), Germany's actions are subject to unusual scrutiny.

Americans too have symbols to which they constantly refer, from Christopher Columbus to the Stars and Stripes—things that define us collectively as Americans. The War of Independence, the Civil War, Pearl Harbor—all provide constantly invoked analogies for contemporary events. Such symbols represent values like democracy and freedom for which Americans proclaim an enduring passion; and they comprise institutions like the Constitution, the Congress, the presidency, and the judiciary—the system of checks and balances which Americans hold sacred, despite their unrelenting criticism of those who occupy the offices.

Through constant restatement, embedded deeply in the consciousness of Americans, these symbols have a special role. They are part of the process of nation building, the development of an agreed identity. Collectively, they contribute to how ideas are collectively formed.

The meaning of particular symbols changes over time. For example, the United States fought extensive wars in seizing land from Mexico but has since enjoyed peaceable relations with its neighbors. Americans see this as evidence of their own benign nature and the beneficial consequences of having the United States as a neighbor. Canadians and Mexicans may recall earlier conflicts and will point out that their behavior is heavily influenced by America. Furthermore, they add, some unintended consequences of American behavior can be highly detrimental to their economic and cultural welfare. U.S. citizens would generally profess no interest in "culturally dominating" their Canadian counterparts. But Canadian concerns about cultural sovereignty are nonetheless genuine and important.

To these neighbors, America is an imposing giant whose policies often limit, if not dictate, their choices. A prime example is furnished by Canadian responses to American pursuit of the North American Free Trade Agreement (NAFTA). Many Canadians suggested that the one option worse than Canadian membership of the free trade zone was Canadian nonmembership. The Canadians were left with a disquieting choice: lose jobs to Mexico if they did join, or lose access to the American market if they did not. (In 1995, Canada seemed to be the biggest winner among the three NAFTA participants, far surpassing the United States and Mexico in benefits derived. However, this in no way mitigates Canada's initial anxieties, which had less to do with actual outcomes than with the awareness of having to make a constrained decision.)

Just as the United States is an imposing presence in North America, so is Germany in Europe. Much of modern European history—conventionally dated from 1815, the end of the Napoleonic Wars—has been heavily influenced by Germany. But here the analogy with the United States ends, because Germany's neighbors have not been able to assume that Germany was not directly hostile to their interests. Even the most ardent of Canadian and Mexican nationalists have focused on the harsh but unintended consequences of American behavior. Germany's neighbors have harbored an assumption of German ill-intent, believing that the primary German aim was to dominate Europe both militarily and economically. Only since the creation of the Bonn Republic have other countries even contemplated that Germany's intentions might be anything but malign.

Germany has shaped the alternatives for European governments, whether Britain's nineteenth-century decision to maintain huge naval forces in order to balance German power; France's early twentieth-century policies maintaining a large land-based army to counter the (justified) fear of German aggression; Stalin's rapid industrialization drive to cope with the growing Nazi threat; or the postwar decision of many countries to join the European Community and NATO in order to contain Germany. This list is not exhaustive; these are simply some of the most notable examples of military or economic policies heavily influenced by considerations about the Germans.[6]

Among many neighbors, Germany's image not long ago was associated with Otto von Bismarck's dueling cudgels, the dreadnaught and the pointed helmets of the kaiser's army, the Nazi swastika, the concentration camps, and a menacing (if admired) degree of industrial prowess. Most of these symbols were seen as intimidating if not outrightly belligerent.

These stereotypes of enmity and the jingoistic ardor they encourage still emerge on rare occasions when the genteel art of diplomacy becomes a bit too strident. During the European Community's 1991 debate on recognition of Croatia, for instance, several British newspapers as well as some politicians referred to the Germans as the "over-mighty Huns."[7] As national pride becomes over-enthusiastic and jingoism develops, whether in soccer or politics, stereotypes come to the fore. A country as economically powerful and historically imposing as Germany demands the attention of its (mostly smaller) neighbors.

Yet while the collective memory of past German aggression exists, so does a contemporary acceptance of the Germans that belies this negative image. The defeat of National Socialism, the Allied Occupation, and the advent of the Bonn Republic led to a stark change in German foreign policy—and with it, over time, a greater acceptance of the Germans as benign members of the international community of nations.

Initial reticence to involve itself in grand diplomacy reinforced the Bundesrepublik's postwar image as an economic giant but a political dwarf, a less hostile country and an economic powerhouse. Indeed, Europe's citizens as a whole have been more sanguine than many political elites about Germany's change of character. Most Europeans have been willing to give the new Germany the benefit of the doubt in the context of unification, despite continued reservations regarding Germany's intentions.

Lingering apprehensions, however, do survive, and not just among Germany's neighbors. Identification with Europe, though growing, has not rendered national sentiments moot. Germany's own citizens have, for example, articulated greater reticence about integrating themselves into a broader Europe than their leaders have exhibited. Public dismay greeted the proposed replacement of the Deutsche Mark, Germany's beloved symbol of economic strength and stability, with a new European currency, the Euro. By October 1992, an Allensbach Institute public opinion poll revealed, a slender 39 percent of Germans supported the Maastricht agreement (which was, according to critics, created in Germany's image).[8] However, the name for the new European currency, the Euro, agreed to in Madrid in 1995, was the idea of Theo Waigel, Germany's finance minister.

Formulations of the German Question

If symbols matter, then none is more powerful for Europeans than those engendered by their understanding of the German Question. We briefly chronicle some historical developments that have contributed to a sense of unease about Germany. These developments and the consequential problems constitute elements of the German Question or—more tellingly, in the French variant—*Les incertitudes allemandes*.

Prussia: Nation-building through conquest.

The German Question often refers to the issue of how Germany's neighbors can contain Germany's prowess. Even before unification in 1871, the German principalities and states were important in defining the military balance and economic structure of Europe. Central to Germany's militaristic image was the gradual growth of Prussia.[9] Following victory over a much larger and wealthier Austria in the Seven Years War (1756–1763), Prussia began a century of successful military campaigns and diplomatic gambits that were eventually rewarded with unquestioned leadership in the German Federation. Emerging from the Napoleonic Wars as one of continental Europe's three conservative powers (the others being Austria and Russia), Prussia became an ardent opponent of democratic impulses throughout the nineteenth century. With a proclivity toward authoritarian government coupled with impressive military prowess, Prussia became known as 'the Sparta of the North."

After defeating Denmark in 1864, Prussia turned on its erstwhile rival Austria in 1866 to determine leadership of the impending all-German state. Prussia's victory presaged the formation of the German Reich (excluding Austria) under its leadership, a process interrupted only by victory over France in the War of 1870/71. United under the aegis of one of its most militaristic states, Germany took on the image of a bellicose and authoritarian nation.

The stereotype of a diligent but warring people was reinforced by two factors. The first was the tremendously rapid growth in German industrial power during the nineteenth century. The second was a succession of turn-of-the-century policies that were clearly imperialistic in intent. These policies were based on the aggressive ideology of *Weltpolitik*, a particularly predatory form of politics designed to compensate for Germany's belated role as an imperialist power.

The relationship between economic modernization and liberal democracy was apparently unresolved. So was the tension between state and nationbuilding, which was to remain a source of much trouble until 1945. The new unified Germany remained under Prussian control, or more precisely under the control of the aristocratic, conservative, antiliberal, statist, and antisemitic agrarian Junker class that controlled Prussia. The distribution of political power in Bismarckian Germany is best captured in Volker Berghahn's statement that "Prussia and the German Empire as a whole was, in effect, ruled by an elite, led by the crown and a 'strategic clique,' whose social and economic power base was the German countryside."[10] The Junkers successfully diverted reformist impulses among the masses into an enthusiasm for foreign conquest, empire, and greater international prestige.[11]

But the effectiveness of the Junkers' strategy in Bismarckian, and then in Wilhelmine and Nazi, Germany, brings us back to the first issue contemplated by the German Question: How, or perhaps why, was Germany able to develop economically without adopting the essential ingredients of a liberal democracy? How could it develop economically but not politically? After all, the liberal theory of modernization assumes that capitalism and democracy are intrinsically related.

The pattern of German development, so different from that of the United States and Britain, defies these expectations. Instead, a large, industrially developed country emerged to menace Europe in part, at least, by dint of having failed to develop a liberal democratic polity.

German culpability for World War I.
The outbreak of war in 1914 resulted in unparalleled horror and suffering in Europe. The victors showed only a limited degree of mercy, imposing retribution in the form of crippling reparations. Some Germans subsequently asked whether they were really culpable as the initiators of war.[12] They (and others) also asked *why* the Germans chose to pursue policies that led to war.

Conservatives fused principles derived from Hegel and von Ranke to emphasize the preeminence of the autonomous, deified state as the synthesis of *Macht* and *Geist*, power and spirit. The *Machtstaat* represented the divine expression of the political spirit of its populace, and its foremost purpose was to survive in an amoral, anarchic, international environment. Unable to impose international law, states maximized their power, and war was the natural outcome of the struggle between states. By being strong, Germany could therefore ensure its survival—denying other states the opportunity to attack it. This approach would supposedly reduce international conflict.[13]

Consistent with this argument, the parochial Junker ideology of *Weltpolitik* justified German expansion as a means of securing national survival through its establishment among the great powers. The Germans could use deterrence to "command the peace."[14] Such an approach rejected the notion that the outbreak of World War I was a consequence of Germany's internal social structure.[15] It legitimated the maximizing of German power through aggressive foreign policy. Security lay in foreign expansion, specifically the defeat of France; the foundation of a Central European federation under German leadership; and the development of Germany as a world power through the acquisition of new colonies.[16] This approach vindicated expansionist Wilhelmine foreign policies in the prewar period and defused postwar accusations of German culpability for 1914. Like other states, Germany had simply pursued foreign policies consistent with its national interest. Miscalculation and conflicting interests combined to spark a war; lack of communication and the failure of leadership explained Germany's defeat.[17]

An alternative response accepted German culpability and concentrated on why the Germans had started the war. Countering the conservative position this view stressed what Eckart Kehr termed the "primacy of internal policy" rather than of foreign policy.[18] The war was a product not of the strictures of the international system but of Germany's internal structure. Various historians and political scientists focused on Germany's class structure, notably the composition and attitudes of its conservative political elites.[19] Largely agnostic on German reparations, this group of scholars explained Germany's bellicosity as a consequence of Germany's failure to establish a liberal democracy prior to 1914.[20]

The collapse of democracy in Germany and the Nazi seizure of power.
The Weimar Constitution was arguably the most democratic constitution written anywhere. The collapse of the Weimar Republic and the Nazi seizure of power was so significant that scholars have debated the causes for over six decades. Indeed, it can be justifiably claimed that the German surrender of liberal democracy to the horrors of National Socialism was the central question in comparative politics in the early postwar period.[21]

Reactions again focused on Germany's economic and political elites. Alexander Gerschenkron stressed the antidemocratic, antiliberal tendencies of the Junker class and its willingness to forge an alliance with other antidemocratic classes. Their strength contrasted with the political weakness of the German industrialists and middle classes who had ceded political power in exchange for economic power. David Abraham argued just the opposite, that major German industrialists were active catalysts for the downfall of democracy.[22]

Other arguments linked the downfall of democracy to the effects of delayed national unification and delayed industrialization—the confluence of factors that Hans-Ulrich Wehler referred to as "social imperialism."[23] But no argument seemed to address satisfactorily the downfall of Weimar. Despite the republic's obvious frailties and the global economic crisis that precipitated its downfall, scholars continue to debate why this advanced industrial state fell victim to that most brutal expression of fascism known as National Socialism.

Why Auschwitz?
Of all manifestations of the German Question, this formulation is at once the most gruesome and the least explicable. How a country could pursue genocide—and then how a country collectively lives with the memory of genocide—has dominated fields of study from political science to psychology.[24] Ultimately, we believe, the enormity of this event will always elude answers.

The conception, construction, and implementation of genocide against Jews, homosexuals, the physically challenged, and other groups remains, in many minds, a unique act in modern European history—more perhaps by virtue of its systematic, comprehensive intent and its design as state policy than by the brutality of its implementation, though in the singularly heinous treatment of Jews, the Germans' actions and policies featured a level of brutality unparalleled in Europe. Auschwitz remains the most elusive question to answer, and so, perhaps, still exerts the strongest influence on the contemporary behavior of Germans—and on the attitudes of others toward them. It is far and away the most continuously horrid component in the ample cluster of destructive collective memories of the twentieth century.

Economic giant and political dwarf?
After two world wars, the German Question appeared to be resolved by occupation and division of the country in 1945. Subsequent Allied attempts to domesticate Germany, turning it into a pacified (though certainly not pacifist)

country, followed to rid Europe of this menace. The process proceeded through the introduction of a democratic constitution and values in the western portion of the country, the stationing of superpower troops on both sides of the border, and West Germany's integration into Europe's broader economy through the EEC. External intervention, extensive domestic socialization, and international integration addressed the security threat and so dispelled any concerns among Germany's neighbors—although the deployment of large armies on both sides of the Berlin Wall complicated this effort.

Indeed, the combination worked so well that the Federal Republic focused on its own economic development rather than on the broader military and political considerations of a superpower. West Germany prospered. Bonn's business elites became international in outlook and education, learned to support the republic's democratic order, and entered into intricate corporatist arrangements with labor as a fully accepted junior partner in Modell Deutschland's quest to become export champions of the world—a goal attained by 1988.

Yet this answer to the German Question created a new enigma. How can a country that was truly an economic superpower remain so politically muted? The answer is that the combination was often tense: the West Germans strained over and debated the contours of their European and global role.

Generally successful in containing themselves, successive West German governments did nevertheless pursue assertive foreign policy positions. Two major issues were intrinsic to their identity and so could not be avoided. The first emerged in the 1950s: reunification. While successive East German governments rejected reunification, the West Germans actively sought it and pressured successive American administrations to express support for the idea.[25]

The second issue emerged in the 1970s: German relations with the Eastern bloc, expressed through the policies of *Osthandel* and *Ostpolitik* (respectively, economic and political policy toward the East). The United States was initially reluctant to support these initiatives, being especially critical of the construction of a gas pipeline between West Germany and the Soviet Union.[26] But Washington, for its own reasons, overcame this reluctance and became an advocate of these policies. Détente constituted a way to tie the Soviets into a dependent relationship with the West and thus to reduce the chances of war.

Although Germany's international involvement was generally confined to diplomatic maneuverings within international organizations, with these two notable exceptions, the pattern of its economic development provoked continuous debate. Modell Deutschland developed a Fordist combination with three elements. First, in a corporatist institutional structure, powerful representative unions negotiated national agreements on a cooperative basis with conciliatory industrialists. Labor was thus well rewarded despite the occasional need for wage restraint. Second, a broad-based and well-financed social welfare system provided comprehensive social benefits to those in need. And third, underpinning this system of wages and benefits, industrial mass production was supported by high-skilled labor to produce high value-added products—such as expensive, high-quality consumer durables and capital tools. This combination became the envy of the industrialized world. Germany appeared to be one of very few advanced industrial states able to weather the economic storms and produce consistent wealth for its citizenry.

For many, the question thus changed in tone. Few considered German military containment an issue, for West Germany was now by consensus a Western country with an enlightened, liberal democratic culture. Indeed, the question became how to emulate the German combination of economic prosperity and peaceful relations abroad.

A new German hegemony?

To call 1989 an *annus mirabilis* might well be an understatement. That year was one of those rare turning points which have altered the course of global history. If a revolution is a fundamental reorganization of existing power relations in state and society, a change in elites, a complete redefinition of what constitutes the private and public, and the introduction of a new economic order, then events in Hungary, Czechoslovakia, Poland, the German Democratic Republic—to a lesser extent Romania and Bulgaria, and somewhat later the Soviet Union— qualify as quintessentially revolutionary. With the exception of Romania—and, of course, the post-Yugoslav wars—they occurred without extensive violence, further enhancing their importance.

The ramifications of the revolutions of 1989 went well beyond their domestic confines and profoundly affected the international order. They signaled the demise of the world system established at Yalta and Potsdam in 1945. Globally, the Soviet Union (then Russia) ceased to be America's equal as a superpower. Yet, instead of returning to *pax americana* of the immediate postwar era, when the United States was the unchallenged power in the world, we seem to be drifting toward an age of multipolarity where—at least in economics, science and technology—Europe and Japan are increasingly becoming America's equals.[27]

The events of 1989 restored Europe to its pre-1945 configuration by allowing a long-forgotten Eastern Europe to join its partners in the West. Most certainly 1989 can claim to be Germany's year. After the fall of the Berlin Wall on November 9, it was only a matter of time before the two Germanys would become one. The unification of the two Germanies and the two Berlins on October 3, 1990, signified the end of two Europes—at least in the Cold War sense. The subsequent widening of the EU has largely institutionalized this return to a single Europe.

Yet these revolutionary changes did not meet with universal acclaim. German unification resulted in a phenomenon rare for scholars: simple declaratory statements that reflected their individual feelings. Most either embraced the event, as a symbol of the demise of the Cold War and the extension of democratic values, or they expressed anguish at the prospects for Europe's economic and political future.

Certainly, the crumbling of the Berlin Wall signaled a new stage, and thus a

new formulation, of the German Question. It added yet another compelling ingredient to the debate in Europe and the United States regarding Germany's
role in a changing environment. *Time, Newsweek, U.S. News and World Report*,
and the *Economist*—to mention but a few English-language publications—ran
cover stories on the changed role of a united Germany in a Europe also scheduled
to be united. After the border opened between East and West Germany, academic
experts of all hues weighed in on the op-ed pages of leading newspapers, opining
about Germany's new position with uncharacteristic candor.

The events of 1989 revealed that traditional forms of the German Question
had been not eradicated but merely suppressed. Once again, the question concerned the role of a unified Germany in Europe. Some Europeans fear German
domination, although few seriously suggest that German power will spread
through force of arms. Others denied that there had been a return to the traditional form of the German Question.[28]

Debate within Germany reflected such concerns. Like their European counterparts, Germans focused their opinions about the present through the lenses
of collective memories. But, as we have noted, collective memory bears an orthogonal relationship to history and is always contested. While not perfectly sym-
metrical with the stages or forms of the German question we have just outlined,
the existing memory maps among Germans mirror many of the fears and concerns generated by successive stages of the German question. The Federal Republic, as Klaus Kinkel suggested in words that preface this book, cannot escape
its past.

Germany's Postwar Memory Map

All societies have problems in reconciling events of the past with the political
realities of the present. Few if any societies experience this task as severely as
does Germany. After all, Germany is the only country in Europe which, in the
course of this century, has experienced an authoritarian monarchy; a failed liberal
democracy; a murderous, predatory fascism in the guise of National Socialism;
a division for nearly half a century into a stable and prosperous liberal democracy
and a politically brutal and economically incompetent Stalinist communist regime; and unification leading to immensely successful continuity of the pre-1989
success story yet also new strains as a consequence. Germany has been a
microcosm of the political developments (as well as tragedies) of the twentieth
century. In no other European country does the memory map exhibit the qualitative complexity and controversial diversity that it does in Germany. Germany's
importance in Europe makes this memory map of more than mere academic
interest to Germans and Europeans.

We distinguish several memory clusters, "generations," in the current German
polity. Not all memories cluster around negative experiences; not all feature vic-

timization and victimhood. In particular, those memories and values which we attribute to the Bundesrepublik are positive in nature, at least for the time being. We argue emphatically that the institutions of the Bundesrepublik transformed society and thus created values that have entered the collective memory of the current German polity. Institutions are constitutive of social practices and ultimately of cultural norms and values. The Bundesrepublik is a prime example of the maxim that "getting the institutions right" is essential to social and cultural transformation. Dominant classes create dominant memories, and the same pertains to institutions. Indeed, institutions fine tune an array of values and memories on behalf of—if not at the behest of—dominant classes. In our opinion, complementarity between classes and institutions is important: a concentration on institutions alone can yield a formal interpretation of power which misses crucial subtleties and historical continuities. Thus, for many, the Bundesrepublik is a new beginning by virtue of the institutional novelties that undoubtedly characterized the so-called *Stunde Null* (Zero Hour).[29] This is not incorrect though incomplete, for "simple" institutionalism omits analysis of classes (i.e., of social actors) and so fails to give agency its due. We need agency to contextualize institutions.

What are the critical memory moments or memory junctures of recent German history? We designate five events: 1945, which featured the defeat (*not* the collapse) of the Third Reich; 1949, which saw the foundation of the two republics; 1968, which witnessed one of the most powerful generational challenges with the most lasting legacy anywhere in the advanced capitalist world; 1985, which marked the events at Bitburg, the first concerted attempt to revive a dormant and partially illegitimate collective memory; and 1989, the system-shattering events that resulted in the collapse of the Berlin Wall and led to unification in October 1990. None of these junctures altered the content of the existing memory map. But each of them created new memory alignments, new coalitions, new configurations.

The Weimar cluster.
A strong collective memory in Germany focused on avoiding the mistakes of the Weimar Republic which in turn helped Hitler attain power. Whether it is the Federal Republic's industrial relations system and the importance of its unions or management's moderation in seeing labor as a junior partner in running the economy, not as a deadly rival, the memory of Weimar still informs the Federal Republic's public discourse. The memory is nowhere more pronounced than in the German sensitivity regarding inflation. As a result, the Bundesbank enjoys legitimacy as Germany's most reliable institution, empowered to fight inflation with all possible means. Its role as "inflation slayer" has rendered the institution a virtually untouchable and perhaps even beloved symbol of the Federal Republic. More generally, Weimar lives as a huge warning system, a larger-than-life caveat that unbridled social conflict, poor economic performance, and irresponsible po-

litical posturing can threaten terrible trouble. Bonn derived immense legitimacy by not being Weimar, and whatever the Berlin Republic becomes, most Germans do not want it to be anything like Weimar.

The Nazi cluster.
The collective memory of Nazism is so overwhelming, so ubiquitous, virtually no aspect of public life is not in some manner affected by its continued presence. Indeed this collective memory crowds out any and all others in the way Germans are viewed by the world and themselves; shapes how they construct their public choices both at home and abroad; and molds the manner in which they implement choices once they have been made. We distinguish four interrelated facets in this complex, continuously present.

   a) Germans as victims of National Socialism. Both East and West Germans portrayed themselves (though not each other) as victims of National Socialism. East German victimization at the hands of fascism reached such mythic dimensions in the East German *conscience collective* that DDR schoolchildren sang the praises of Germany's "progressive forces" who, together with the Red Army, liberated Germany from fascism.[30] The East Germans were victimized by capitalism, of which National Socialism was merely a particularly heinous manifestation. The West Germans viewed National Socialism as an evil perpetrated by a handful of ruthless men who somehow bamboozled the German nation to follow them on a path of adventure and conquest, ending in destruction and political emasculation. If anything this collective memory of Germans as victims of National Socialism has received additional support from the Bitburg events, the fiftieth-anniversary celebrations of D-Day in June 1994, and the worldwide commemoration of the end of World War II in August 1995.

   b) Germans as perpetrators of National Socialism. Public opinion polls corroborate the presence of this collective memory. With the passage of time, more Germans came to view National Socialism as a criminal regime in which Germans participated, with at least tacit complicity if not outright enthusiasm. In the 1950s there developed what Theodor Adorno termed an atmosphere of "cold and empty forgetting"; but things began to change with the Auschwitz trial in 1963, continued with the parliamentary debates over the expiration of the statutes of limitation for genocide in the late 1960s and late 1970s, supported by the airing of the television series *Holocaust* in 1979, and culminated in Richard von Weizsücker's speech to the Bundestag on May 8, 1985, commemorating the fortieth anniversary of the end of World War II. The popular view developed that the Germans had something to do with National Socialism's crimes; that those crimes were not only the machinations of an evil coterie of thugs, or of capitalist rule, but resulted from developments in which the German people were active participants instead of passive bystanders or innocent victims. This collective memory identifies with National Socialism's victims, both domestically and abroad. The people for whom this collective memory remains salient are the ones who join

Aktion Sühnezeichen Friedensdienst (Sign of repentance/Service for peace) and perform their national service where Nazis behaved with special cruelty; they take field trips to Auschwitz; visit Israeli kibbutzim; enjoy the sound of klezmer music; learn Yiddish; fight racism; and come to the aid of persecuted foreigners. In short, they are the thousands of Germans who exist in every metropolis and village, and who continue to speak out. In many ways, the active presence of this collective memory rejects the possibility that a nightmare similar to National Socialism might recur in contemporary Germany.

c) Germans indifferent to National Socialism. There also exists a collective amnesia. We might call it an actively sought nonmemory, a collective effort to forget the past. This amnesia does not deny the Nazi regime's atrocities or the Germans' involvement, but prefers to remain silent and "let byegones be byegones." This is the collective memory of the *Schlußstrich* (endpoint of history).

d) Germans approving of National Socialism. Numerically the smallest of our four memory clusters, Germans who approve cannot be dismissed as completely insignificant. This collective memory appears in various guises, ranging from the widely held view that National Socialism was basically a fine idea but poorly implemented to the many Holocaust denials that have enjoyed growing popularity. Revisionist historians in the 1980s attempted to legitimate this response.[31]

Each of these four facets of the Nazi cluster closely follows the political allegiances and sympathies of the German population. Facet (b) is prevalent among adherents of social democracy and various other manifestations of Germany's political Left; the collective memories of Germans as victims of Nazism, of amnesia and of approval, have always been more at home on the right of the German political spectrum. Like all collective memories, these too have consistently furnished important ammunition for contemporary political battles.

The Bundesrepublik cluster.
In this area we also distinguish several facets. In a context as temporally immediate as the Federal Republic, collective memory blurs with values and norms. Memories and experiences are simply too close to allow a meaningful distinction to be drawn. Even though the Bundesrepublik is almost the present, however, its inhabitants have formed certain opinions about it, share certain values with it, and express feelings toward it which are in part shaped by memories. The Bundesrepublik, too, has developed its myths and collective memories.

a) The Bundesrepublik as an economic success: the saving and investment story. Beginning with the reconstruction period of the late 1940s and early 1950s, there developed the collective memory of hard-working Germans, the *Trümmerfrauen* who combed the bombed ruins, scrimped and saved, eventually beginning the Federal Republic's successful economic recovery. This collective memory features the "economic miracle" and proclaims that no adversity, regardless of magnitude, could stop the Germans from becoming the economic envy of the world. It portrays the German as hard worker, as ascetic, as profoundly apolitical, as private. It focuses on deprivation, saving, frugality, and investment—a sort of collective memory of the Protestant ethic.

b) The Bundesrepublik as an economic success: the consumption story. By the late 1950s, there developed a *Wohlstandsideologie* (ideology of affluence), a memory of abundance and comfort based on unprecedented levels of consumption. The Bundesrepublik became identified with six weeks of paid vacation; shops in even the smallest German towns filled with exotic fruits, state-of-the-art electronic gadgetry, and the latest in international fashion; Germans traveling the world in record numbers (Germans have consistently been the world champions in international tourism); the obligatory second car; a nice small house or a condominium in a squeaky-clean neighborhood; no material wants unfulfilled. This collective memory portrays the Federal Republic as secure provider of material abundance, as procurer of the "good life."

c) The Bundesrepublik as Germany's most successful democracy. Economic success, particularly in a troubled country with a weak polity, possesses a great potential for democratizing and legitimating what was previously a barely legitimate political order.[32] The Bundesrepublik is a perfect case in point. Hardly accepted by the population in the late 1940s and much of the 1950s, the Bundesrepublik was a rump Germany occupied by the victorious (and much disliked) Allied powers. Germans did develop a substantial affection for these Allied forces, particularly the Americans, during the dark days of the Berlin blockade in the late 1940s. The German population also exhibited a certain tolerance for them simply because they were not Soviets. The Bundesrepublik, however, was hardly loved in the beginning. With the exception of a few members of the largely Catholic political elite, the citizens of the Federal Republic only tolerated this new political construct. They had little choice, so they made do with something which, whatever it was, was certainly *not* "that thing over there"—the much despised Eastern Zone, dominated by the hated Soviets. Thus developed one of the Bundesrepublik's most powerful pillars: its opposition to anything Soviet, its deeply ingrained anticommunism. With economic success, the West Germans gradually began to appreciate their non-Soviet construct. The Federal Republic's profound political legitimacy was built almost exclusively on the success of its economic power.

Constitutional patriotism, *Verfassungspatriotismus*, which by the 1970s had developed into a genuine political reality well beyond the narrow world of intellectuals such as Jürgen Habermas, had its origins not in the still elusive bourgeois revolution, nor in the particular affect that citizens conveyed toward the Basic Law, but in the Bundesrepublik's economic performance. Perhaps of greater importance than the economic miracle has been its unheralded political miracle: in the course of its nearly fifty-year existence, its institutions of liberal democracy, constitutionalism, and *Rechtsstaatlichkeit* (liberal democratic mores) have become acceptable to a large majority of Germans. Only through this lengthy process of successful democratization propelled by a powerful economy are Germans now developing a genuine, proud collective memory of the Bundesrepublik.

The affect expressed by Germans vis-à-vis the Bundesrepublik continues to be tainted by the immense shadows of the Nazi clusters—and thus cannot express itself with unbridled emotions resembling those of the French toward France, of the Americans toward the United States. But a strong republican consciousness is proud of the Federal Republic because of its deep anchoring in the good liberal values of the West: republicanism, constitutionalism, parliamentarism, free speech, and an independent judiciary, to name a few key items. This collective memory celebrates Germany as a thoroughly Westernized society whose values convey the triumph of Western liberalism over all previous German arrangements of illiberalism. Flag-waving remains largely confined to fans of the successful national soccer team, but pride in the Deutsche Mark has become a legitimate expression of affect for the Bundesrepublik. "D-mark waving" has become an unusual but telling manifestation of pride in the Bundesrepublik's economic prowess as well as its full integration into the world of western political values.

d) The Bundesrepublik as a powerful player. A related collective memory is rooted in the West as a community of power. It depends on the Bundesrepublik's being an integral, indeed indispensable, member of the North Atlantic Treaty Organization. The memory focuses on the struggles of the Cold War in which the Bundesrepublik developed into the bulwark of the West's determined defense against the communists. The major carriers of this memory are the Federal Republic's Atlanticists; institutions such as the venerable *Atlantikbrücke* (Atlantic Bridge, which fosters U.S.-German understanding); those few remaining policy makers who still feel indebted to the United States for rebuilding and protecting the western part of postwar Germany. This group's identity centers around the Federal Republic as an integral player of a common security alliance and a powerful defense community and is best personified by Michael Stürmer. To others the West constitutes the core values espoused by the French and American revolution, but to this collectivity the West means NATO. In this among other communities of collective memory, Helmut Kohl is firmly anchored.

e) The Bundesrepublik as the heart of Europe. The Bundesrepublik was active, indeed central, in all matters concerning the construction of a new Europe. Beginning with the grand old Catholic men—Konrad Adenauer, Charles de Gaulle, Robert Schumann, Jean Monnet, Alcide de Gasperi—formed by the collective memories of World War I, the Weimar experience and, of course, World War II, enthusiastic engagement on behalf of a new and integrated Europe attempted to eradicate anything which perhaps might lead again to something resembling National Socialism. "Europe" for Germans developed into a surrogate identity, replacing German nationalism. While it was unacceptable to express German nationalist sentiments, it was commendable to develop into an enthusiastic European. Germany, more than any of the other large European countries, always pursued an inclusionary strategy in Europe. Driven by economic and political interests, this *largesse* was also a consequence of deeply felt notions that any inclusionary politics would diminish the chance of new, terrible wars.

At the very core of this European identity lay a special relationship with France. It was fraught with symbolism at every corner: Mitterrand and Kohl holding hands at Verdun in 1984; the exclusion of the Germans from D-Day festivities in 1984 and 1994; the inclusion of German troops on the Champs-Elysées in the special ceremonies celebrating V-E Day in May 1995. Reconciliation with France has developed into a sacrosanct and politically unchallengeable tenet of the Bundesrepublik's collective identity.

f) The Bundesrepublik as gate to the east. The East remained anathema to the collective identity of the Bundesrepublik. It served as both lesson and deterrent, as everything the West could have become if not for the prudent leadership of the Federal Republic. Much of this changed in the mid-to-late 1960s. Acceptance of the East—culminating in the *Ostpolitik* and *Osthandel* of Willy Brandt and the social liberal coalition—established in a curious way the natural order of things for Germany, its bridging function between western and eastern Europe. This new collective memory began to distance a large minority of West Germans from the iron-clad Westernism that defined the Federal Republic's dominant postwar discourse. Coupled with an increasing criticism of and distancing from the United States, Germany's affinities with eastern and central Europe developed into a viable political identity.

Although far less pronounced than in the Nazi cluster, the Bundesrepublik cluster also features variants of victimization. One frequently encounters the argument that the Bundesrepublik's Westernization was, in fact, performed against the will of the Germans, or that the Germans would not have opted for such a course had they been totally free to choose. Even the collective memory of economic success emphasizes victims in the so-called two-thirds society: success favored only two-thirds of the populace, who enriched themselves at the expense of the lower one-third, the forgotten Germans, the losers of Modell Deutschland.[33]

The GDR cluster.

Nowhere is victimization more central than in a completely new collective memory that entered the political discourse after 1989: that of the GDR. Two dimensions of victimization define competing political identities that vie for public recognition, sometimes with great acerbity. The first stresses the victimization of thousands, perhaps millions, of East Germans at the hands of a brutal regime that never enjoyed the support of its subjugated population. In almost complete contrast, and to the surprise of many, a second, and politically more potent collective memory features the victimization of virtually all East Germans at the hands of the allegedly callous, rapacious West Germans. In this GDR nostalgia, a powerful collective memory accords the GDR posthumous legitimacy that the regime did not come close to attaining during its forty years.

In contemporary Germany we are witnessing a memory war, pitting all five memory clusters (and their numerous variants) against one another in fascinating competition. This phenomenon is accompanied by newly constituted, precarious coalitions that feature the strangest of bedfellows. The eventual outcome is anybody's guess. At this moment we can observe only the deconstruction of existing collective memories; we are still far from the establishment of a permanent memory map in which one cluster of memories will enjoy a dominant position. Currently, we are witnessing an equation of Nazi Germany with the German Democratic Republic which enjoys much support among right-wing Germans. In one of the most cynical moves in recent German history, some West German Rightists want to punish the East German perpetrators for crimes lest they, too, are absolved of their heinous acts—as were thousands of top Nazi officials during the Bundesrepublik's establishment in the late 1940s and early 1950s.

This memory clash was visible in the elaborate festivities surrounding German commemoration of the fiftieth anniversary of V-E Day. In Chancellor Kohl's official statement one could easily detect a clash among the Nazi cluster, the Bundesrepublik cluster, and the GDR cluster. More important, one could also discern intracluster discrepancies. For example, Kohl mentioned the victims of National Socialism while also characterizing the Germans as victims of the war, especially at the hands of communism. His speech all but equated these two victimizations. Largely as a consequence of the Bundesrepublik's success, V-E Day had become for many Germans a day of liberation from Nazi dictatorship. This memory was in stark contrast to the historical reality of V-E Day 1945, which most Germans viewed as a day of shame, defeat, and occupation by two hated enemies—one of which, however, was preferable because its soldiers dispensed chewing gum, cigarettes, and chocolate instead of revenge.[34] It took the collective memory of the Bundesrepublik to arrive at two developments in the collective memory of many contemporary Germans: first, being able to admit that National Socialism, with very minor exceptions, enjoyed the unequivocal support of the vast majority of Germans; and second, that fifty years of hindsight, buttressed by the collective identity of a successful Bundesrepublik, developed in the Germans a collective memory that was nothing short of a distortion of history. Here one can gauge the Federal Republic's immense success in creating a new way of thinking *and* feeling.

Such distortions have conspired to generate a sense of envelopement among Germans; of Germany as best when focused on domestic matters, timidly venturing out into international politics as a good European. Leadership is equated with aggressiveness and power, and so leadership is a role that Germans are reluctant to assume.

Collective memories are pluralistic and often clash; they are neither uniform nor generally complementary. The collective memories of pre- and post-Auschwitz (and even of a few who relish the memory of National Socialism) compete for dominance in the psyche of the Federal Republic. That the past is far from resolved in Germany was again demonstrated by the immense discussion triggered by Daniel Jonah Goldhagen's *Hitler's Willing Executioners: Ordinary Germans and the Holocaust*. Even *before* it appeared in German, in August 1996, there was hardly a German periodical which did not carry lengthy pieces on Goldhagen, his book, its thesis, and their reception in the United States. Initially, reactions were mainly negative, harshly dismissive of Goldhagen and his work. But following the appearance of the book's German edition and Goldhagen's triumphant tour of Germany, the opinions of the German public—in notable contrast to that of the academic experts—switched in favor of Goldhagen and his views. It is very telling of the still "unmasterable" nature of the German past in the public discourse of the contemporary Federal Republic that one single academic book can cause such an extensive debate and such profound soul searching. Most Germans, regardless of their political preferences, thus conveyed the message that no moving Richard von Weizsäcker speech, no contrite Roman Herzog appeal to collective responsibility, has yet exculpated the Germans from their Nazi past.[35] But, while the status quo is not guaranteed to last, it does exist. The present, stable, and dominant consensus in Germany emphasizes a German culpability and responsibility for past actions. While acknowledging and occasionally celebrating the consumption and investment story of the Federal Republic, it remains fearful that foreign engagement may threaten Germany's prosperity and the foundations of German democracy. The wrong form of engagement may also cause unease among Germany's neighbors and partners.

These twin concerns congeal into an ideology of reluctance; one that fears for domestic prosperity and democracy when faced with an activist foreign policy and potential adverturism. Collective memory thus becomes the foundation for a debate about the trajectory of future German engagement. Which historic incarnation is the new Germany most likely to resemble? Is it to be Germany's dictatorial past or its democratic present?

CHAPTER TWO

Optimists and Pessimists

The division of Germany, although often pronounced unnatural, provided for a
good night's sleep during the past 40 years.
—Unnamed Dutchman, quoted in *NRC/Handelsblad*, December 27, 1989

The phenomenon, aftermath and likely consequences of German
unification kept observers and politicians busy since 1989. We divide reactions
to German unification and the new Germany's role into two categories. The first
is optimistic: basically, unification and Germany's new role are a boon to Germany, Europe, and the world. The second is pessimistic: a united Germany may
not actually repeat the mistakes of its past, but it will certainly prove to be a
problem. Both voices have, in fact, been responding, at least implicitly, to the
legacy of Auschwitz.

For the optimists, the collective memory of Auschwitz was so decisive in shaping the political culture of the Bonn Republic that it reliably inoculates the world
against renewed German arrogance of power. In the optimists' assessment, the
country has attained a perfect mixture, just the right amount of voice to be an
effective but not overbearing leader, just the right amount of loyalty to play on
the European team without surrendering its own autonomy. The exit option,
according to the optimists, has been exorcised once and for all. *Sonderwege* are
neither wanted nor feasible in today's Germany.

In contrast, the pessimists believe that the collective memory of Auschwitz has
had a completely different effect. Auschwitz, for the pessimists, has never been
exorcised. The Germans themselves would never have renounced Auschwitz had
Allied armies not forced them to confront their past. Because the Germans'
coming to terms with the past was involuntary, the pessimists believe that the
Bundesrepublik's values—albeit wonderful and commendable—still await their
true test. Once the shame of Auschwitz disappears, moreover, the collective
memory of National Socialism may become more positive. The pessimists fear
that Germany's voice could easily command the rest of Europe; they worry that
Germany's loyalty to the European Union and to the West might prove ephemeral, and that the Germans will uphold it only as long as it suits their interests.
Finally, the pessimists do not exclude the possibility of a German exit, though
such an exit is unlikely as long as Germany derives all it needs from current
arrangements.

The Optimists' View

Arguments stressing the benign effects of German unification reflect one of three key ingredients: functional, institutional, or sociological. In all three, the optimists find supporting evidence in Germany's postwar history. The Bundesrepublik's shining success exemplifies this view of Germany's future role in Europe. Optimists focus on three points:

1. Germany has been burned so badly by the mistakes of its history that it will never commit similar ones again. This notion assumes the acuity of collective memory will act as a continued deterrent.

2. Germany's interests are not served by upsetting comfortable European arrangements. This is an interest-centered argument.

3. Even if Germany is willing to use its power more freely, its power threatens nobody. This position contributes a power-centered approach to the optimists' overall view of Germany's role and position in Europe.

The functional analysis of Germany's presence in Europe has been popular among scholars studying the development of the European Union (EU). The argument focuses on the taming of German power and influence through Germany's involvement in international organizations such as the EU and NATO, the World Trade Organization (formerly GATT) and the United Nations.[1] The crux of the argument is that, in Stephen Kinzer's words, "Germany, once an aggressively nationalist country, [is] now more ready than any of its neighbors to surrender sovereignty to a strengthened [European] community."[2]

There are least two assumptions behind this approach. First, involvement in such institutions has bred interdependent rather than dominant relationships between Germany and its partners, and such relationships are likely to promote friendship rather than friction. This assumption lay behind the initial American promotion of French-German collaboration, back in the early 1950s.[3] Some observers identify this as part of America's postwar "double containment," aimed against Germany and the Soviet Union. Just as a policy of military containment successfully constrained Soviet aggression, proponents suggest, so it will continue to limit German imperialist ambitions.[4]

Second, states are interested in absolute rather than relative gains, and Germany's trading arrangements with its partners are positive-sum in effect—that is, they benefit both Germany and its partners.[5] Germany's involvement in organizations such as the EU will allow its economic strength to act as a locomotive for broader European development, as its foreign investment grows and it reciprocates in foreign trade. Hence, as Ronald Tiersky says, "France in the new Europe may well continue to be 'only' the second-ranking power. But France in the new Europe will be relatively stronger and more prosperous than it would have been over the long term in the old Europe."[6] As this claim suggests, successful German development can occur only within the context of European growth. Europe and Germany have two options: they can prosper together or fall apart.

This simultaneous liberation of and constraint on Germany through international institutions result, proponents claim, in a Germany tamed by international ties. Such constraints make war, with France for example, unthinkable.[7] Indeed, the prospects for further Franco-German cooperation appear good.

How did international organizations affect French and German policies, and their bilateral relationship, during the late 1980s? According to Tiersky, once François Mitterrand accepted the inevitability of German unification, the crucial point became

> to imbed German unification firmly in the Atlantic Alliance and the European integration process. Consequently, French policy firmly supported unified Germany's full membership in NATO. . . . To assuage a French concern that unification might lead German policy eastward and away from plans for EC monetary and political union, Kohl agreed with Mitterrand that German unification and further EC "deepening" must go together. The Germans, in turn, understood well that legitimacy for German unification required deeper EC integration, that German unification and the unification of Europe were two sides of the same coin.[8]

In the 1990s, even after the departure of Foreign Minister Hans-Dietrich Genscher, the German government has worked assiduously to remain a model European, mediating among contentious members, deepening and widening the community, playing the moderator and anchor in an increasingly turbulent sea.[9] To be sure, Germany suffered some setbacks but it remains embedded in a series of functional relations and so is prone to peace and cooperation. Optimists can point to the thorough Europeanization of Germany, which, beginning with Helmut Kohl at the very top and reaching deep into German public opinion, is a major element in the identity of the Federal Republic. Kohl's speech at the first congress of the reunited Christian Democratic Union reaffirmed that Germany is inextricably embedded in Europe: "For me German unity and European unity are two sides of the same coin . . . in truth we are German patriots and convinced Europeans . . . Europe is our future, Germany our fatherland."[10] Both Kohl and Genscher repeatedly emphasized in 1990 that any exit from the West's main institutions, NATO in particular, was out the question. To advocates of Germany's international bond, the news is unequivocally good: Germany's Europeanness and Western ties are so overwhelming that the country's leaders would likely have forgone unification in 1990 had the price been Germany's exit from the postwar compact.

The second, institutional argument, supporting a benign image of the effects of unification among certain Americans and Europeans, focuses on the postwar development of Germany's political system. Advocates point out the evident success of federalism and democratic values as the new Germany assimilates the old Federal Republic. They argue that the new Germany will be merely an institutional extension of the highly successful and well-adjusted Federal Republic. Unification thus bodes well for the continuation of a Germany both democratic in the domestic sphere and tamed in the international arena. Indeed, in this view it is the democratic nature of domestic reforms which will continue to temper German foreign policy. The Federal Republic's success has once and for all exorcised the demons of the *Sonderweg*. The Federal Republic's successes—the profoundly Western orientation of its elites, the commercialization of its culture, its decided republicanism, its constitutional as opposed to romantic or *voelkisch* (ethnic German) patriotism, in short its profound bourgeoisification—make analogies to Weimar unnecessarily alarmist. Accordingly, the new Germany can— indeed should—be divorced from the history of the predatory Germany of the 1870–1945 epoch. Germans today seek enjoyment from wealth not power.[11]

Evidence to support a claim of peaceful German behavior is twofold. The first hails from a general proposition: democracies like contemporary Germany do not fight wars against each other. Germany, as a fully established member of the club of liberal-democratic states, will not go to war against other liberal democracies; domestic arrangements and values would never permit it. The Bundesrepublik has eliminated the Clausewitzian paradigm as a legitimate component of German thinking: war is no longer the continuation of politics by other means.

A complementary point notes the disappearance of the Junker class from postwar Germany. The feudal landlords of Prussia were the major proponents of German imperialism. Fearing a loss of political control, they fermented expansionist, nationalist, antiliberal, and racist ideologies to deflect domestic discontent and ensure their own brutal hold on power. The activities of the Junker class, according to this position, thus formed the social and economic basis for German imperialism and led to two world wars.[12] But the Junker class was destroyed by World War II. Its devastation was a watershed in German development, profoundly altering the German propensity for war by removing perhaps the primary obstacle to institutional reform. With the Junkers gone and the Allies predisposed toward institutional change, the foundation was laid for a peaceful Bonn Republic—to be maintained in the reunited Germany.[13]

Both of these arguments share a benign view of the effects of German unification on the rest of Europe. They mainly differ in which element they stress. The institutional approach concentrates on internal constraints to German dominance, whereas the functional approach emphasizes external impediments. But both have an optimistic diagnosis of Germany's role in Europe.

The third argument concentrates on sociological and cultural elements within Germany, focusing on the evolution of both elites and masses. The central premise is an evolutionary perspective of "knowledge through learning." German elites, acutely aware of their responsibility for Germany's terrible past, stand vigil against the reemergence of militarist, antiliberal, xenophobic, and crypto-fascist tendencies in the new united Germany. German foreign policy, such optimists suggest, emphasizes humanitarian values and is conducted in a responsible manner. Any shift toward a "normalization" of German foreign policy would thus benefit Germany's neighbors, for it would create what Philip Gordon calls "a better and more reliable partner in its Atlantic and European alliances."[14]

Education, through schools and mass communication, now ensures a healthy ambivalence about German nationalism. Indeed, all opinion polls testing German reactions to unification conveyed a picture almost identical to those in the United States, Britain, France, and Italy. Those favoring this fortuitous event far outnumbered those who did not, but Germans exhibited no nationalist fervor in the process. Even at the very moment of unification, on October 3, 1990, there were no popular expressions of nationalism by the German population, rather the leisure-like enjoyments of a work-free day. These calm manifestations of a Westernized republican culture suggested that the dangers of renewed German nationalism are unlikely in the foreseeable future.

Many problems have since plagued the united Germany and clearly led to an indifference, even hostility, to German unification on the part of a substantial minority of Germans (both East and West). Unification as a moment for the revival of German nationalism has been all but discredited. The Bundesrepublik's educational system has proved effective in heightening awareness of German culpability for the Holocaust and, simultaneously, alienating Germans from the military and economic adventurism of their past. Far from the entrenched militarism of pre-1945, today's public opinion is informed by a deep skepticism about German adventures in foreign policy and ambivalent about Germany's position in Europe.

The underlying belief of this position, and indeed of the optimists' view in general, is epitomized by Tiersky's comment that

> old worries about Germany have not entirely dissipated but no one can believe that forty years of Federal Republic history have not created a modern Western political culture, including as in France and elsewhere, a too-often apolitical or apathetic youth, or that all the sturdy safeguards in the new German system are about to spring loose.[15]

In broad historical terms, the new German elites represent, for the optimists, the postwar triumph of the bourgeoisie. Victorious bourgeois values stress a cosmopolitan culture within a European economy in which Germany and its trading partners benefit from Germany's adherence to free trade.

It is important to establish that the primary motive for this cultural evolution is, in fact, economic self-interest. As a result of export orientation, Germany's new and thoroughly commercialized economic elites recognize the country's dependence on the willingness of foreigners to purchase German goods. These elites advocate policies that enhance free trade. The representatives of German business understand that such policies can be implemented only in an environment that adheres to the principles of reconciliation and mutual trust.

Perhaps the Federal Republic's greatest asset in the security of its democratization is the profound Westernization of its economic and business elite. Cosmopolitan and bourgeois, the Federal Republic's captains of industry are perhaps the most fundamental difference between the Weimar and the Bonn republics. In Weimar, the business class as a whole adhered to hypernationalism, was profoundly authoritarian, detested the republic's democratic institutions, and tried to cow labor. In marked contrast, the Bonn Republic's business elites have been internationalized in outlook and education, have accepted and supported the Republic's democratic order, and have entered intricate corporatist arrangements with labor in the widely praised Modell Deutschland.

The new Germany's elites have created a culture of commercialism which is congruent with the exigencies of a trading state or Handelsstaat. Ironically, the Germans have become the very "mercenary creatures" or Krämerseelen—one of the worst epithets once associated with allegedly venal England and the Jews— that they formerly despised. This development is now celebrated as a major component in Germany's triumphal embrace of democratic values and peaceful policies.

Two more optimistic interpretations deserve mention. The first pertains to Germany as a trading state, the second to that of a new civilian power. The trading state—in contrast to the Machtstaat, which is territorially rapacious, expansionist, nationalist, and in a sense provincial—is disinterested in power, if not downright antimilitarist, and profoundly international because its very essence is defined by trade and commerce.[16] The peaceful Handelsstaat requires an enlightened, international, and interdependent foreign and security policy.

The Handelsstaat is virtually embedded in an extensive web of international relations and international organizations. This interdependence renders national adventures all but impossible. Germany, so this view suggests, has become completely interdependent with the advanced industrial world, particularly with Europe. As a result, Germany cannot lead in any meaningful sense of conventional Machtpolitik, even if it so desired.[17] Moreover, German exit is not only anathema to the dominant postwar political class; it is structurally impossible.

Interdependent and pan-European arrangements fit Germany's needs very well. What makes them so attractive is that Germany's needs are more often than not completely congruent with those of other European countries. German power, though perhaps not completely innocuous, is most certainly benevolent in effect.

The concept of the Handelsstaat and the debate surrounding it in Germany are nothing new. At least since the publication of Johann Gottlieb Fichte's Der geschlossene Handelsstaat [The closed trading state] in the fall of 1800, the question how commerce and business might constitute a political order in relation to other collective identities has been prominent in German debates.[18] International embeddedness, according to this view, need not abrogate national interest and national power. Contemporary Germany is the center of a European core which defines the content, form, speed, and results of European integration.[19]

Fichte's book is transitional between his early rationalist phase and his late romantic-nationalist incarnation, so the book contains elements of both. It has a clearly positive assessment of the liberating aspects of commerce, but it also includes passages critical of commerce's destructive tendencies for traditions. Fichte's ambivalence has remained a mainstay of German debate to this day. The *Handelsstaat*'s allegedly negative aspects predominated in the discussion until 1945, its positive aspects emerging after 1945 and particularly among its advocates since 1989. Fichte understood that the *Handelsstaat* embodied a form of political domination which was, if anything, superior to other states in its projection of power.

Regarding Germany's identity as a new "civilian power," the comparison with Japan is enlightening. This characterization is by Hans Maull, one of the most eloquent exponents of this view:

> Even after unification, Germany will be anything but a reborn Bismarckian empire. It will be a democratic and federal state, economically integrated; solidly anchored in the European Community and preoccupied with internal and regional problems of reconstruction and development, to which traditional military power has no relevance whatsoever. The webs of interdependence tying Germany to its partners in Europe and across the Atlantic are much more varied and broad than those between Japan and the West—the importance of European integration can hardly be overestimated. . . . To expect a revival of traditional militarism in Germany or Japan at present requires a considerable leap of imagination; it is hard to construct plausible scenarios for such a return of history. Even if domestic developments were to evolve in this direction, however, it would be enormously difficult for either country to extricate itself from the complex web of integration to which they have allowed themselves to be bound and to develop their own, independent military capabilities. Such moves would also immediately trigger powerful reactions and no doubt involve very serious economic and foreign policy costs. In short, those fears simply seem unrealistic . . . Germany's new identity will have to be supranational and European.[20]

The optimists see a bright future. Germany's leadership of Europe is a cause for celebration. The EU is an institution of "pooled sovereignty," where no country is a clear and consistent leader. In some issue areas Germany will lead Europe and shape the visions of the future; in others it will follow. Above all, for the optimists, Germany's democratic institutions and Western culture, its continued emphasis on being a good European citizen, predestine it for solid but unobtrusive leadership of Europe. And even if Germany's domestic checks and balances were to fail, even if the country's collective memory about Auschwitz were to erode and be replaced by aggressiveness, the international web of institutions would not permit Germany to exit. Germany's taming is irreversible.

The Pessimists' View

The pessimists range from British Tory backbenchers and Euroskeptics to radical Marxists; from French, Polish, Czech, Dutch, Danish, and other European policy makers to a majority of German Left-wing intellectuals; from liberal American scholars to conservative politicians. It would be well-nigh impossible to give a comprehensive account of their suspicions and worries, so we discuss only those points which we see as common to most of these groups. Two factors are ubiquitous in the world of the pessimists. The collective memory of Nazi atrocities remains so vivid, so palpable, that it simply crowds out any other way to interpret German intentions. And pessimism—though obviously reflected in many publications and public statements—is (with the notable exception of the German Left) primarily articulated in private. It is not "politically correct" in the European capitals and Washington to express misgivings about Germany.[21] Pessimism manifests itself away from the office, in the pubs and the coffeehouses.

We note several points in the pessimists' view of Germany.

German power has never been innocuous.
It is even less innocuous now. Pessimists agree with the optimists that postwar Germany became an integral part of various multilateral arrangements. But they disagree about Germany's role in these networks and institutions. The pessimists argue that European institutions always served German interests, mainly economic but also political. The EU permitted Germany to accelerate its legitimation and become a leading player in Europe much faster than would have been possible otherwise. The EU helped make Germany acceptable; it also provided Germany with a structure it could come to control.

To the pessimists, it was not the EU which embedded the Bundesrepublik; rather, it was Germany which used the EU to exert unrivaled influence. With the collapse of the Soviet Union, the fall of communism, and German unification, the pessimists believe that Germany's already formidable power can only grow. Germany will use the EU's widening to the east to create an old-fashioned sphere of influence (it already dominates virtually every aspect of economic life in the east). Culturally, too, the pessimists perceive a special link between Germany and the German-speaking world, on the one hand, and the countries of east central Europe, on the other. Can political domination be far behind? Austria's joining the EU in 1995 was tantamount to *Anschluss* (annexation). A European framework never hindered Germany; it was merely a matter of good taste to disguise German power as "European" as long as shame for Auschwitz prevented the Germans from displaying their national interest. Now Germany will exert its power overtly.

The disappearance of the Soviet Union and the changes in Europe's political topography since 1989 have enhanced Germany's power, but the post–Cold War era will do something more substantial: it will change the subjective articulation of power on the part of the Germans. In short, the pessimists see the Germans' intentions as far from European and benign; instead, they view Europe as a convenient conduit to pursue German interests and exercise German power. Above all, they regard the Germans' identification with Europe as merely an ersatz nationalism. Leftist and conservative pessimists agree that Germany's power was always formidable; that Germany used Europe as a structural as well as cultural construct to further its own interests; and that future developments will make these undesirable features even more pronounced.

Two examples give weight to the pessimists' argument. The first pertains to Germany's rule-setting and agenda-defining role in the creation of a common European currency. If Europe is to have a single currency, it is going to be on Germany's terms: the new currency will be called the Euro; the members' budget deficits should actually be no more than 1 percent of GDP in periods of economic growth, so that deficits do not exceed 3 percent during recessions; each member's total public debt will not exceed 60 percent of GDP; and countries whose budget deficits rise above 3 percent must pay a deposit equal to 0.25 percent of GDP as a penalty. If the deficit is not reduced within two years, the deposit is forfeited.

In early 1996, only Luxembourg and Germany fulfilled these stringent requirements, and there is little hope that even a substantial number of members of the EU will meet these criteria by 1999, as stipulated in the Maastricht Treaty, let alone all of them. Proposals and papers emerged to advocate the creation of a multilayered Europe, a Europe of different speeds. All had one thing in common—Germany lies at the core, it is the heart and head of Europe.

One paper advocating the creation of a multilayered Europe offers a second example to support the pessimists' assessment. "Überlegungen zur europäischen Politik: Position der CDU/CSU Bundestagsfraktion vom 1. September 1994" ("Reflections on European Policy: Position of the CDU/CSU parliamentary group in the Bundestag") is of particular importance because its principal author was Wolfgang Schäuble, the CDU/CSU's parliamentary leader and often mentioned as Helmut Kohl's likely successor. In this fascinating document, the CDU/CSU makes it explicit that if Europe is to unite successfully, then Germany, together with France, will have to be "the core of the hard core." The CDU/CSU calls for the institutionalization of a "variable geometry" and the establishment of "different speeds" in the formation of Europe.[22] It is clear that Germany (together with France and the Benelux countries) will determine the rates of speed involved. Germany is to become the pacesetter for the whole process of integration.

If other countries can stick with Germany, all the better. Those who cannot or prefer not to will be left behind, although the CDU/CSU generously concedes that they will always be welcome to catch up. Germany has often been called the engine of Europe, the locomotive of European integration. The important task, as Mary Hampton notes, is to determine who is the engine driver.[23]

Whether prompted by public disquiet or anticipating it, German pessimists have begun to find a voice—indeed, an effective one. Many respond to the Schäuble initiative and its like by asserting that the whole debate about Germany's normalcy and the responsibilities it now has to shoulder—including military obligations, in Europe and perhaps elsewhere—is nothing but a wedge to open a hitherto closed discourse. The Gulf War emphatically demonstrated that warfare in the post–Yalta world need not be of the nuclear (thus total) variety. Germany could once again learn to wage war without having to destroy everything. Albert Statz, a most eloquent critic of the dangers of German power, argues that it would be a serious error to believe that a *Handelsstaat* is peaceful by nature. He concludes that "international commerce and economic interdependence have by themselves never created peace."[24]

The return to normalcy is cause for concern.
Germany became formally sovereign when the Soviet Union ratified the Treaty of Moscow on March 15, 1991. To many pessimists this was a watershed for Germany in the European and global arenas. Politics, in the pessimists' view, is still dominated by nation states, even in a world of interdependence. After the Allied victory, Germany never quite possessed the most coveted asset that continues to define the nation state: sovereignty. Unification gave Germany this asset. Now Germany can behave like any other nation state. It need not feel bridled by loss of autonomy, and German nationalism can once again become acceptable. Pessimists can point with some conviction to the precipitous rise of "acceptable" voices of nationalism since German unification, whether in the editorial pages of *Die Welt* and *Frankfurter Allgemeine Zeitung* or the increasingly nationalist editorials penned by Rudolf Augstein for Germany's leading weekly *Der Spiegel*.

The "new," acceptable, nationalist Right centers around such intellectuals as Rainer Zitelmann and Karlheinz Weissmann and former Leftists such as Tilman Fichter and Karl-Heinz Bohrer. Friedbert Pflüger's insider account of the growing acceptance of nationalist sentiment in the CDU only confirms the pessimists' fear concerning the rise of nationalism in postunification Germany.[25] *Junge Freiheit*, a lavishly funded national-conservative student newspaper that extols Holocaust revisionists, attracts growing attention and legitimacy; the German Right barely disguises its enthusiasm for Austria's Jörg Haider as its much-missed leader—pessimists' suspicions about normalcy in the Germany of the 1990s warrant some credence.[26]

The return to normalcy substantially lowers the threshold of shame regarding Germany's past. Normalcy, to the pessimists' horror and the delight of the German Right, implies removing the Nazi albatross from the Germans' neck and reclaiming the good parts of German history, including some from the 1933–1945 era. This lowering of the threshold can be dated from 1985 and the comments by Günther Rühle, then head of the Frankfurt Schauspielhaus theater. He coined an apt phrase when producing Rainer Werner Fassbinder's overtly anti-semitic play *Garbage, the City and Death*: "Die Schonzeit ist um!" (The no-hunting season is over!).[27]

Germany's anchor in the West is far from certain.
The pessimists are fixated on Auschwitz but also on earlier aspects of German history. Notable among them is *Schaukelpolitik* (seesaw politics), the jockeying for advantage between East and West, and the concomitant *Zwischenkultur* (hybrid between East and West) which claimed a special cultural niche for Germany. Of course Germany has become totally Westernized on such superficial levels as fashion and rock music, Hollywood movies and American fast food chains. On the material levels of commodification, the pessimists concede, Germany has become fully Westernized. Even on the overt levels of politics, the flawless functioning of a parliamentary democracy, a lively multiparty system, an independent judiciary, and the vibrancy of a civil society full of social movements testify to a healthy pluralist Germany. It is on the level of values and culture that pessimists remain skeptical about Germany's Westernization. To be sure, what Jürgen Habermas termed *Verfassungspatriotismus* has been shared far beyond a handful of Frankfurt's left-liberal intellectuals. But how deep is this constitutional patriotism? How prevalent is it in the new Germany? Marxist pessimists decry the growth of "D-Mark Patriotismus," a spin on Habermas' equally derisive "D-Mark diplomacy." Certainly German skepticism about Europe has expressed itself in a vigorous defense of the D-Mark as perhaps the most untainted symbol of national prowess. Making matters worse, this D-Mark patriotism has been articulated not only by members of the German Right, such as CSU leader Edmund Stoiber who has repeatedly called Europe a "delusion," but also by certain key social democratic leaders, notably Gerhard Schröder and Rudolf Scharping.[28] To Marxist pessimists, crude D-Mark patriotism will become more prevalent in the future.

Liberal and conservative pessimists fear the thinness of the veneer of Westernization among some leading intellectuals of both the Right and the Left. Since unification the attacks against Germany's ties to the West and on its Westernized culture have become more pronounced. The neorightist intellectuals around Rainer Zitelmann who, after all, is one of the principal editors of one of Germany's leading daily, *Die Welt*, contributors to the editorial columns of the prestigious *Frankfurter Allgemeine Zeitung*, and other conservative intellectuals have openly questioned Germany's postwar ties to the West, and to the United States in particular.[29] But on the Left, too, criticisms of Western values have grown louder. (The Left, of course, has always decried Germany's ties to Western capitalism.) Rudolf Augstein's columns in *Der Spiegel* have often disintegrated into vitriol, particularly against the French. Brigitte Seebacher-Brandt, the widow of Willy Brandt, has bemoaned the absence of national identity among Germans, blaming the problem mainly on the country's thorough Westernization. And large elements of the Greens and the SPD have recently augmented the hostility toward the United States which they expressed in the 1980s protesting the deployment of medium-range nuclear missiles on German soil.[30] Joschka Fischer, the brilliant leader of the Greens, terms this view among his friends and colleagues "the negative obsession USA."[31] Both the Left and the Right conveyed their deep dislike of the West in their criticism of the Dayton Accords, which, under American leadership, established at least a temporary cessation of hostilities in Bosnia.[32] In short, the pessimists see Germany's Westernization as shallow and transitory.

Germany has always had special ties to the East.
This point entails two different but mutually supportive, components. A German tradition has always seen Germany's affinities to the "noble" and "romantic" values of the East as stronger than its affinities to the commodified and "rational" West. In this vein, Gorbymania was far stronger in Germany than in any other Western (and for that matter Eastern) European country. Also in this vein, the West worried about "Genscherism," which revived fear of the Germans' latent admiration for Russia and the East. Both the neutralist German Right and the Left have—since the middle of the 1980s—constantly emphasized that Europe is not only Western Europe. The pessimists see instances across the German political spectrum of a normative allegiance to East over West.

    The second component of this attraction for things eastern is the fact that there German economic and political domination will be unconstrained. There is no NATO or EU, no vigilant France, jealous Britain, or patronizing United States, to embed Germany in various structures of containment. Of course there is Russia—but it is in Germany's interest to pursue a deal with Russia. Germany does not want a hostile and recalcitrant Russia interfering with its enormously lucrative business prospects in the region. In eastern Europe there is Königsberg (Kaliningrad) and other areas that might once again ignite the flames of German irredentism. At the moment, no respected member of Germany's political class voices geographical revisionism. This is still the stuff of the extreme Right, but there is no guarantee that it will stay that way. Who would have thought it possible that Sudetenland controversies might lead to serious diplomatic confrontations between Germany and the Czech Republic in the early spring of 1996?[33] As long as expellees and their German-born children embrace the former German territories as an important issue, and as long as they articulate their political wishes through a key German party (the CSU), it is premature to declare the former German territories irrelevant. After all, it was Helmut Kohl, perhaps the most astute German politician of the postwar period and a brilliant reader of the German pulse, who hesitated to recognize Poland's Oder-Neisse borders with Germany after unification. If the eastern territories were truly a nonissue in Germany's domestic politics, Kohl would not have waited to be forced to sign the treaty.

Consensus in a Polarized Debate

Who is right, optimists or pessimists? We believe they both are. There is simply no doubt that, as the optimists have it, the Federal Republic is one of the world's most democratic, Western, and politically stable countries. Again, there is no question that the Federal Republic has used power in a circumspect manner that furthered Germany's interests but also benefited others. Most notably, we agree with the optimists that Germany's loyalty to Europe and the West is beyond question and that the country is not interested in bailing out of current institutional and political arrangements. In short, we agree with the optimists on loyalty and exit. As long as Helmut Kohl is in charge, Germany's anchor in Europe and the West—in terms of both culture and institutions—is immutable. One can hardly imagine a more ardent Atlanticist and Europeanist than Kohl, and he has long regarded Germany's complete immersion in Europe as one of his foremost tasks. But what happens after Kohl?

We disagree with the optimists predominantly in the area of voice, meaning the effect of Germany's power, whether it is purposively exercised or not. We do believe that some of the Germans' activities and policies might have and have had adverse consequences for others in Europe. Germans speak with a voice far louder than they care to admit. They are still hiding comfortably behind their alleged smallness. How often have we heard Germans assert that poor little Germany is a medium-sized power at best, barely the size of Oregon—the former West Germany—and Indiana—the former East Germany? The wish to be a slightly larger Austria or Switzerland is still real for a considerable proportion of the German political class, particularly on the Left. Today's Germany might still be "peaceable, fearful and green", and favor a low profile in world affairs, but the objective fact is that Germany is already Europe's premier player and is on course to enhance its already dominant position in the years to come.[34]

Germans also hide their power in various international institutions, where they are fine team players but individual stars all the same. They see to it that the rules of the game suit their every need. To be sure, the Germans lose on occasion; they do not have all their wishes fulfilled all the time. But at the end of the day their power carries more weight than that of any other player on the European team. Put bluntly: on most, though certainly not all, important issues affecting European politics, Germany matters more than any other European country.

Ultimately, though, in the debate between optimists and pessimists we believe that the latter's fears, though justified, are misplaced. German power will expand inadvertently rather than willfully, economically rather than militarily. National aggrandizement is not part of the German agenda, and it is not likely to be in the foreseeable future. The Germans remain ambivalent and hesitant about using their power; but power ignored, even unwanted, does not become nonexistent. German power is a byproduct of Germany's central position in Europe. It will grow even if Germany remains unwilling to tackle the responsibilities and adverse side effects associated with power.

Germany thus has limited structural power and, bound by ideological constraints, lacks purpose. Germany has no hegemonic aspiration (which comes as a welcome relief to its neighbors). Furthermore, Germany lacks the resources to assume a hegemonic position. It could at least conceivably develop militarily and so dominate Europe, but it does not have the cultural resources necessary to assume the mantle of a hegemon.

Constraints on German hegemony appear insurmountable for reasons that are both indigenous and external. In the ensuing chapters of this book, we have two goals. We justify the claim that hegemony is not feasible by demonstrating that Germans reject power and that the European and American acceptance of German integration is limited. We then juxtapose these ideological limitations with German structural power, and discuss the vacuum created by the necessary shortcomings of German cultural power.

Part Two

COLLECTIVE MEMORY AND
PUBLIC OPINION

CHAPTER THREE

Germans and Germany:

A View from the United States

I heard that the UN recently expressed reservations about the unification of Germany. I don't know why, there are more Nazis in Idaho nowadays.

—Jeff Cesario, HBO Special

Of course, the "American mind" is so sweeping and general, so comprehensive and amorphous an idea that it is limited in its explanatory value. Although we might not be able to provide even a vague definition of what constitutes the American mind, we have no doubt that it exists—amorphously, undefinably, ambivalently, full of contradictions. The *conscience collective*, precisely because of its amorphous nature, is a powerful whole that is much more than the sum of its parts. Yet any presentation will of necessity fall victim to either the Scylla of a huge generalization or the Charybdis of a falsely important niche.

Establishing a baseline of American attitudes is of fundamental importance for our project. The attitudes of Germany's neighbors are crucial in defining the contours and limits of potential German power. The importance of America's perceptions of Germany is threefold. First, the United States is the only genuine superpower in the post–Cold War world. As a result, the American view of anything and anybody matters. Second, American perceptions of Germany attain added importance by dint of the United States' special responsibility for the construction, maintenance, and protection of the longest and most stable democracy in German history, as well as its central role in facilitating unification in 1990. Third, power rivalry is extremely unlikely in the foreseeable future, but it seems reasonable to suggest that political relations between the two nations will become a lot more complicated and contentious than they were before 1989.

This proposition may not be pertinent to global politics for years to come, if ever, but it will undoubtedly attain growing relevance as far as Europe is concerned. For the trajectory there is unmistakable: America's power and influence is waning, Germany's is growing. Hegemons and their aspiring rivals, Robert Gilpin tells us, often end up going to war,[1] having grown to distrust each other— as the British and the Germans did in 1914. We have suggested that Germany is not a hegemon but, rather, a reluctant hegesy. Studying U.S. attitudes may add credence to this claim, by demonstrating that Americans do not fear Germans as growing rivals. Yet the very fact that Americans see no need to block German power may provide an avenue for Germany to grow more powerful within its region.

We propose to discuss the mind of America's mass publics and their interpretations of Germany. Any serious discussion of how a country collectively interprets another distinguishes between mass and elite opinion.[2] Our discussion of optimists and pessimists in Chapter 2 covers elite opinion on Germany as far as the American academy is concerned. Here we rely on a brief summary of Germany as understood by a few "papers of record" and the country's security elite. For the mass segment of the American view of Germany, we systematically evaluate different public opinion polls, covering the attitudes the American public has held of Germany since the early 1950s. We studied opinion polls and the quadrennial surveys on the American public's view of U.S. foreign policy published by the Chicago Council on Foreign Relations. We also used anecdotal evidence gathered from audience reactions, questions, interventions, suggestions, and observations in connection with our research and teaching on Germany over the past twenty years.

Public Opinion

Findings generally confirm the pragmatism, thoughtfulness, and intelligence of American public opinion regarding the complex issues associated with the German Question. U.S. public opinion characteristically abstains from extremes of all kinds and commits itself to a safe (if boring) and moderate centrism. The Chicago Council on Foreign Relations calls this phenomenon "pragmatic internationalism."[3] At the same time, however, one can frequently detect an emphatically moralizing tendency in U.S. public opinion, which Europeans often dismiss as naiveté. This mixture of pragmatic "can do-ism" and moral mission— usually full of contrasts and contradictions—characterizes the American public as predictable and balanced but devoted to absolute moral values. Abstract knowledge, however, differs from concrete experience, particularly with such an emotionally charged topic as the unification of the two Germanies. The realism and pragmatic optimism demonstrated by American public opinion combined with its sense of justice confirm the persistence of democratic culture and the high degree of public tolerance in this country.

Since German unity became an issue in the fall of 1989, an overwhelming majority of Americans has consistently favored the unification of the two states. The ratio of those who supported unification vis-à-vis those who rejected it never fell below 3.5 to 1, while values of 7 to 1, even 8 to 1, depending on the formulation of the relevant questions, have not been unusual.

In a CBS/*New York Times* poll of March 30, 1990, 76 percent of American respondents favored the unification of East and West Germany, with only 13 percent expressing opposition. Americans welcomed, by 9.5 to 1, the opening of the Wall and demanded by 4 to 1 that the U.S. government help the Germans as best it could. By 3 to 1, Americans were not afraid that a unified Germany might threaten world peace. By 5 to 1, Americans thought it completely inappropriate to keep Germany divided lest it again become a military threat to its neighbors. By the even higher ratio of 6 to 1, American public opinion emphatically rejected Germany's continued division to impede even greater economic domination by Germany of its European neighbors. Indeed, Americans seemed utterly convinced that a unified Germany "would be a good thing for the United States and its Western allies" (73 percent agreeing with this statement, only 10 percent opposing it).[4]

Americans believed by a ratio of almost 3 to 1 that a united Germany would be good for future world peace and prosperity, and by a ratio of 4.5 to 1 they were convinced it would not exert excessive dominance in Europe. However, 29 percent exhibited some skepticism on this matter. Queried further about their skepticism, 37 percent of this minority feared a reemergence of National Socialism, and 26 percent showed apprehension about excessive German power in the economy.

The number of Americans who suspected that a unified Germany would be an aggressor was not quite half the number of those who perceived no such danger. Reflecting the mood of the times, 51 percent of those who saw a potential aggressor in a united Germany envisioned aggression in the realm of the economy; only 33 percent feared military aggressiveness. Fifty-six percent of Americans agreed with the statement of a CBS/*New York Times* survey of October 1990 describing "Germany as a peace-loving nation, willing to fight only if it thinks it has to defend itself," and only 26 percent concurred with the second part of the statement that depicted Germany as "an aggressive nation that would start a war to get something it wants." Thirty-three percent of respondents to an NBC/*Wall Street Journal* survey conducted in March 1994 believed that relations between the United States and Germany had improved "since the fall of the Berlin Wall and the end of the Cold War"; 52 percent thought they remained about the same as before November 9, 1989, and only 5 percent thought they had gotten worse. As to Americans' trust in Germany, here too the tally is largely positive. In a CBS/*New York Times* poll of March 1994, 13 percent of respondents indicated they had a lot of trust in Germany; 51 percent had some; 23 percent not much; and 9 percent none at all.

Some of the negative data may stem from the fact that a good number of Americans perceive Germany as an economic rival as well as a political ally of the United States. This economic rivalry nowhere engenders the levels of apprehension and antipathy that Americans feel for Japan, but the post–Cold War axiom of economic competition certainly shapes German-American relations in the 1990s. In a survey conducted by the Associated Press in March 1991, 14 percent of respondents saw "economic competition from Germany" as a very important problem for the United States, and 44% classified it as somewhat important. Confirming that economics is the most likely area of friction between the United States and Germany are data from an NBC/*Wall Street Journal* survey of March 1990. What most concerned those Americans who expressed apprehensions about a united Germany, its military or economic strength? Thirty-three percent chose the former, 51 percent the latter. In a similar subgroup of apprehensive respondents, a *Los Angeles Times/Economist* survey of January 1990 found the following justifications for maintaining American troops in Europe: 37 percent, to help maintain the alliance; 31 percent, to defend against the Soviet Union; 16 percent, to help offset Germany's new power.

Still, 60 percent of Americans believed that the Germans had changed substantially since the end of World War II. These respondents were of the opinion that the Germans had finally learned their lessons. By a ratio of 8 to 1, Americans saw World War II as completely behind them. They regarded it as conclusive, its legacy as resolved. By an overwhelming majority, Americans consider Germans partners and not enemies, even though a poll commissioned by the International Policy Opinion Survey in September 1993 reported that 63 percent of respondents thought that "guarding against a resurgent Germany" should be one of the American government's priorities (17 percent viewed it as a top priority). Partnership, of course, does not exclude rivalries and irritations which may have been the source of this particular response.

A certain healthy skepticism also informed the American public's view of the new Germany's relations with the rest of Europe. An ABC/*Washington Post* poll of May 1990 reported that 6 percent of respondents viewed Germany as posing a lot of danger for Europe, 13 percent a good amount, and 35 percent only some, thus yielding a slight majority who viewed Germany as at least remotely "dangerous" for Europe. (Forty-five percent responded that they saw not much danger at all for Europe.) A similar question was asked by ABC News in the week preceding Germany's formal unification on October 3, 1990. The tally was: 5 percent a lot of danger; 7 percent a good amount; 26 percent only some; and 52 percent not much danger at all.

Do Americans worry that Germany will become the dominant power in Europe? To a question posed in a survey conducted for the *Los Angeles Times* and the *Economist* in January 1990, 29 percent stated that they were worried, 62 percent were not. In a CBS News/*New York Times* poll of March 30, 1990, 67 percent of American respondents said they were not concerned that a united Germany would threaten peace in Europe; 22 percent were concerned.

Assessing the situation in Europe, 36 percent of respondents in the same survey said they believed that "Germany would try to dominate Europe economically," with 49 percent expressing no such concerns. In a *Los Angeles Times/ Economist* survey of January 1990, which measured how people assessed a united Germany's impact on close political ties in the European community, 36 percent believed German unification would have a positive effect, 47 percent thought it made no difference, and 4 percent saw it as detrimental.

Americans had realistic estimations of this new united Germany. By a ratio of almost 3 to 1, they wanted the military forces of the new country subject to a strict size limit. By an even larger ratio, nearly 4 to 1, American interviewees hoped that the Germans would forego all nuclear weaponry. On the other hand, twice as many Americans wanted united Germany to maintain a powerful conventional military as favored complete disarmament. Americans preferred, by a ratio of over 6 to 1, united Germany's firm integration into the European Community. By only slightly less impressive a margin (75 percent in favor, 17 percent opposed), Americans wanted Germany to continue its membership in NATO.

This pragmatism and evenhandedness has an important moralistic core. Asked for the most important reason for supporting unification, the overwhelming majority of Americans chose the simplest answer: because the German people belong together if that is what they want. The response is another manifestation of the continued vitality of Wilsonian ideas and ideals in the American public psyche.

This sense of the world has its precursors in the 1950s. American public opinion toward Germans and their politics has remained remarkably constant over the last forty years. In 1955, Americans favored German unification by a ratio of almost 4 to 1. They did so as much on moral, altruistic grounds as on pragmatic, selfish ones. Those who then rejected German unity did so not because they feared the reemergence of National Socialism (20 percent) but because they worried that communist influences would carry greater weight in a united Germany than in the divided status quo (52 percent).

That a perceived communist threat determined, until recently, most American public opinion vis-à-vis foreign affairs is no surprise. Thus, in the 1950s American public opinion held the following preference scale regarding Germany's political position in Europe: the largest majority of Americans favored a united Germany within NATO (5 to 1). As a result, a large majority welcomed West Germany's actual participation in NATO (3.5 to 1). American public opinion rejected a united but neutral Germany by 2 to 1, whereas a united Germany allied with the Soviets was decisively opposed by a ratio of 8 to 1. Little changed in forty years. Germany's unity, as well as its strong ties to the West, remain very important in the eyes of the American public.

The American population's pragmatic anticommunism is also revealing. Most things involving the terms communism/communist (or what are for Americans the largely indistinguishable terms socialism/socialist) have had a negative connotation in the American mind, but we recognize two different patterns in this distrust. First, it is striking that the American public has, on the whole, been positively predisposed toward the actual content of communist and socialist programs—provided they appear under different names. Second, despite animosity toward communism/socialism and its most important representative, the Soviet Union, Americans by a ratio of 3 to 1, consistently rejected military intervention against the Soviets. The same is true of the American position regarding Eastern European countries, whose communist regimes the American public considered for decades, by a ratio of 6 to 1, to be Soviet-imposed and hence illegitimate.

Despite this obvious antipathy, a significant majority of Americans never wanted to rectify matters in a military manner. Even for the defense of West Berlin following a Soviet occupation, only 52 percent of Americans favored any kind of military response. And this feeble majority was attained only once, in early 1980 shortly after the Soviet invasion of Afghanistan and the beginning of the so-called Second Cold War. No majority of Americans ever favored risking a hot war with the USSR—even for Berlin. Most Americans were prepared for a military conflict with the Soviets only under two conditions: direct Soviet attack on North America (the United States and Canada, though not Mexico), and direct Soviet attack on Great Britain. The "special relationship" has clearly reached far beyond the personal friendships of different heads of state, whether Roosevelt and Churchill or Reagan and Thatcher, deep into the American public.

A few words are relevant concerning the general American image of Germans and Germany, since the affect or antipathy for a country and its people might in a democracy establish an important framework for policy. The American public's image of Germans is by and large quite positive. In a Gallup poll conducted in February 1992, 17 percent of respondents had a very favorable view of Germany, and 57 percent a mostly favorable one. Only 14 percent indicated that they had a mostly unfavorable view of the country, with 6 percent choosing the category "very unfavorable." In a Harris poll of March 1991, 16 percent of respondents had a great deal of admiration for Germany's economic success, with 46 percent reporting some admiration. Nineteen percent of respondents had not very much, and 15 percent had none at all. Interesting, too, are responses to a question posed in the same survey asking people how much admiration they had for Germany as a "real world leader." The result: 7 percent had a great deal of admiration, 35 percent some, 33 percent not very much, and 24 percent none at all. A large majority of Americans (68 percent vs. 19 percent) approved of Germany's becoming a permanent member of the United Nations Security Council in a poll conducted for CBS News/*New York Times* in December 1994.

A majority of Americans see Germany as friendly and a close ally of the United States. In a Harris poll conducted in February 1991, 28 percent of respondents categorized Germany as America's close ally, and 50 percent viewed it as friendly. Only 14 percent classified Germany as unfriendly to the United States, with 3 percent viewing it as an enemy. The same poll and the same question was repeated in February 1994. The results were very similar: 22 percent close ally; 54 percent friendly; 16 percent not friendly; and 3 percent an enemy. In an ABC News/*Washington Post* poll of May 1990, 53 percent of respondents preferred Germany as a member of NATO, 43 percent wanted it to be neutral. A *Los Angeles Times* survey of January 1990 offered the following responses on the same topic: 50 percent preferred Germany as a member of NATO; 27 percent would like it to be "outside NATO as a neutral country"; and 21 percent were not sure.

Gallup has questioned Americans regularly since the early 1950s about how they see the different peoples of the world. The scale, from +5 (absolutely positive) to −5 (absolutely negative), shows Americans disposed toward Germans at a constant +2 for decades. Whether during the Eichmann trial in the early 1960s, or twenty years later during the controversy about basing medium-range missiles in the Federal Republic, these moderate but solidly positive values have hardly deviated for forty years. Other surveys substantiate this picture of an unenthusiastic but positive disposition. In a survey conducted by Princeton Survey Research Associates in September 1990, Americans were asked to rank Germany on the same preference scale, and the results confirm Gallup data: only 5 percent of respondents scored Germany on the very unfavorable minus 4–5 another 14 percent ranked Germany in the unfavorable category of minus 1–3. Fifty-seven percent of respondents gave Germany a "favorable" rating of plus 1–3, with 17 percent ranking it "very favorable" (plus 4–5).

The Chicago Council on Foreign Relations also measures how Americans feel about an array of nations and their leaders. The results are different from, yet fundamentally complementary with, the data just mentioned. On the council's "feeling thermometer" from 1991, which ranged from zero to 100 degrees, Germany's 62 scored a distant third to Canada's 76 and Great Britain's 74 but was well ahead of Italy (59), France (56), Israel (54), Japan (52), and twenty-three others. On the thermometer that measured the American public's feelings about world leaders, Helmut Kohl shared a position in the middle with Nelson Mandela (both at 53), ahead of François Mitterrand (50), Jacques Delors (47), Toshiki Kaifu (46), and Yitzhak Shamir (44) but well behind the leader Pope John Paul II (67), runner-up Margaret Thatcher (66), and third-place finisher Mikhail Gorbachev (64).[5]

The 1995 thermometer was consistent with the 1991 findings. Americans' feelings toward Germany had slipped to a 57 rating, which tied Germany in fourth place with Mexico. Italy had edged ahead of Germany into third place, with a 58 rating. Canada maintained its lead with 73, followed by Britain with 69, confirming their hold over the hearts of the American public. Interestingly, American affection for all of these foreign countries declined between 1991 and 1995, and Germany was no exception. Helmut Kohl also maintained his standing in the middle, sharing his 51 rating with Yitzhak Rabin. Pope John Paul II continued as leader with a 65 rating, followed by Nelson Mandela (58) and Boris Yeltsin (53). François Mitterrand and Jacques Delors still trailed Helmut Kohl with a shared 48.[6]

Whether pollsters ask which country Americans like to visit, or which people they can trust as a friend, they hear that only the Canadians, British, and Australians surpass—although by quite a substantial margin—the Germans. Compared to other European peoples and countries, Germans and the Federal Republic (although certainly not the GDR) have on the whole done quite well.

Americans do not love the Germans as they do the British. Rather, they respect and trust them, not as friends, but as equal partners who can occasionally also be rivals. That Americans respect Germans but do not love them is nicely supported by time series data compiled by the Gallup Organization. Repeatedly, Gallup questioned the American public about which adjectives best characterize a people's qualities. In the case of the Germans, "hard working" ranked consistently in first place (around 70 percent of respondents), followed by "intelligent" (about 50 percent), "progressive" (approximately 35 percent), "practical" (around 25 percent), "honest" and "brave" (both 20 percent). Negative impressions, such as quick-tempered, warlike, and arrogant, followed, averaging slightly less than 20 percent. An ABC News survey conducted on March 13, 1990 confirmed these Gallup findings. Tellingly comprising part of a large survey on U.S.-Japanese relations, which have been much more openly tormented than U.S.-German relations, the ABC poll also asked a few questions about how Americans viewed Germans and other Europeans. Concerning each of the six characteristics on which respondents had to compare Germans "to most people"—efficiency, friendliness, creativity, arrogance, intelligence, and regimentation—a majority categorized Germans as like most people (54 percent for efficiency, 67 percent for friendliness, 66 percent for creativity, 63 percent for arrogance, 80 percent for intelligence). Only "regimentation" attained a mere plurality of 47 percent.

But among the minority who scored Germans as different from most people, the stereotypes were obvious. Thirty-two percent believed the Germans were more efficient than everybody else, as opposed to 11 percent who believed them less efficient than most people. Twenty percent thought the Germans less friendly than most people, whereas 11 percent held them to be more friendly. On creativity, the tally was even, with 17 percent believing the Germans were more creative and 16 percent less creative. As to arrogance, 23 percent viewed the Germans as more arrogant than most people whereas 11 percent believed them less so. Fourteen percent of respondents thought the Germans more intelligent, only 5 percent less so. It was on the issue of regimentation that the stereotype was most pronounced: 41 percent of respondents believed the Germans were more regimented than most people whereas only 8 percent saw them as less regimented. The picture that emerges is clear: to American public opinion, Germans are mainly like most people. To the extent that they are different, they are above all regimented and then, in descending order of prominence, efficient, not particularly friendly, slightly arrogant, a tad more intelligent than most people, and about as creative as everybody else.

Anyone who sees even a few American advertisements knows how the German image continues to be sold to Americans: serious, disciplined, and competent men, wearing white smocks and glasses, the reliable engineer of an even more reliable Mercedes or BMW somewhere on a test track deep in the Black Forest. (This is the personalized reproduction of Modell Deutschland. No Junkers here, just fine engineers producing the "ultimate driving machine.") In the American mind, few phrases identify more closely with top quality than "German engineering."

In notable contrast, the image of the Japanese clearly shows that the American public does not unconditionally accord positive meaning to hard work, competence, intelligence, and practicality. It has become a cliché but seems true: throughout the 1980s and 1990s, Japan has become, to the American people, the major economic and technopolitical rival of the United States. In a CBS/*New York Times* poll of June 1990, Americans were asked which country represented the strongest competitor of the United States today. The response is revealing: 58 percent listed Japan, followed by the Soviet Union with 19 percent, China with 3 percent, Germany with 2 percent, and Britain with 1 percent. Nearly 75 percent of those questioned in 1985 believed that American trade difficulties were solely the fault of Japan. Only 4 percent listed the next country as the Federal Republic.

In the same year, this "Japan fixation" led to notably incorrect answers. For example, 62 percent of Americans cited Japan as the country with which the United States has the highest level of trade relations, and only 15 percent correctly mentioned Canada. One year later, 46 percent of the American public saw Japan as a very serious threat to America in global trade relations; the Federal Republic was listed by a mere 12 percent. Almost 70 percent of those questioned in 1989 saw Japan as the largest challenger to the United States in the world market (only 1 percent perceived the Federal Republic in this role); 35 percent claimed Japan was America's most important trade and technology partner (Great Britain 9 percent, Canada 7 percent, the Federal Republic 1 percent); 42 percent thought Japan had the best technology in the world (the United States got 47 percent, still leading by a narrow 5 percent). One must add that the American public had consistently given the United States an overwhelming lead—an 80 to 1 margin—on this matter until the mid-1980s. Perhaps most revealing of all, 54 percent claimed that Japan was absolutely the strongest economic power in the world (United States 29 percent; USSR 3 percent; Federal Republic 1 percent).

Japan has achieved so dominant a position in the consciousness of the American public, as far as economic and technological affairs are concerned, that all of the American public's many antipathies in this matter concentrate on the Japanese and away from everybody else. One can legitimately speak of a "crowding out" of antipathies and prejudices in the American mind, in which the Japanese have attained an unenviably dominant position.

Whether the Germans will continue to conduct their business in the relative obscurity of the past, which helped them avoid the wrath of the American public, no one can predict. However, one thing does seem clear today: on the level of American public opinion one can talk only about the "ugly Japanese." The "ugly Germans," if they exist at all, do so only for Jewish and Polish Americans (for whom public opinion data are unfortunately not available). Yet, while the ugly Germans do not exist for the American mind, there are residues of caution and apprehension concerning Germany. American public opinion draws a fine but discernible distinction between Germans (unproblematically positive) and Germany (accorded a cautionary distance but still in a framework of respect and trust). For example, the percentage of Americans who worried that Germany could endanger peace in Europe increased from 31 percent to 41 percent between 1991 and 1993. The residue of World War II conditions American images of Germany. Thus 54 percent of American respondents believed in 1993 that there could be a revival of National Socialism in Germany, one-third of Americans saw Right radicalism as a major threat in Germany, and over 50 percent of Americans categorized the Germans as antisemitic.[7]

Clearly, surveys provide what is at best only a superficial—and often misleading—view of the truth. On matters of great sensitivity, controversy, and potential embarrassment, there exists a significant gap between manifest reality as evinced in the answers given to survey researchers and unspoken reality reflecting people's feelings, fears, and prejudices. Whether issues related to how Americans really feel about Germans belong to such an unspoken reality is very difficult to tell. Moreover, it is quite certain that the gap between a *pays réel* and a *pays légal*, that is, between the public's opinion and the official view of the Germans is considerably smaller in the United States than in some European countries.

Yet a distinction exists here, too, between what people think and what they say. As is to be expected, the *pays réel* carries a heavy load of negative images, all of which concern Germany's Nazi past. The Hun of World War I days has been completely overwhelmed by the image of the Nazi. This is true not only among Jews but also among gentile Americans. Thus, for example, one of the authors of this book, Andrei Markovits, was a guest of the Armenian community in Watertown, Massachusetts, in April 1990. Even though he did not once mention the Nazi genocide in his keynote address, which concentrated exclusively on the Turkish genocide against the Armenian people, almost all questions after the lecture concerned events in contemporary Europe and Asia Minor. Surprisingly, worries about renewed German power, dominated by the memory of Auschwitz, were more prominently voiced than fears about Armenian losses (and possibly a new genocide) in Nagorno Karabakh.

This pattern of concern has repeated itself in every single forum in which we have spoken about the new Germany since 1989. Even though we always emphasize the phenomenal achievements of the Federal Republic, which we portray as definitive protection against anything vaguely resembling the establishment of National Socialism in contemporary Germany, without fail we encounter more than a negligible number of skeptics. While the number is larger and voices its worries more vocally among the North Shore Jewish Sisterhood or the B'nai Brith annual convention in the Catskills, it is also present among 300 middle managers of Fortune 500 firms and an assembly of high-school social studies teachers from Georgia, Florida, and the Carolinas. The German Question has also captured the American mind.

Auschwitz and the Nazi atrocities have not disappeared from the collective memory of the American public. Although this aspect of the Americans' assessment of Germany appears marginal on the level of public opinion surveys, it is very real in the world of the local bar, the office water fountain, and the dinner table. There seems to be a major discrepancy between the world of public opinion as ascertained by survey research and the world of real feelings as expressed in the vernacular. National Socialism's enormity has become synonymous with evil in the contemporary American mind. It has also become synonymous with fascism, humiliation, pain, sadism, expansion, occupation, authoritarianism, and the abuse of and obsession with power. And to a certain extent German has become synonymous with Nazi.

When the brilliant journalist Molly Ivins derided Patrick Buchanan's speech at the 1992 Republican party nominating convention, in which he declared cultural war on America's alleged permissiveness, she wrote that the speech sounded "better in the original German."[8] When America's New Leftists characterized the U.S. government, as well as the country itself, as "fascist," they spelled it "Amerika," the German way. The word "Nazi," denoting the ultimate evil, is often used in absurd and offensive ways, as when the radio commentator Rush Limbaugh rants about Feminazis. The general point is obvious: Nazism, more than any other political regime or ideology including Stalinism, epitomizes evil for contemporary American culture and political discourse, even after nearly half a century of anti-Communism.

The world of comedy is perhaps the least encumbered voice of the *pays réel*. It is a realm of political and cultural discourse which need not worry about decorum and inhibitions—indeed, its essence is to shed them, to articulate what people *really* feel and think but are afraid to tell survey researchers. The formerly transitive verb "to offend" has become intransitive: where once one offended or did not offend something or somebody, today one must not offend, period. Comedy is the last refuge from this neo-Puritan universalism in contemporary America, and in this world the Nazi experience monopolizes representations of the Germans. The comedians constantly evoke the collective memory of World War II, and in the category of the ethnic joke, the Nazi experience dominates ideas about the Germans and things German.

It is fascinating that, contrary to expectations, the presence of Auschwitz has if anything grown in America's mass perception. Over the years, Auschwitz has developed into the epitome of immorality and pure evil in the minds of Americans. The power of this impression remains so overwhelming that no other consideration can challenge its validity. When Ronald Reagan tried to legitimize his visit to the Bitburg cemetery in the name of current American interests, his popularity fell to an all-time low and his arguments were dismissed as immoral. Whenever matters relate to Auschwitz, the politics of interest becomes completely subordinated to the politics of morality. In heated debates such as the conflict about abortion, each side tries to delegitimize the other by denouncing it as Nazi-like. Invocation of the Shoah is calculated to push the opponent into the corner of absolute evil, thereby changing the debate from the politics of interest to that of absolute morality. Auschwitz has become universalized in contemporary America.

Elite Opinion

American elites, like their counterparts in other countries, have a much greater knowledge of and interest in Germany and Europe than does the general public. Unlike French and British elites, American decision makers are remarkably supportive of Germany in virtually all respects. Indeed, as the Chicago Council on Foreign Relations has shown in its quadrennial surveys, Germans and Germany are viewed more favorably inside Washington's Beltway than in the rest of the country. But as we will see, the split between public and private which we found in the American population's views also pertains to elite reactions.

American leaders see Germany favorably. They want it to play a more active military role in the world, and they also would like to see Germany hold a permanent seat on the United Nations Security Council.[9] American leaders perceive Germany as more central to American interests than does the public. Thus, in a regular feature that ranks countries according to how the American public and American leaders perceive them as vital interests of the United States, the Chicago Council on Foreign Relations found in 1986 that 77 percent of the American public but a whopping 98 percent of the elite viewed West Germany as vital to American interests. The leadership figure tied for first place with Japan and was 2 points ahead of Mexico and Canada (both at 96) and 4 points ahead of Britain (at 94). In 1990 Germany and Japan remained in first place in the leaders' assessment, but the score had slipped slightly to 95 percent, leading Mexico at 94, the Soviet Union at 93, and Canada at 90. Britain had slipped to only 86 percent. A comparable slight decrease also occurred in the popular perception of Germany, to 73 percent.[10] The 1995 rankings show an interesting shift in the perception of American leaders. Germany, still boasting 91 percent, had slipped to seventh place behind countries such as Russia and Mexico (tied at 98 percent), Saudi Arabia (94 percent), and Canada (93 percent). In the perception of the public, Germany had slipped to tenth place with a 66 percent ranking; Japan was number one for the first time, with an 85 percent score.

One thing is obvious from an epoch-making decade in global politics: alongside Britain, Germany is perceived as far and away the most important European country to America's vital interests. Countries such as France (59 percent), Poland (46 percent), and the Ukraine (66 percent) do not even come close.[11] Also, affect defines assessment much more for the public's perceptions than for the elite's. The public consistently ranks Britain ahead of Germany as of vital interest to the United States, whereas the reverse was the case for the elite views in 1990. Only 4 percent of leaders and the public expected Germany to develop into a "main adversary of the United States in the next 10 years."[12] Yet, 56 percent of leaders and 45 percent of the public predicted a greater role for Germany in the year 2005.[13] Also, there were some telling changes concerning economic competition. Germany, as Europe's economic powerhouse, must have played a considerable role in respondents' replies: 41 percent of leaders and 30 percent of the public believed that Europe posed a critical economic threat to the United States in 1990. Four years later the figures had diminished substantially, to 11 percent on the elite side and less dramatically to 27 percent among the public.[14] Washington insiders shed initial fears of Fortress Europe in the course of the 1990s. They seemed to gain confidence in the U.S. ability to hold its own in world markets; they also saw the latter-day GATT and its immediate successor, the newly established World Trade Organization, as auspicious for the global economy and America's role within it.

This confidence is amply borne out by numbers on Japan which—on the elite level—mirror those on Germany. In 1990, 63 percent of leaders and 60 percent of the public perceived Japan as a critical threat to the United States in economic competition. By 1994, the tally sank to 21 percent among leaders but *rose* to 62 percent in the eyes of the public. American mass opinion had constructed an image of the ugly Japanese which not only was openly expressed but was largely based on contemporary events. To be sure, Pearl Harbor and other encounters from World War II continue in America's collective memory about Japan. But the destruction of Toyotas in the parking lots of Detroit's Big Three car manufacturers owes little to Pearl Harbor and everything to the contemporary insecurities of millions of American workers—who blame the Japanese for their travails.

Let us return to the world of humor. Jay Leno's and David Letterman's frequent jokes about the Japanese concentrate almost exclusively on the present; on rare occasions they lampoon a Japanese-controlled future; but never do they invoke Japan's past. Yet given the nature of World War II, Japan was arguably a more immediate adversary than Nazi Germany for the United States. Still, the horror of Auschwitz is much more potent than Pearl Harbor or any other encounters with the Japanese in the course of a long and brutal war. It bespeaks the magnitude of the evils of Nazi rule that even in the United States, whose citizens suffered more at the hands of the Japanese than those of the Germans, the present defines the negative image of the former and the past accounts for the negative perception of the latter.

Ronald D. Asmus is one of the most pro-German policy experts in the United States. In a fascinating paper, he clearly discerns a consistent apprehension about Germany in the American security elite. Written for the German Ministry of Defense, his study exemplifies the many attempts by experts to tell the Germans what it is that makes them less liked than they desperately want to be. Asmus identifies (to his great chagrin) a sense of discomfort with, even distrust of, the Germans among American policy makers. Embarrassed by and dismissive of such realities, he offers no explanation other than stating that "Germany, rightly or wrongly, is still often seen through a different optic and measured by a different standard than other countries."[15] From opposite ends of the normative spectrum, he and Marc Fisher confirm the same thing: in many a Georgetown dinner party and at power lunches in the capital's fine restaurants, virtually any conversation on Germany will sooner or later include the questions "Are you really that sure . . . ? Do you trust them that much . . . ?"[16]

What of the image of Germany and Germans offered by some of the country's leading newspapers? We offer a short summary of Karin Böhme-Dürr's pioneering work.[17] Böhme-Dürr started her research with the assumption that Americans' views of Germany deteriorated substantially after unification. She hypothesized that the shift came from the changed pictures Americans were receiving. She analyzed in meticulous detail all front-page articles and editorials on Germany in 115 American newspapers between 1976 and 1993. Among them were such papers of record as the *New York Times*, the *Washington Post*, the *Los Angeles Times*, and the *Boston Globe*. Though fully aware that most Americans obtain most political information from television, the author excluded—correctly, in our opinion—television news on Germany in favor of print media: "*Newsweek* columnist Jonathan Alter cites a high-ranking government official saying: 'You campaign and win on TV, but you govern in print. Ultimately, people think through print. That's the way the issues get framed.' Habermas conceives it similarly: ' . . . The print media are still at the core of any media we have now. . . . Print is a necessary source for maintaining the public sphere.' "[18]

Böhme-Dürr's data convincingly bear out a deterioration in the image of Germany following unification and throughout the 1990s. She ascribes this trajectory only marginally to the notion that unification enhanced Germany's strength. Instead, she sees the press as newly preoccupied with Germany's Nazi image— manifested in the prominent coverage of violent xenophobia and the radical Right in newly unified Germany. The Manichean worldview of the Cold War years has resulted, she suggests, in disorientation for America's leading journalists and their spiritual soulmates (and perennial lunch partners), the country's foreign policy elite.

Why should such a sense of disorientation lead to a revived fixation on the imagery of National Socialism in things German? Böme-Dürr has no answer. Still, we find the message of her empirical work utterly convincing. Auschwitz remains real in the collective memory of many Americans: policy makers, journalists, editors, humorists, even the large majority of respondents who offer a favorable characterization of Germans in public opinion surveys. The past will not release the Germans, as Klaus Kinkel so aptly put it—not even in the United States.

It is striking that the American image of Germany more or less corresponds to that held by Germany's European neighbors. Just as in Europe, a significant majority of the American population favored the unification of the two Germanies. Similarly, in every country only a minority is negatively disposed toward the Germans. But also clear is the immense tenacity of Auschwitz in the collective memory of Americans. One detects an ambivalence about things German. On the one hand is the good and clean and democratic Germany, America's ally and partner. On the other hand is a continued dread of National Socialism as evil incarnate, an evil so immense that it often seems to exist apart from history, devoid of social content, only tangentially linked to today's Germany.

One cannot speak of simplistic, widely held anti-German prejudices among the American public. Of course, there are reservations, and one can identify a variety of fears. The American image of Germany thus follows a fairly pluralistic, balanced, mature pattern which we will find throughout the Western democracies.

CHAPTER FOUR

Reactions among the Europeans

Michael Jackson has just returned from Europe where—among other places—he played at Fantasy World, the German equivalent of Disney World. What makes this Fantasy World such a special theme park is the fact that in the Germans' fantasy, Germany also includes France, Poland, and the Czech Republic.
—Jay Leno, *Tonight Show*

How did public opinion in fifteen countries react to German unification? We understand the limits of this research. No matter how rigorous our methods, we cannot measure how each country's population feels about Germany and the Germans at any given point in time, especially during such turbulent moments as the late 1980s and early 1990s. Publics have become too diverse for us to characterize, for example "the French view of the Germans." Which French? Parisians or provincials? men or women? young or old? working class or bourgeois? blue or white collar? elite or mass? southern or northern? urban or rural? Even the best-designed survey cannot convey with certainty collective views of such complexity.

The value of this exercise is in illustrating broad trends rather than microdistinctions. Just because these feelings and attitudes cannot be presented without a reasonable doubt does not mean they do not exist or they are not important. Opinions do influence people's behavior and so their politics. Even though to speak of a people's collective attitude vis-à-vis the Germans reduces complexity to a simple cliché, we know that such distortions exist in reality and influence collective behavior.

Societies are becoming increasingly fragmented in terms of their opinions, habits, and milieus. But still, in every society, collective characteristics are more than just the sum of individual parts. We agree with Ludwig Fleck that "we look with our own eyes but we see with the eyes of the collective."[1] Stereotypes and preformed judgments based on history may be an unfair way to guide contemporary behavior. Alas, they form a real if unfortunate ordering mechanism in an increasingly disorderly world.

Why confine ourselves to responses to German unification? The answer is a combination of the pragmatic and our belief in the explanatory power of extraordinary, indeed epoch-making, events. Confining ourselves to particular events allows for a semblance of comparability between frequently incomparable phenomena. Moreover, public responses at this time are interesting because German unification represents a generational change, an event that occurs rarely but leaves an indelible imprint on people's views, opinions, and outlooks. Here we follow

74

Karl Mannheim's interpretation of the "generation" as a decisive determinant of social and political life.[2] Mannheim believed that certain events—the French and Russian revolutions, for example, or the Great Depression, or the student revolts of the 1960s—were of such experiential importance that their contemporaries (not just immediate participants) formed a common collective around the shared experience, often for life. In other words, the event's impact on its collective lasts well beyond the event itself. And it shapes the collective's identity: "*soixanthuitard*," "sixty-eighter," "baby boomer," "cold warrior." The events of 1989 and 1990 created just such a Mannheimian moment.

German unification and the events of 1989/90 were epoch-making phenomena that ended one era—that of 1945 and the Cold War—and began a new one. Like 1945, 1989/1990 were watershed years that define generations. It is appropriate, we believe, to explore how people immediately affected by such resonant events felt about them.

We use data from three sources: public opinion surveys; a large number of newspaper and magazine articles; and secondary materials written by country experts.[3] We concentrate on five key periods that proved of major significance to German unification and the restructuring of postwar European politics.

Period one is the week November 10–17, 1989, the week after the opening of the Berlin Wall (arguably the single most important event in the unification of Germany). Period two concentrates on the week between Christmas and New Year's 1989/90, when the Brandenburg Gate was opened and many newspapers carried extensive retrospectives on the events of 1989. Period three centers on the week of February 14–21, 1990, in which the actual unification of Germany was decided and the "2+4" agreement devised for its implementation by the international powers in Ottawa. The week of March 19–26, 1990, is period four. This week followed the first and last democratic election in what was then still the German Democratic Republic. Lastly, period five features the first two weeks of July 1990, which witnessed the monetary unification of the two Germanies, guaranteeing that the former East Germany would develop under capitalist conditions set by West Germany's market economy (so died the "third way"); NATO's historic London conference, which officially acknowledged the end of the Cold War; the annual meeting of the G-7 countries in Houston; and, perhaps most significant, the Soviet Union's unexpected concession that a united Germany could remain in NATO.[4] In slightly less than nine months, the world had changed to a degree not witnessed since 1945. And just as in 1945, Germany was both object and subject of this enormous change. We believe that with these five time periods we can gauge in a meaningful way the reaction among Germany's European neighbors to the events that transformed Germany and its politics in 1989 and 1990.

Several questions guided our investigation. Were reactions to German unification and the new Germany positive or negative? If the former, how did they express themselves? If the latter, how was fear or apprehension expressed? Was it mainly dominated by memory, by a historical fear, or was it contemporary? If the latter, was it more economic or political? Were there worries about Germany's turning away from its commitments to western Europe due to the sudden opening to the east? Were there significant inter- as well as intracountry differences in reactions to the German Question? Did reactions differ in small as compared to large countries, in the west as opposed to the east? What about countries that suffered German occupation in World War II and those that did not? In terms of intracountry differences, we were particularly interested in any visible Left-Right cleavages or variations between elite and mass opinion.

We cover prevailing attitudes only in fifteen countries. These, we believe, represent a reasonable cross section of European states—the small and the large, the distant and the close. We here summarize our seven main findings, which follow in more detail in the next five separate chapters.

1. Germany may be unique in the degree to which it engenders strong feelings on the part of all Europeans. It is as futile to deny this, as some German officials have wished, as to fight it by claiming that the Germans are like everyone else and that Germany is little more than an oversized version of Switzerland.[5] By virtue of the size of its population, its economy, its history, and its geographic location, Germany matters. European elites and European masses have strong opinions and feelings concerning Germany which are qualitatively different from their views of smaller, less powerful countries.

2. Collective memory matters in how Europeans formulate their views of Germany. Collective memory is not the sole lens, but it is a very powerful one, more powerful than what Europeans use in gauging other nations. Instances are legion: the Italian public regularly labels German soccer players *panzeri* and calls the German national team the Wehrmacht; Finns use the endearing term *Aatus*, the diminutive of the German "Adolf," to refer to Germans. Germany's Nazi past continues to cast a long shadow over contemporary Europe.[6] No other European country's recent past plays a comparable role in terms of its assessment by its neighbors. Of course, immediate neighbors have a heightened awareness of each other, whether in innocuous relations between small countries such as Austria and Hungary or tragic interactions like those between Serbia and Croatia. What makes Germany so interesting, and what bespeaks its importance, is the fact that it engenders strong opinions and feelings both on the elite and the mass levels in countries that are not contiguous with Germany. The geographic and political reality is that no other country in Europe is surrounded by as many neighbors—nine—as is Germany. Moving clockwise, they are Denmark, Poland, the Czech Republic, Austria, Switzerland, France, Luxembourg, Belgium, and the Netherlands.

We encountered no country in which Germany's past did not play a significant role in shaping the country's view of things German. Particularly striking is the tenacity with which images of victimization continue to define European collective memories about the Germans. Even if these negative associations are not readily expressed, they lurk just beneath the surface, to be called up by any conflict involving Germans, be it on the soccer field or in the corridors of national ministries. As we have argued already, victimhood appears to be a crucial dimension of collective memory.

3. At the same time, the past is receding everywhere. And the faster it receded, the more enthusiastic was support for Germany. In all cases a decisive majority had positive associations with the Bundesrepublik. Nearly everywhere—the notable exceptions were Poland, Czechoslovakia, and Denmark, with the Netherlands a distant though significant fourth—an equally impressive majority welcomed German unification. Warmth and enthusiasm varied widely, but the data from opinion polls are decisive: Europeans welcomed unification and respect the Bundesrepublik, though at the same time they are somewhat apprehensive about Deutschland.

4. We discerned two levels in the Europeans' reaction to German unification and to things German. The first might be labeled the "official" or "legal" level. Propelled by reason, it is the reaction which respondents voice publicly, which they find acceptable and *salonfähig* (suitable for polite company), in sum "politically correct." Prejudices and fears are generally concealed; it is this manifest level which public opinion polls have no difficulty in measuring quite accurately.

The second, less official, level is a good deal more difficult to ascertain. Generated by fears instead of reason, this level is voiced in private and it is barely gauged by opinion surveys. Yet it exists, even beneath the reiterated admiration for the impressive achievements of the Federal Republic. One cannot help feel that repeated assurances about the democratic nature of today's Germany, the reliability of its institutions, the stability of its economy, the pacifism of its youth, its deep commitment to Western values and its moorings in NATO, are whistling in the dark. Such assurances sound too much like hopeful claims in a situation of acute uncertainty.

5. Four major factors explain variations in countries' reactions to German unification and by extension in their views of Germany: geographic distance from Germany; the country's role as a player; the nature of historical linkages with Germany; and the country's degree of economic integration with the German economy. As a rule, the further away from Germany, the less intense are collective feelings about Germany. Thus the Dutch and the Danes have more intense and negative attitudes toward Germany than do, for example, the Greeks, the Irish, and the Portuguese.

"Player" is, of course, a loose term. It refers to a combination of size and importance. The more a country is or has been a player, as for example Britain and France, the more rivalry will propel its public and especially its elite to hold negative views of Germany. Here, too, distance is a significant variable. American attitudes on the elite and mass levels have favored Germany more than has been the case in either France or Britain, reflecting a greater security—as well as indifference—on the part of the American public.

An appreciation of history is critical to understanding the dynamics of public opinion. Perhaps more surprisingly, it is not simply the history of the 1930s and 1940s that is influential in this regard. Pre-Nazi relations with the Germans also shape contemporary attitudes, though not always in a consistent way. The historical legacy that continues to influence the present reaches well beyond the trauma of National Socialism. Nazi occupation was very brutal in Greece, but it seems to have left few traces on current Greek opinions about Germany. Much more hostile attitudes prevail in Denmark and the Netherlands, but they are also connected to Danish-German and Dutch-German relations before the Nazi period. The animosity exhibited by the Danes has almost as much to do with 1864 as it does with 1940.

This is not to discount the effect of the Nazi image in contributing to the fears of Europeans. Of course there were occasional articles, and swastikas appeared in the odd cartoon. On the whole, however, National Socialism did not appear as an explicit expression of fears associated with German unification.

These fears will not in any way alter Germany's new role in Europe as far as the substantial issues of politics and the economy are concerned. They will, however, make an important subjective difference as to whether Germany's new power will operate in an atmosphere of congeniality and acceptance or one of suspicion and reticence.

Finally, the degree of economic integration proved to be important in explaining attitudes, and the linkage is counterintuitive to liberal expectations. Small states that have the most attenuated economic links with the Germans are enthusiastic about integrating their economy with Germany's (Portugal, Greece, Ireland), and are among the most politically accepting of German unification. In contrast, the countries whose economies are closely integrated with the German, such as Denmark and the Netherlands, harbor the greatest emotional hostility to Germans, German unification, and broader integration with Germany. Proximity, history, and degree of integration overlap, and it is difficult to discern their relative significance.

6. Shifting to intracountry differences, one generally sees in each country clear differences in reactions by age, education, position, and political allegiance. Everywhere, for example, mass opinion has been much more favorably disposed toward the Germans than elite opinion.

Indeed, were it not for the intellectuals and the political classes, the climate of opinion in all countries would be more favorable. The following sentiment might be a bit extreme, but it certainly bears some truth: "Were it not for the educated classes, nothing would impede the mutual understanding of peoples. A well-established prejudice on the part of teachers, lawyers, journalists and politicians is more durable than marble."[7]

7. The political Left has consistently exhibited greater hostility than the Right toward Germany. Tellingly, its antipathy has nothing to do with Germany's Nazi past. Rather, it concentrates on its current economic might and its emerging political power in the new Europe. Even in Greece, where the political Left has been consumed by anti-Americanism and welcomed Germany as a possible replacement of American dominance in Europe, an apprehension exists. The Left, to nobody's surprise, dislikes any economically powerful player as an agent of capitalism.

Our findings were neither consistent nor unequivocal. But they do indicate an openness toward the Germans that an aspiring power could clearly exploit. Some small countries that are hostile nevertheless are subject to the structural power of the German economy (Austria is our key exception). Small states that are politically friendly to the Germans but do not share immediate linkages with the German economy want what they perceive as the benefits of dependence. And the big states, at least in principle potential rivals to the power of the German economy, are fraught with a sense of frailty created by their own inadequacies. German political openings to the East and the West appear largely unconstrained by the attitudes of neighbors. It testifies to Germany's power that it matters almost nothing what their partners think of them and toward them: Germany's partners have few if any options. What difference does it make to Germany that Germans are well liked in Austria, despised in the Netherlands and Denmark? Key economic decisions for all three countries are made in Berlin and Frankfurt, and the Dutch and the Austrians have hitched the fates of the Guilder and the Schilling to the D-Mark. Affect in one case, antipathy in the other—they matter little in terms of actual behavior. Still, attitudes have profound effects on outcomes, even if they appear marginal at first glance.

Abiding Concerns

How are we to interpret these data? In general we urge extreme caution and much qualification. Circumspection, even more than the habitual etiquette of scholarly reserve, is of particular importance because of the political sensitivity of the subject.

Trends are not clear and results are not definitive. Yet we conclude that there exists no deep-seated fear, no comprehensive aversion to German unification or to Germany itself on the mass level anywhere in the European Union. With few exceptions popular opinion in Europe responded favorably to German unification and the new Germany's role on the Continent. Intercountry differences have to be taken with a grain of salt (84 percent of Spaniards and 82 percent of Britons purportedly favored some kind of unification), but surveys are helpful in painting a general picture of Europe's attitudes. Most telling about the existence of such a Europe-wide attitude is the fact that West German data regarding German unification are congruent with the rest. In a survey conducted by the Belgian daily *Le Soir*, 80 percent of respondents in the Federal Republic favored German unification—in fact, *lower* than the score for British, Spanish, Italian, Portuguese, and Greek respondents. In a CSA survey published in the *New York Times*, only 30 percent of the West German public expressed a very favorable opinion regarding German unification, in contrast to nearly 50 percent of Spaniards and 40 percent of Italians. Moreover, 17 percent of respondents in Germany were either very or fairly opposed to German unification; the corresponding Spanish and Italian figures were 6 percent and 13 percent. These results hint at two important developments: first, the German Question has to a considerable degree become subsumed under a larger European question; second, the West Germans have become Europeans in ways that pertain even to an issue as historically and psychologically charged as German unification. In Europeanizing the West German public, the Bundesrepublik proved an unmitigated success.

This is, obviously, not the whole story. Something substantial is afoot here, something that leads to surveys in the first place. *Les incertitudes allemandes*, as the French call the phenomenon, have led to cover stories in *Time*, *Newsweek*, and the *Economist*, countless articles in the world's leading newspapers, even a substantial piece by playwright Arthur Miller in the *New York Times Magazine*. Elites in Western as well as Eastern Europe and the United States were at least deeply preoccupied with, if not negatively disposed toward, the German Question. Every newspaper we investigated had something substantial to say about German unification. This amazing phenomenon and its immediate consequences, the transition from the Bonn to the Berlin Republic being the most significant, clearly remain central to the political classes of many European countries. Simply stated, Germany matters to its neighbors, to all Europeans, more than does any other European country. We encountered so many accolades about the new Germany's stable democracy that we became at least somewhat suspicious of what we call "whistling in the dark." What can we conclude about elite opinion on German unification?

Fears may be present only selectively, but uncertainties and ambivalence are certainly not. They come in a variety of forms with varying degrees of urgency. Most prevalent are worries concerning a larger, stronger Germany. This apprehension has three interrelated dimensions. First, the economic dimension manifested itself in concern that a united Germany will be an even more formidable competitor. On Europe's rim, in Spain, Portugal, and Greece, there emerged a worry that potential economic advantages might now move eastward.

The second dimension centered on politics. Worries concentrated on Germany's inevitable emergence as the most important political actor in all of Europe just as Europe was becoming increasingly independent of the superpowers. Germany's dominance will be bought at the direct cost of France and, to a lesser extent, Britain.

The third dimension concerned Germany's reliability as a European and Western country. In this context emerged a ubiquitous urge—powerful in France but also palpable in Italy, Spain, and Britain—to bind Germany to Europe at all costs. Europe, of course, had become synonymous with the continent's western half. With Germany at the geopolitical center of Europe, worries emerged that the traditional pull of the east might rival ties to the west.

Yet the abiding conclusion is that, faced with German unification and the growth of German influence, Europeans did not choose to circle the wagons nor even resort to that kind of rhetoric. If one decisive factor renders the project of a united Europe so difficult, it must be the absence of a collective European memory. Yes, Greeks and Danes, just like Germans and French, see themselves as Europeans and are representatives of the Judeo-Christian tradition. But in a more immediate sense, in the sense of offering an operative *conscience collective*, little ties Europeans together. In contrast to the United States, no common memory unites Europe. Rather, Europe has a memory of division, of negation, of the "other." In this collective negative memory, in Gian Enrico Rusconi's words, "there appears to be a black thread which runs through the collective minds of the otherwise divided memory of the Europeans, and that is a negative image of the Germans."[8]

Europe has only national memories, and those are often significantly fragmented by factors such as class and political allegiance. As a result, when asked about the Germans, some respondents are openly optimistic, many are apprehensive, few are ready to curtail German engagement. Indeed, preponderant is the view that greater integration with the new Germany might be the appropriate solution. Public attitudes among Europeans therefore do not appear an impediment to the widening and deepening of German structural power. This is all the more so because Europeans—no matter how apprehensive some might be in the *pays réel* of their private sphere—are simply unable to enter any kind of anti-German coalition. This, too, bespeaks the Germans' position as *primus inter pares* in the new Europe.

Any study of the effect of collective memory on how foreigners think about the Germans has many candidates to examine. But logic and sentiment suggest that no more profound a case exists than that of Israel.

It is fascinating that, at least on the level of public opinion, the country whose population one would expect to be the most hostile to Germany anywhere in the world reacts just like Europe. Israeli opinion vis-à-vis Germany is so split between the present and the past that one of the leading Israeli interpreters of German politics speaks of an "Israeli schizophrenia."[9] Israeli views of German unification and of the old Bundesrepublik have been surprisingly normal, given the Holocaust and its centrality in the political socialization of Israeli society and the identity formation of the modern Jewish state. Moshe Zimmermann and his colleagues at the Hebrew University conducted a poll in March and April 1990, and the findings show that a majority of Israeli respondents were either positively disposed toward Germany's (then prospective) unification or expressed neutrality. Only a minority voiced fears. Concretely, 26.3 percent favored German unification with no qualifications; 40.4 percent expressed no opinion or responded with various contingencies and qualifications; and "only" 33 percent expressed outright opposition. A subsequent study by the German public opinion research group EMNID, conducted at the end of 1991, confirmed this mildly positive inclination of the Israeli public regarding German unification: on a scale of +5 to −5, the Israeli public's view of German unification averaged out at a lukewarm +0.3. These numbers speak a level of generosity, of forgiveness, perhaps even of forgetfulness which is nothing short of remarkable. The finding is borne out by a time series that sought responses to the question whether Israel's relations to Germany were "normal." Here are the findings in percentages:

	1982	1990	1991	1992	1993	1994
Yes	31.3	62.5	51.9	56.8	58.1	58.2
No	30.0	21.8	35.9	33.5	25.4	24.6

Another question tried to ascertain whether Israelis believed that there existed "another Germany," a good, non-Nazi Germany:

	1982	1990	1991	1992	1993	1994
Yes	64.0	63.6	55.7	52.2	50.3	57.2
No	13.0	23.1	34.5	38.4	34.4	30.8

This finding suggests the schizophrenia which Zimmermann describes and which we also found, at least to some degree, in virtually every other nation. Although the percentage of Israeli respondents who believed in "another Germany" remained virtually constant over this twelve-year period, the percentage who denied its existence more than doubled in the 1990s. Zimmermann attributes this increase—in our view correctly—less to German unification than to Germany's role in the Gulf War, in which the German peace movement's antiwar activism often exhibited openly anti-Israeli and antisemitic sentiments.[10] The Gulf War also witnessed Iraqi SCUD missile attacks on Israel, which rekindled anti-German sentiments. It was well known that German companies and engineers had been actively engaged in Arab countries since the early 1950s in such endeavors as missile construction, the production of chemical weapons and other lethal measures aimed against the Jewish state. German corporations were prominent in constructing Saddam Hussein's personal bunkers, in improving the ballistic trajectories of his Soviet-built SCUD missiles, and in stockpiling chemical and poison-gas weapons that SCUDs were to carry straight to Tel Aviv and Jerusalem. Thus developed a truly frightening but realistic scenario: barely fifty years after Auschwitz, German-made gas could again cause mass destruction among innocent Jewish civilians. Israel was spared this ultimate nightmare, but sitting every night in sealed-off apartments with gas masks at the ready triggered the Israelis' collective memory concerning Germany. The image of a new and benign Germany experienced serious deterioration among the Israeli public in the course of the 1990s.

Germany's image among Israelis did not vary much by gender, class, or—interestingly—age. Moreover, as further evidence of the centrality of the Holocaust in the identity formation of all Israelis, studies discerned no differences toward Germany between Israel's Ashkenazic (occidental and European) Jews and its Sephardic (Oriental, Mediterranean, and Middle Eastern) Jews. The Sephardim, too, have come to appropriate the Holocaust as an essential icon of their existence. In contrast to other countries, it was the Israeli Right rather than the Left which exhibited disproportionately negative attitudes toward Germany. The decisive variable is the degree of religiosity, which in the last two decades has increasingly come to define Right and Left in Israeli politics. Rightists are much more openly religious and "orthodox" than Leftists, who pride themselves on their secularism. Religious Israelis as a rule view themselves much more consciously as Jews than do their secular counterparts and so bear greater animosity toward the Germans.

CHAPTER FIVE

The European Rim:
Greece, Portugal, Spain, Ireland

Challenged by memory, you could move forward.
—Elie Wiesel, *From the Kingdom of Memory*

Greece

One might have anticipated negative feelings toward Germany in a country that suffered brutal occupation by the Nazis, but in this event the Greek public overwhelmingly favored German unification. In polls carried out in the autumn of 1989, 83 percent answered that they were "personally in favor of the unification of the two German states," while only 3 percent were opposed and 14 percent offered no reply. The percentage of those in favor had slipped to 74 percent by the spring of 1990, and the numbers of those opposed had risen to 11 percent (no reply 15 percent), but these numbers indicate that the Greek public had no problem with the idea of German unification.[1]

What impact would German unification have on Greece? Questioned in June 1991, 11 percent of those polled said that unification made them very hopeful about the future of Greece, 36 percent somewhat hopeful, 24 percent rather fearful, 6 percent very fearful, and 24 percent did not know. Again, those who believed that German unification would have a positive impact on the future of Greece, 47 percent in all, were a majority of those holding an opinion, although it was not as large a majority as had favored German unification one year earlier.[2]

On the level of elite public opinion, in a country as highly politicized as Greece, it was not surprising to find clear-cut differences between the editorial positions of Leftist and Rightist publications on the German Question. However, the differences themselves were often counterintuitive. Publications close to PASOK, the left-wing party of former prime minister Andreas Papandreou, and the Eurocommunist KKEes (Communist Party of Greece—Internal), repeatedly ran positive articles about a resurgent Germany, to be welcomed as a long-overdue antidote to the American presence in Greece, the Mediterranean, and Europe. Anything that might lead to a departure of the much-hated American troops, whose government was perceived as leaning toward Turkey, met with the enthusiastic support of the Greek Left. The PASOK and Eurocommunist Left also rejoiced in the demise of the repressive GDR state.

If the center-left welcomed a united Germany as potentially liberating from

84

decades of American domination, the center-right worried about the same scenario. One author feared that Germany's rise would lead to an inevitable decline of American involvement in Europe, leaving a vacuum in the eastern Mediterranean. Uncertainty would ensue, and Turkey—spurred by increasing radicalization throughout the Muslim world—would be likely to assume an expansionary position vis-à-vis the Balkans. German unification, another suggested, was tantamount to the creation of a multipolar world, which would throw Europe eighty years backward. Publications close to the New Democracy of then prime minister Constantine Mitsotakis worried about German unification because it might spur U.S. disengagement from European affairs.

Much more prevalent than political concerns were various economic ones. Articles expressed what turned out to be a prophetic fear that a united Germany's involvement in eastern Europe would siphon away much-needed financial resources that could otherwise have been used to Greece's benefit. Worries also existed that East European countries would directly compete with Greece as low-wage attractions for German manufacturing. These fears were compounded by the notion that East European workers, though not working with state-of-the art technology, were better educated and had a more efficient work ethic than their Greek counterparts. Another source of anxiety concentrated on the weakening of the D-Mark as a consequence of its becoming East Germany's currency. As Greece had to pay for most of its imports in dollars, this development, it was argued, could ratchet up inflation in an already inflation-prone economy.

In contrast to its political fears, the right was optimistic about economic issues. In particular, it construed German unification as a means to diminish Margaret Thatcher's power in Europe, a happy occasion for Greece's pro-EU forces who saw the Iron Lady as the major obstacle to completion of the Single Market—a completion they hoped would bring immense benefits to Greece's ailing economy. Surveys did not reveal any fear about German unification; somewhat surprising to us, there were no manifest apprehensions about Germans as Nazis in contemporary Greece. The collective memory of World War II appears to have receded, at least on the level of opinion polls.

The Greeks thus were predictably divided between the Left and the Right. But that division was complicated by the reversal of positions regarding economic and political issues. Much concern in general rested on the possibility of German neglect of Greece rather than attention devoted to it.

In the wake of the wars in and the disintegration of the former Yugoslavia, some tensions developed between Greeks and Germans. They focused on the Greeks' bellicosity toward the newly founded state of Macedonia, which—after a lengthy indulgence of Greek animosity—the European Union proceeded to recognize at the end of July 1991. The Germans, in full accord with other EU members, decried Greek intransigence on the Macedonia issue. They were in the forefront of finding a solution that let the EU accord Macedonia full diplomatic status while exacting a substantial symbolic price. Among the changes the Germans negotiated were Macedonia's official name (it is now the Former Yugoslav Republic of Macedonia), passages of its constitution, and its official emblem. These concessions appeased the Greeks, although they were still far from happy. Moreover, for reasons of history and shared Orthodox Christianity, the Greeks were active supporters of the Serbs throughout the various Balkan wars of the 1990s.[3] As the Germans were the Croats' loyal allies and consistent supporters, Germans and Greeks found themselves on the opposite ends of the EU spectrum on matters relating to Serbia, Croatia, and Bosnia.

Portugal

Rich in history, proud of its former colonial empire, Portugal is now with Greece the European Union's poorest member. On virtually every indicator of affluence and economic comfort, Portugal, Greece, and occasionally Ireland share a permanent hold on last place in the EU rankings. Encouraging developments in 1989 rendered Portugal's unemployment rate the lowest and its annual growth rate the highest in the European Union, but Portugal remained among the union's poorest and least developed countries.[4]

Like Greece and Spain, Portugal had a troubled political past accompanying—some would argue causing—its economic retardation. Only in 1976 was liberal democracy of the parliamentary variety established successfully as Portugal's form of government. Geographic distance from the heart of Europe, continued longing for its Lusitanian possessions in Africa, the special relationship to Brazil, and failure to part with its fascist-authoritarian regime after 1945 placed Portugal apart. It is mainly through an enthusiastic embrace of the European core that Portugal hopes to shed its peripheral character in the twenty-first century. Germany is crucial to this vision.

It is hardly surprising, then, that we encountered no fear in Portuguese reactions to the German events of 1989 and 1990. We anticipated that traditional animosities would be quite low in Portugal since Hitler was too busy elsewhere to carry out his plan to invade the Iberian Peninsula in 1942. Moreover, Portugal has developed over the years affective feelings for Germany as a powerful rival of France, an occasionally troublesome partner, as well as Britain, its most consistent but also overbearing and capricious ally. There was no evidence of fear that unification would begin a replay of Germany's troubled past. Like their Greek counterparts, an overwhelming majority of Portuguese—83 percent—polled in the autumn of 1989 stated that they personally favored the unification of the two German states. Only 7 percent were opposed, and 10 percent had no reply. The numbers in favor slipped a little by the spring of 1990. Despite the slight decline—74 percent of Portuguese now favored German unification, 5 percent opposed, and 21 percent had no answer—the Portuguese were still friendly to the aspirations of the two Germanies to become one.[5]

Just as in Greece, there were fears regarding Germany's preoccupation with eastern Europe to the direct detriment of Portugal. When asked what effect a united Germany would have on Portugal, 10 percent of those questioned replied that this development made them very hopeful about Portugal's future, 49 percent rather hopeful, 16 percent rather fearful, and 2 percent very fearful (23 percent did not know). Thus the majority, 59 percent, felt German unification would ultimately be beneficial to Portugal, compared to 18 percent who believed it would ultimately hurt Portugal.[6] However, some commentators feared that developments could easily lead to even further marginalization of Portugal. As one editorial writer suggested: "What is happening is the shift in the center of European gravity further east . . . and this will inevitably accentuate the peripheral character of Portugal. . . . The question now is how to become Europe, how to be Europe, without ceasing to be Portugal. . . . The worst error would be to find refuge in historical nostalgia. Our history, our Portuguese universe, our Atlantic relations and links with Africa and Brazil give substance to our identity as a people, a nation, a state . . . But they are not our destiny. Our big chance is further integration into Europe."[7] The article exhorted its audience to fight the Portuguese propensity to view Portugal as a periphery—that becomes a destructively self-fulfilling prophecy. Periphery is not so much geographic location as state of mind. After all, Portuguese pride focuses on an epoch when Portugal was the center of the world and many current power holders were part of the periphery.

Portugal, too, devoted much attention to the end of bipolarity, but unlike in Greece, it evoked little anti-American *Schadenfreude* (joy in another's pain). Instead, much of the debate centered on the new role accorded Portugal in this imminently multipolar world. All answers focused on the need for Portugal to integrate into Europe with even greater vigor. In this context fears regarding Germany's new strength came to the fore. Most commentators emphasized that Germany's new position will strengthen her not only economically but politically as well. All suggested a further consolidation of the European framework as the most effective mechanism to contain German power. *Expresso* asked: "Would the future Germany of 80 or 90 million people and a powerful economy be able to unbalance the European Community? Yes and no. Or rather, it depends on the degree of integration which the Community will have achieved."[8]

Spain

Similar sentiments informed commentary in Portugal's Iberian neighbor. Here, too, we found no evidence of fear colored by Germany's Nazi past. Spanish commentators said little about "German characteristics" one might associate with authoritarianism or antidemocratic propensities. Apprehensions were almost entirely contemporary, with a virtually exclusive focus on such instrumental issues as the consequences of a united Germany for Spain's financial fate. We discerned awe for, rather than fear of, the emerging German juggernaut.

When asked whether they approved of German unification, 84 percent of those polled in Spain in the autumn of 1989 answered in the affirmative, with only 7 percent saying that they were not in favor, and 9 percent with no reply. In the spring of 1990, there was still great approval, with 81 percent percent personally in favor of unification, 5 percent opposed, and 13 percent unsure.[9]

On the mass level, Spaniards had little concern that German unification would be problematic for Spain. Questioned in the spring of 1991, 16 percent of Spaniards replied that a unified Germany made them feel very hopeful about the future of Spain, 48 percent rather hopeful, 9 percent rather fearful, 1 percent very fearful, and 27 percent did not know.[10]

On the elite level, however, as in Greece and Portugal, we encountered "periphery phobia" in Spain. There was much concern about Germany's rerouting of desperately needed investment to the former GDR and other eastern countries. Various responses were discussed. Articles in Spain's leading daily El País, consistently close to the PSOE-led governments of Felipe González, offered Germany a quid pro quo: Spain promised to support vigorously Germany's quest for unification in every international forum in late 1989 and 1990, especially within the European Union, as long as Germany continued to fight for a European central bank, helped create one European currency, and guaranteed that German investments to Spain would continue unabated. West German economics minister Theo Waigel's repeated assurances in March 1990 that investments already promised to the Iberian countries would not be rerouted testified to the clout of Spanish lobbying.

Spanish articles arguing for a united Germany in the context of a strengthened and united Europe abounded. The Spaniards did not want an isolated Germany and voiced support for the frequently sputtering process of European unification. The PSOE line, repeatedly articulated by Felipe González, was to back a united Germany (self-determination of any people is an inalienable right) in the framework of a united and secure Europe. González went so far as to argue that European unification now had four instead of the conventional three statutes: a single market, monetary union, political union, and a united Germany.[11] By welcoming a united Germany into the EU, the Spanish Socialists and the business community hoped (and still hope) to insure a smoother and irrevocable European unification and a Europeanized Germany. It should be noted that Spain's fears, confined to the realm of the instrumental and pragmatic, were the fears of an educated elite. As an editorial in El País of February 19, 1990 noted, German unification seemed to be a "universal trauma" for political analysts, but it provoked little concern on the part of the mass public.

Ireland

Like their counterparts in Spain, Portugal, and Greece, the vast majority of the Irish favored unification of the two German states. In the autumn of 1989, 81 percent of the Irish said they were for unification, 7 percent were opposed, and 13 percent did not have a reply. In the spring of 1990, 75 percent were in favor, 8 percent were opposed, and 18 percent did not have a reply.[12] A year later, when asked about the results of German unification for Ireland, 19 percent were very hopeful about the future of their country, 42 percent were rather hopeful, 14 percent were rather fearful, and 7 percent were very fearful, while 19 percent replied that they did not know what effect a unified Germany would have on the future.[13]

Commentaries in the Irish press identified opportunities as well as dangers for Ireland. Whereas some worried about further marginalization, others hoped that the new Europe would lead to a much-needed economic boom, spurred by a rejuvenated European Union. However, nobody seemed to doubt that the events of 1989/1990 shifted power relations within the European Union substantially in Germany's favor, a point that worried nobody in traditionally anglophobe Ireland. The country, after all, adopted a neutral stance vis-à-vis Nazi Germany during World War II.

Yet a number of articles stressed that Ireland was to all intents and purposes an English-speaking country, a clear competitive advantage in a global economy in which English had become the lingua franca. This advantage was underlined vis-à-vis countries in eastern Europe, Poland in particular, which some in Ireland viewed as potential rivals for German investments. Ireland's middle position between the United States and Europe was mentioned as a special advantage in the new economic and political world order. Thus Ireland, it was argued, should do everything in its power to become better known to German investors, German business, and the German public at large. Knowledge of Germany and, most important, a far better mastery of the German language were urgently desirable.

Most attention focused on the hope that a unified Germany would be a much-needed counterweight to the traditional dominance exerted by Britain over Irish affairs. Although Ireland's economic dependence on Britain had decreased markedly in the previous thirty years (80 percent of all Irish exports went to Britain in 1958, for example, only 33 percent in 1989), dependence on Britain remained both an objective and a subjective reality for many Irish. Opinions such as the following, from the *Irish Times*, were not uncommon:

> The new Europe may well be a union of small and large nations and pseudo-nations pursuing their own ends within the framework of a great federation, using the bigness of the Union for the purposes of a modern economy and the smallness of its components for the purposes of communal life. But the patterns formed by the

European historic experience will not have been erased. We can be certain that within the new Europe, for example, Britain's stance will be as adversary to the greatest Continental power in the Union, Germany. Ireland's interests are and will be in a great many matters quite different from those of Britain. In the balance of power and influence within the Union it will be in our interest generally to align with Germany rather than Britain. . . . The principal difficulties we may encounter, especially in a greatly enlarged European Community, will arise from the constant danger of marginalisation. . . . Our relationship with Britain is an important and valuable one . . . But it is a relationship that can reinforce marginalisation: it can come, as it has, between us and the rest of Europe. Britain is economically, socially and politically very different from Ireland, with some major interests that are contrary to ours. We need to establish new direct relations with the centre, and the centre of the new Europe will be Germany. This is not a matter of liking Germans, or of Ireland being friends with Germany. The first is desirable but not essential; the second is all but meaningless. It is a matter of intelligently consulting our national self-interest.[14]

The Irish reaction, like those in other countries, injected views into the German Question which had little if anything to do with German unification. The Irish reaction was, rather, conditioned by issues with which the Irish were preoccupied. Thus, for example, a few articles noted that unification might change the balance between Catholics and Protestants. Lothar de Maizière's notion that the new Germany would become more northern, eastern, and Protestant than the old Bundesrepublik was ignored in the rest of Europe but recognized in Ireland. It is noteworthy that religion served as a prism through which new developments in Germany were gauged. The religious dimension of German unification attained greater salience because Ireland, too, remained divided in the eyes of its Catholic citizens, with the division being justified in religious terms. Yet the religious cleavage between Protestants and Catholics has barely any political significance in contemporary German politics, so the issue offers a stark example of the projection of local realities shaping perceptions of German unification.

German unification, in sum, was accelerating the construction of a new Europe in which Ireland had to find its niche, establish its role, and forge a new identity. The best way to do so was for Ireland to expand and fortify continental (i.e., German) contacts, reduce dependence on Britain, and emphasize its geographically, culturally, and linguistically advantageous position between Europe and North America. In short, to the Irish public, German unification offered an unlimited opportunity.

CHAPTER SIX

Four Small Northern States:

Belgium, the Netherlands, Denmark, Finland

Soccer is a game where twenty-two men chase a ball for a long time and the Germans always win.

—Gary Lineker, English soccer player quoted in *Kurier*, June 28, 1996.

Belgium

According to the pan-European survey published in the Belgian francophone daily *Le Soir*, Belgian attitudes toward the new Germany were more or less in line with European averages. Seventy-five percent of Belgian respondents in 1990 favored German unification; the European average was 78 percent. Sixteen percent of Belgian respondents had no opinion and 9 percent opposed unification, with the latter characteristically overrepresented in the older (60+) category. These numbers are similar to those found by the Eurobarometer in a flash poll of November 1989. In answer to the question: "Are you for or against the unification of the two German states?" 71 percent of Belgians replied that they were in favor, 15 percent were opposed, and 14 percent had no reply. By the spring of 1990, when the Eurobarometer conducted a second survey, the numbers of Belgians in favor of German unification had slipped to 61 percent, 19 percent opposed, and 19 percent had no reply.[1] Similar patterns emerge for the Belgians' view on European integration (68 percent in favor compared to the European average of 70 percent) and the opening of the European Union to eastern countries (77 percent of Belgian respondents in favor compared to 75 percent of Europeans).[2] Belgians have become Europeans: torn between the Flemish north and the Walloon south, they have opted for the Brusselian solution of the golden mean in international politics. Brussels has developed into a suitable European capital as far as its immediate political surroundings and the political culture of its inhabitants are concerned.

Surprisingly, *Le Soir* ran no editorials or major articles on Belgian views of German events after the opening of the Berlin Wall. In none of the five time periods on which we concentrated could we locate much on Germany in editorials or interpretive pieces. There were many detailed news reports, to be sure, but virtually nothing to help us understand how the Belgians, or at least *Le Soir* reporters and columnists, felt about Germany. There were interviews with an East German writer, a West German literary critic, the British secretary of defence and a few asides concerning François Mitterrand (e.g., in connection with the Strasbourg conference of early December 1989), but no detailed debates about unification and nothing concerning Belgian attitudes. Yet Belgium was the only country to announce at that time that it was recalling its troops from former West Germany. All other Western allies maintained troop contingents in the western zone, albeit in substantially reduced numbers, well into the 1990s.

Belgium suffered twice from German aggression in this century. Belgium fought heroically in World War I and built up its defenses in the interwar period (including the "impregnable" fort of Eben-Emael), only to see all resistance crumble in the face of an overwhelming German onslaught in May 1940. The experience profoundly marked the Belgian psyche. Belgians realized that no matter how well they prepared, they would never be a match for the Germans. Their best hope therefore lay in pursuing reconciliation with Germany and in constructing a "common European house." We assume that the German mood must have attained great significance for Belgium.

Britain, a long-time ally and guarantor of Belgian independence since the country's inception in 1830, is another country whose opinion has historically mattered to Belgians. Relations between the two countries have varied enormously, but on the whole they remained good. Britain came to Belgium's rescue in both world wars, and Britain still commands respect in the country, particularly as a counterweight to France and Germany. This factor may account for the special attention accorded to British official opinion in *Le Soir*. The scant mention of the French point of view can perhaps be explained by the fact that Belgians, especially francophones, know France intimately. It was more startling to see virtually nothing about American and (then) Soviet responses to the new phase of the German Question.

When asked in the spring of 1991 how German unification would affect the future of Belgium, 9 percent of respondents answered that they were very hopeful (the lowest score of any EC country except France), 42 percent were rather hopeful, 25 percent were rather fearful, and 6 percent were very fearful, while 18 percent replied that they did not know.[3] Clearly, the majority of Belgian mass opinion saw German unification as beneficial to Belgium. The only instance of fear we found was a cartoon in which a huge Helmut Kohl towered over a group of European midgets. The midgets were voting for the German right to self-determination, closely watched by Kohl. The caption says, "We are together forever." One midget, Margaret Thatcher, walks away dejectedly.

The Belgian attitude toward unification can be characterized as silent acceptance bordering on normalcy. Occasional irony tinged with some bitterness did not amount to any noticeable fear of German unification. Fear seemed to be absent in its expected variants: Germans as Nazis, as economic giants, as political bullies, as large and powerful partners. Developments after November 9, 1989, changed little if anything in Belgium's position. It is almost as if the absence of Belgian views regarding the changed geopolitical order conveys Belgium's impotence and irrelevance. Belgium is comfortable in its European role, which means being resigned to playing second fiddle to Germany however constituted.

The Netherlands

David Cameron once called the economy of the Netherlands "Germany Inc.," so closely is the Dutch economy integrated with and dependent on that of its larger neighbor. Yet the Dutch image of Germans remains unremittingly negative, filled with mistrust, anger, rejection, and a certain contempt. It continues to be overdetermined by the Nazi occupation of 1940–45. Not even the still-despised and feared Count Alba, empowered by Philip II of Spain to defeat the Dutch rebellion of the sixteenth century, compares in levels of antipathy to those the Dutch continue to exhibit to their dominant neighbors to the east.[4] Although the image of the ugly German is not as prevalent as it used to be, the pejorative *mof* (the Dutch equivalent of "Kraut" or "Boche") has not yet disappeared.[5]

The *mof* is a rough character who is loud and pretentious, a know-it-all who is brash about his country's power. The Dutch see the Germans as arrogant bullies; Germans are replete both with obsequiousness and with bossy authoritarianism and a propensity for militarism.[6] Above all, Germans are uncouth, unrefined, in essence uncultured, again traits that weaker groups often associate with the strong (the German view of Americans is an excellent case in point).[7] The syndrome is characterized by an inherent superiority that the weaker group imputes to itself. What it concedes in strength and importance, it compensates through superiority of culture, sensibility, and other refinements.

Perhaps more surprising than the existence of this image is its demographics. It was generally thought that a generational change had taken place in the Netherlands, and that this view of Germans was confined to older people. But recent research suggests that Dutch teenagers have an antipathy, even hostility, toward the Germans. A survey of 1,800 Dutch 15- to 19-year-olds in the period November 1992 to January 1993 revealed a clearly negative view of the Germans. When asked what they spontaneously associated with the word "Germany," 18 percent of the youngsters replied "the First or Second World War," and 20 percent replied "racism, right-wing extremism and violence against foreigners." Sixty percent saw the Germans as arrogant (compared to 25 percent who thought the French arrogant, 19 percent the British, 12 percent the Dutch, and 5 percent the Belgians). Seventy-one percent saw the Germans as power-hungry, and 47 percent regarded Germany as a land that wanted to rule the world.[8]

The Germans view their *Kultur* as superior to Anglo–American civilization; so too the Dutch see themselves as inherently culturally superior to the Germans by virtue of being liberal, bourgeois, and an integral part of the West. Small states often do not trust their larger neighbors, particularly those with a penchant for predatory behavior. This phenomenon is certainly exemplified in Dutch perceptions of Germany. The Dutch feel and fear the German presence regardless of what Germany actually does.

The Dutch perception of Germany was and is based not only on actual events but also on a structurally conditioned situation in which the larger state appears threatening merely as a consequence of discrepancy in size. Negative sentiments under these conditions emerge in periods of crisis and extraordinary circumstances. The unification of Germany was one—indeed a unique—event that qualifies as extraordinary. Others fraught with crisis and its imagery are soccer games between Dutch and German clubs, most notably, of course, between the two national sides. These games have triggered ugly nationalist sentiments on both sides, with German reactions bordering on racist attacks against Dutch players of Surinamian origin and the Dutch invoking crypto-Nazi imagery. One rather telling gaffe by the German chemical and pharmaceutical giant Bayer received wide attention in the Dutch press: harnessing the German national soccer team's dramatic "sudden death" victory in the European Nations' Championship final against the Czech Republic in London in late June 1996 for marketing purposes, the company touted the potency of one of its insecticides in Guatemala by claiming that "sudden death is a German speciality."[9]

Many Dutch reactions provided a startling contrast to the Belgian. Mass opinion in the Netherlands seemed to favor German unification. In the Eurobarometer survey of autumn 1989, 76 percent of the Dutch surveyed were for unification, 12 percent were opposed, and 12 percent had no reply. In the spring of 1990, 59 percent of the Dutch surveyed were in favor of German unification, 21 percent were opposed, and 20 percent had no reply.[10] A year later, in the spring of 1991, when asked whether a unified Germany made them feel hopeful about the future of the Netherlands, 8 percent were very hopeful, 52 percent were rather hopeful, 22 percent were rather fearful, and 4 percent were very fearful, while 14 percent said that they did not know.[11]

On the elite level, however, reactions to German unification were loud, unequivocal in expressing concern, and insistent in comparison to the muted Belgian response. Yet it is the Dutch economy that is more integrated with the German.

This difference in reactions resulted in part from the fact that the Dutch were defeated only once by the Germans in recent memory and so find themselves emotionally at the stage the Belgians occupied in the interwar period (when Belgium was actively and openly anti-German). Moreover, the Netherlands had historically been a Prussian and then German ally. The brutal attack of 1940 was thus seen as a great betrayal, a stab in the back. Belgium, for its part, never had illusions about German friendship (or anyone else's, for that matter).

Relatively early in the process of unification, on December 8, 1989, the Dutch minister of foreign affairs Hans Van den Broek called the vagueness characterizing discussions on German unification "alarming" because the problem was international, far beyond the confines of the two Germanies.[12] Van den Broek seemed particularly irked that Kohl failed to give his allies advance information on his plan for unification.

At the 1990 conference in Strasbourg, the Dutch prime minister Ruud Lubbers would ask Kohl directly whether "the German people" also applied to Polish citizens of German origin. The Dutch seemed particularly concerned about Poland's western borders and its German minorities because, in the Dutch assessment (shaped by vivid memories of World War II), that is where trouble was most likely. Kohl's insistence that clarification of Germany's stance on the Polish frontiers had to await a democratically elected parliament of a unified Germany and a peace treaty with Poland caused a storm in the Netherlands.

On December 12, 1989 there was a heated debate in the Dutch parliament. This debate consolidated the Dutch position on the inviolability of Poland's western frontier, German unification only within the context of European unification, and subsumed the German Question under the larger European umbrella. Dutch concern with Germany's rush toward unification was obvious in press accounts. "While nervous neighbors sigh over the 'German question . . . ' " started an article in *NRC/Handelsblad* (December 14, 1989), which spoke of the "spooky dream of the looming unity" of 80 million Germans. German unification did not elicit an enthusiastic response in the Dutch press.

The growing Dutch concern over German guarantees to Poland prompted the West German ambassador to the Netherlands, O. H. Von der Gablentz, to declare on December 15 that "Poland's western border will remain Poland's border." The Dutch were upset about German attitudes and the German tone on all of these developments. They were indignant about the harping on German rights, and they distrusted the hurried nature of West German reactions to developments in the GDR.

In yet another contrast to Belgian silence, the Dutch were also vocally assessing the implications of German unification for broader geopolitical relations. In particular, they found Mitterrand's "Florentine diplomacy" embarrassing and ultimately ineffective.[13] Even if the French kept the Germans commited to the European Union, they would have to accustom themselves to playing second fiddle to a strengthened Germany. The Dutch seemed to get particular joy from Mitterrand's Freudian slip when he mistakenly called the Bundestag the "Reichstag." Even the Dutch Left adopted a pro-NATO position in which the Americans had to be given a leading role. Overall, Dutch sentiment toward the prospect of German unification was best summarized by a sentence from the *NRC/Handelsblad* of December 27, 1989: "The division of Germany, although often pronounced unnatural, provided for a good night's sleep during the past 40 years."

The image of the ugly German remained prevalent among the Dutch Left, the political and cultural elites, and the young. These antipathies were no different from those typically expressed by the political class, and especially the Left, in other small states. The content differed little from that expressed with regularity by Canadian (especially Ontarian but not Quebecker) Leftists concerning the United States: Germany for the Dutch left-wing intelligentsia, like the United States for its Canadian counterpart, is conceived as bullying, brutal, domineering, exploitative, and inherently imperialist. These negative assessments of Germany are sharpened by the particular aversions arising from the continued memory of the Nazi occupation.

In few other countries in Europe can one perceive such a glaring discrepancy between overwhelming structural integration with Germany and a lasting antipathy toward the Germans. Germany is far and away the Netherlands' most important economic partner. Cooperation on an institutional level goes well beyond linkage of the Dutch Guilder to the D-Mark. The most important symbols of national sovereignty—the two countries' military establishments—have begun to construct a military partnership to reinforce the European pillar of NATO.[14] But just beneath the surface of this institutional initiative, one again confronts the vivid images of collective memory. The past lingers. "Why is Waterloo history, and the Second World War an experience?" asked a Dutch general involved in this project, echoing the distinction we draw between history and collective memory. "How many years does it take?"[15] Kohl's subsequent threat to block Ruud Lubbers's candidacy for presidency of the Commission unless Lubbers ceased opposition to the location of the new European central bank in Frankfurt—a threat Kohl carried through—reminded many Dutch of earlier episodes when the Germans abridged Dutch sovereignty and autonomy.[16] For a large number of Dutch, even today, encounters with Germany still evoke reactions that are characteristic of collective memory and not of history.

Denmark

If anything, Germany's image has been even more negative in Denmark. All the connotations of the word "German" (*tysk*), whether literal or figurative, are negative.[17] Just as in the Netherlands, the Germans are disliked because they are a big power and because they occupy a particularly negative position in the Danes' collective memory. We know that the issue of small vs. big state plays a role in these relationships because Danes express some of the same negative feelings toward the Swedes as toward the Germans: they characterize both neighbors as displaying an arrogance of power, imperial demeanor, loudness, and uncanny efficiency.

Part of this big vs. small syndrome is magnified through tourism, and Denmark does indeed receive a massive infusion of German and Swedish tourists every year. What makes these intruders so unwelcome in the eyes of the natives is the fact that they are an economic necessity or at least a substantial boon for the local economy. Yet tourists are loud, inconsiderate of local customs, and a general nuisance to the alleged tranquility of local life. Adding to German unpopularity in Denmark is what the Danes label "yellow peril," meaning that they take particular umbrage at Germans running around Denmark's beaches in yellow ponchos and yellow rainhats in weather that makes Danes retire to the living room to play cards and enjoy a beer. In sum, Danish antipathy for the Germans is seriously overdetermined.

Further accentuating the Danish dislike for the Germans is a twofold historical trauma: in addition to 1940, the Danes carry the memory of 1864, when Prussians and Austrians attacked Denmark in the name of the German Federation and stripped it of the duchies of Schleswig, Holstein, and Lauenburg. Denmark's misgivings about German power are refracted through a continued memory of Denmark's decline from major-power status occurring at the hand of the Germans. The Danes clearly bear a feeling of inferiority vis-à-vis the Germans. The feeling emerges partly in resentment, partly in a false sense of superiority.

The Danes were somewhat more ambivalent about German unification than many of their European counterparts. Only 59 percent of Danes replied in the affirmative when asked in November 1989 whether they were for the unification of the two German states. Twenty-two percent were opposed, and 19 percent offered no reply. By the spring of 1990, 56 percent were in favor, 26 percent opposed, and 18 percent offered no reply. These rates of approval were lower than in any other EC country except Luxembourg—even lower than those in the Netherlands.[18] In a survey from January 1990, 51 percent of Danish voters thought German unification had negative implications for European development, only 26 percent saw it as positive, and 23 percent offered no opinion.[19]

In Denmark, too, the political class exhibited more pronounced reservations than the mass public about unification. For example, Danish prime minister Poul Schlueter expressed his feelings with almost Thatcher-like abandon in November 1989, hoping that there would remain two German states.

If we disaggregate the negative responses and analyze motives, we find that in Denmark the fear has been defined less by the past as manifested in German military might than by the present, in German economic power. Thus, 58 percent were worried about the potential economic domination of Denmark whereas 24 percent had no such concerns, and 18 percent expressed no opinion. The Danish political class has long resented the fact that Danish monetary policy is totally subject to policy decisions reached in Frankfurt. One newspaper headline expressed it poignantly, and in German no less: "Bundesbank über alles."[20] As in the Dutch case, the more dependent the country was on the German economy, the greater the resentment.

Even the Danes, however, considered unification as a positive development for their own country. When questioned in the spring of 1991, 10 percent of the Danes polled said that a unified Germany made them personally feel very hopeful about the future of Denmark. Forty-eight percent were rather hopeful, 29 percent rather fearful, 4 percent very fearful, and 9 percent did not know.[21]

Even though economic apprehension was prevalent, military fears had a sizable presence in the Danish reaction. Forty-three percent of those polled believed that a united Germany might be a military threat again, with 41 percent disagreeing and 16 percent having no opinion.[22]

Danish concern was significantly greater than anywhere else except Poland. The parallel confirms that a nation's feelings toward Germany are only partly related to the brutality of German occupation during the Nazi period. In Poland, German brutality was greater than in any other country the Nazis occupied (excepting perhaps the Soviet Union). In Poland, antipathy toward Germans is obviously overdetermined by, if not rooted in, the horrors of occupation.

The Danish case, however, was different. While obviously humiliating to the Danes, German occupation was not particularly brutal, partially because the Danes signed a mutual nonaggression pact with the Germans in 1939 (as if the Danes were going to attack Germany at some point!). Thus, the reaction of the Danes to Germany is a complex composite of interdependent phenomena: current German domination, particularly in the economy; collective memory pertaining to World War II and before; and a general dislike of anybody who is larger and more powerful.

Many Danes have felt that the only way to prevent the reemergence of an even more powerful Germany was to domesticate it through the European Union. An equal number of Danish citizens, particularly those on the left-liberal portion of the spectrum, fear that Europe will be little more than an extension of German power. The issue was of more than academic interest, as amply demonstrated by the Danish referendum on the Maastricht Treaty. A slight but nevertheless clear majority of Danish voters opted not to ratify the treaty in June 1992. Never mind that in a subsequent vote, barely one year later, the Danish public reversed itself and narrowly approved Denmark's participation in a European Union governed by Maastricht. The Danes initially refused to approve European unification because of their profound suspicion of Germany. At least half of the Danish population worried that any politically united Europe would be a German-dominated Europe.

Soccer once again offers a fine gauge of uncensored sentiment. When Denmark played Germany in the European Nations' Cup Final in June 1992, the analogy of David meeting Goliath extended far beyond the immediate game. For the Danes, and vicariously for many other European countries, their team's improbable victory against the heavily favored Germans was nothing short of a symbolic statement of Danish autonomy, sovereignty, and independence. The soccer team did what neither the Danish army nor the Danish economy ever could, it defeated the Germans. This symbolic victory helped the Danes exorcise some of their fears of Germany and may actually help explain why they then approved Denmark's participation in Maastricht in the spring of 1993.

It may all come down to the following anecdote. A reporter for the left-wing Danish newspaper *Information* described in shocked terms how members of the

Bundestag sang "Deutschland, Deutschland über alles" at their session on November 10, 1989, the day after the Berlin Wall had opened. A German professor corrected him: the Bundestag members had of course sung the third stanza of the Deutschlandlied, "Einigkeit und Recht und Freiheit" (Unity, justice, and freedom). The Danish reporter responded that he certainly knew this, but that he automatically associates the melody of the German national anthem with its first stanza.[23] In a history of domination and unequal power, melodies render lyrics moot. Whatever the Germans sing, many Danes hear something quite different—and sinister.

Finland

Finland's association with Germany has been among the most positive in Europe. Indeed, together with the Hungarians, the Finns have been the most favorable to German unification in particular, and Germany in general, among the populations surveyed.[24] The differences on this score between Finns and Danes lie entirely in different historical experiences and resulting collective memories. What Finns and Danes have in common is a dislike for the Swedes. They differ about the Germans.

The Finnish struggle for independence was inextricably tied to a refusal to recognize Finnish as a legitimate language by the Swedish-speaking upper class, who generally referred to Finnish as the "language of the devil." In the nineteenth-century movement for autonomy, German universities and German romanticism played crucial roles in educating the Finnish literati, providing them with an intellectual counterforce against Russian political rulers as well as Swedish cultural and economic elites. Since Finland, ruled by Russia until December 6, 1917, did not have its own army, Finnish officers had to turn elsewhere to receive military training. Sweden refused as a consequence of its strict neutrality, and it was Germany which trained the Finnish officer corps. Finnish soldiers and units fought alongside the Germans on the Russian front in 1915, and German troops, in turn, intervened in the Finnish civil war in 1918. The Finns' gratitude to Germany was so profound that they elected a Hessian prince as their first king. Even though the kingdom was never constituted, in good part because of the demise of imperial Germany in 1918, the Finnish Republic remained extremely grateful to the Germans throughout the interwar period.

The winter war of 1939–40 between the Soviet Union and Finland reinforced anti-Russian sentiments that the Finns had developed during the years of tsarist rule. Throughout World War II, it was the Soviets and Stalin, not the Nazis and Hitler, whom the Finns feared. Hitler is still the best-known German politician in Finland, by a fivefold margin over his closest contemporary competitors (Hitler known to 75 percent of the Finns; Brandt, Adenauer, Schmidt, and Kohl to perhaps 15 percent), but few Finns view him in a particularly negative light. It is in the context of this uncritical Hitler image that the nickname "Aatu"—a diminutive of "Adolf," as mentioned—is employed in an endearing rather than a pejorative manner.[25]

The Finnish reaction to German unification followed the European pattern. According to a survey published in the magazine *Suomen Kuvalehti* on March 16, 1990, 67 percent of the Finnish respondents favored unification with 21 percent opposing it and 11.5 percent having no opinion. By the summer of 1990, opposition to German unification had become negligible, and a unified Germany was fully accepted.

This is not to say that there is no criticism of Germany. In Finland, too, the Left has been much less willing than the population as a whole to embrace Germany. The reasons are plentiful. First, the Finnish Left has always had a strong, rather pro-Soviet communist component. Second, the Left, even more than other Finns, resented the fact that the German Right derided their unique arrangement with the Soviet Union as Finlandization, a pejorative term that became synonymous with an exchange in which a small country abdicated full political sovereignty to a large and dominant neighbor while maintaining its freedom to conduct economic and social affairs. Third, like the Left everywhere, the Finnish Left remained suspicious of German economic power which, even before unification, dominated the Finnish economy. Fourth, the Left, as well as other Finns, exhibited the usual small-state syndrome in which the pristine character of their own small country is extolled and defended against the noisy intrusion and commodified intervention of the large state's tourists. The usual fears of beer-swilling, uncouth Germans disrupting the serenity of the Finnish wilderness is a variation of a theme we have encountered among the Dutch, the Danes, and the Belgians.

CHAPTER SEVEN

Austria: Germany's Junior Partner

Although many Austrians would like to see Hitler go down in history as a German and Beethoven as an Austrian, it was the other way around.
—Frederick C. Engelmann, "The Austro-German Relationship"

This will be the world's most powerful economic bloc in which the Germans will have their place with open borders to Czechoslovakia, Poland, and Hungary.
—Helmut Kohl, *Der Spiegel*, 26 February 1990

Austria may be the only one of Germany's nine contiguous neighbors where German tourists can relax without feeling guilty. Even though the Austro-German relationship (an intra-German relationship until 1806 arguably 1866, perhaps even 1871, quite possibly 1945) had its ups and downs, it has been continuously cordial throughout the twentieth century. Most important, the Nazi era whose legacy still burdens Germany's relationship with so many European countries saw the closest and most harmonious interaction between Germans and Austrians this century. Even though Austrians have been magically successful in selling to themselves and the world the notion that they were Hitler's first victims, the Nazi past does not divide Austrians from Germans. It unites them. Thus Austria's relationship to Germany is unique in Europe.[1]

Culture

The German presence in Austria's culture is nothing short of overwhelming. It is hardly an exaggeration to say that the production, financing, and channeling of contemporary Austria's mass culture has become the prerogative of German media giants. In the print media, its electronic counterpart, advertising, book publishing and all other aspects of mass culture, Germany's influence is so pervasive that Austria's leading student of the country's media calls Austria a "media colony."[2]

Here are some data to illustrate the point. German media giants have controlled, either directly or indirectly, 70 percent of Austria's daily newspapers since the mid-1980s. The Federal Republic's second largest newspaper company, the *Westdeutsche Allgemeine Zeitung* has acquired a 45 percent interest in the two largest Austrian dailies, the *Neue Kronen Zeitung* and the *Kurier*, thus not only exerting decisive financial control but in effect ending competition by uniting them under one foreign owner. With the *Neue Kronen Zeitung* reaching 2.7 million Austrian readers, 43 percent of Austrian readership, and the *Kurier*, though a distant second, still reaching 941,000 Austrian readers on a daily basis, 15 percent of Austrian readership, the "Kronen-Kurier" has a prominence which is proportionally speaking far and away the highest in any advanced industrial democracy. Among Austria's highbrow papers as well, there exists a considerable German presence. Germany's largest newspaper company, Axel Springer AG, owned 50 percent of Austria's paper of record, *Der Standard*, until 1996, and still has a 45 percent interest in a leading regional newspaper, the *Tiroler Tageszeitung*. To be sure, some important Austrian daily newspapers, *Die Presse* and *Salzburger Nachrichten* among them, are independent of German capital, and Austria's main weekly newsmagazine, *profil*, is also financially independent of German sources. However, most leading German publications enjoy a major presence in Austria. As Hans Heinz Fabris notes, "approximately 93 percent of imported journals come from the FRG, and 80 percent of exports go there, which illustrated Austria's extreme degree of dependence on the FRG in this particular sector of the market."[3]

In electronic media there are many cooperative arrangements in programming and production between the Austrian state-owned television and radio network ORF and the two German public networks ARD and ZDF. With the increasing diversification of Austrian television, German-owned private channels such as SAT1 and RTL have enhanced their reach over the Austrian viewing public.

German dominance in Austria's book market is equally pronounced, as Fabris makes clear. "More than half of the books sold in Austria originate in the FRG. The readers' association Donauland, which is predominantly owned by [the German publishing house] Bertelsmann, the world's second largest media concern, dominates the channels of distribution. Every third household in Austria is a member of Donauland. Imports from the FRG account for 84 percent of the total book imports by Austria. . . . Conversely, only 17 percent of all books imported by the Federal Republic come from Austria."[4]

Only in motion pictures is Austria's production and consumption of daily culture not overwhelmingly dominated by German products. Here, the United States is still the market leader, with nearly 37 percent of the Austrian film market. Germany is a distant second with 15.3 percent, followed closely by France with 13.9 percent and Italy with 12.1 percent. The figures for all other countries are negligible.[5] But even here there exists a far from unimportant, albeit indirect, German influence on Austrian mass culture: with very few exceptions, American-made films are shown in Austria dubbed into German. This dubbing is done exclusively in Germany, with German actors, German voices, German accents, and German translations. In short, Austrian film viewers see American films with German accents, translated into a discourse that is distinctly German not Austrian. The nuance may be slight but it exists nonetheless. It must be strange for Austrians to hear Arnold Schwarzenegger dubbed into *piefkisch* north German. The German presence in Austria is ubiquitous.

Perhaps even more important than the sheer quantitative weight of this German presence are its qualitative implications. Germany's dominance over Austria's culture can be illustrated by the following fact: any Austrian who is vaguely interested in anything beyond the narrow confines of her or his own little local world has to read German publications such as *Der Spiegel, Die Zeit, Süddeutsche Zeitung, Frankfurter Allgemeine Zeitung,* and *Frankfurter Rundschau.* With the exception of a handful of scholars who make their living studying Austria (usually in some kind of comparative context), very few Germans have ever heard of, let alone read, *Der Standard, Die Presse, profil* or other Austrian publications. Even on their holidays in Austria, Germans read their own newspapers, which are readily available. Austrian intellectuals and scholars have to write for German publications, and so much of Austria's voice "occurs" abroad. An Austrian who really wants to be heard, read, seen, or otherwise received has to make his or her talents work in German ways sooner or later: publishing in German periodicals and newspapers, writing books published by German houses; appearing in German theaters and movies; being listened to by German audiences; receiving a paycheck written by a German or German-dominated company. Austrians have very few options to avoid the German dominance of virtually every aspect of their cultural scene.

Yet curiously, it is precisely in the realm of culture that Austrians view themselves as the Germans' equal, indeed often their superior. Austrian authors, actors, artists, intellectuals, and scholars have profited immensely from the presence of a huge neighbor with a similar culture, an overlapping if not identical history, and of course a shared language which is—despite localisms and differences in pronunciation—the most potent link between the two countries.[6] For many Austrians in the arts, sciences, journalism, and literature, "making it" really means being accepted in Germany. Intellectuals in many other small countries, neighboring Hungary for example, do not have the luxury of using their mother tongue to be readily understood by 80 million people in a neighboring country. In addition to the enormous financial and psychological rewards that the huge German market provides, the profound advantage of not having to have one's work translated, of writing for a larger German audience in the language in which one was taught in school, is simply priceless.

Knowledgeable critics of the Austrian cultural scene see in this combination the origins of Austria's self-identification as a global power in the realm of culture.[7] For a country that has gained legitimacy in the family of nations by touting its smallness, Austria often claims to be one of the world's giants in the area of culture.[8] To be sure, Mozart, Schubert, the Vienna Philharmonic, the Salzburg Festival, and the Burgtheater—among many other cultural icons—are singularly important in their contributions to European culture. But there is obviously more at work. Only in the realm of culture can Austria attain three key elements of legitimacy.

First, cultural primacy allows Austria to reminisce about its past and glorify its former political importance, well aware that the latter can never be attained again. Thus, wallowing in Strauss (of any kind, Johann, Josef, Richard et al.) is a safe and legitimate way to extol the alleged virtues of the Habsburg Empire and to create a direct link between the empire and the current Austrian republic.

Second, cultural primacy permits Austria to separate itself from its heinous Nazi past yet still be proud of its history. Austrians have appropriated Beethoven and made Hitler a German. In short, by dwelling on Mozart and the icons of Austrian culture, Austrians make National Socialism the sole prerogative of the evil Germans. As a cultural giant and a political dwarf, the Austrians pursue a remarkably successful strategy of exculpation vis-à-vis their recent history. Their strategy paralleled the Germans' postwar self-understanding, though the Germans projected themselves as an economic giant and a political dwarf. To be sure, the German gambit was a good deal more difficult to accomplish than the Austrian, if for no other reasons than that culture is a lot less threatening than the economy and that Germany is about ten times the size of Austria.

Third, Austria's identity as cultural giant and political dwarf also offers a clear position of strength vis-à-vis contemporary Germany. For it says loudly and clearly: we might not be your match in economic might and political importance, but we are certainly your equals in the finer things in life that reflect a country's real worth: culture. At this point Austrians habitually start enumerating the famous Austrian writers, actors, artists, and journalists who became successful in Germany (often because they were neglected, vilified, misunderstood, or mistreated by their fellow Austrians). No matter how much Thomas Bernhard or Peter Handke were abused in their native Austria, the Austrians were quick to claim them as soon as Germans dared to call them German authors. Austrians harness a rich tradition in the realm of culture which, at least in the Austrians' eyes, renders them equals of the Germans in an otherwise heavily imbalanced relationship.

Politics

If in the areas of culture and the economy Germany's presence in Austria is nothing short of ubiquitous—rendering Austria obviously dependent vis-à-vis Germany—the situation does not pertain in politics. Quite surprisingly, in politics there coexist two separate, independent entities with virtually no issues between them but also no dependency as a consequence of unequal power relations. At least until Austria joined the European Union, two discrete, separate sovereignties shaped the political relations between the Federal Republic and Austria.

To be sure, a bird's eye view would identify substantial similarities and overlaps between the political systems of these two neighbors. Both in form and in content, structural parallels abound. The number of parties represented in the respective national legislatures was identical until 1990. The names of the parties, their ideologies, the histories of their origins, and their role in each country are very similar, if not identical. The colors denoting political allegiances (black, red, green, blue, and parts of the *pays réel* of both countries, brown) bespeak a common political culture.

Both political systems are federal. Both are profoundly permeated by political parties that help characterize individuals: what matters are name, address, profession, and party color (which can denote anything from dyed-in-the-wool activist to vague sympathizer). Austria and Germany continue to be party states. Both political systems are corporatist; both are deeply committed to a politics of stability. Of course, there are important differences. Austria is more corporatist than Germany, and the Austrian state is far more interventionist and active. Though substantially weakened since the late 1980s, Austria's two dominant parties—the SPÖ and the ÖVP—still exert a more substantial presence than do their German cousins, the SPD and the CDU/CSU. Germany's obsession with its constitution and the legitimation bestowed by the Basic Law, which reaches almost American proportions, is virtually unknown in Austria. The concept of a "constitutional patriotism" (*Verfassungspatriotismus*), crucial to the political process and the formation of political identity in the Federal Republic, is meaningless in Austria. The Bundesrat, parliament's upper chamber, is more significant in Germany than in Austria. The Austrian president, unlike the German, is elected directly by the Austrian people; and Austrian postwar politics has conducted referenda on issues of fundamental controversy whereas its German counterpart has not.

Differences and similarities abound, and they most certainly matter to the people involved. Of greater interest to us is that, despite substantial similarities over the past century and despite the immense German importance for Austria's quotidian culture and economic welfare, the area of politics until 1995 witnessed a profound separation between Germany and Austria.

The Federal Republic of Germany and Austria had very little political contact other than regular diplomatic relations after 1949. Relations that had been "special" in the economy and culture were simply "normal" in politics: two neighboring states that had few conflicts but no special ties. This separateness is best illustrated by the following phenomenon: whereas thousands of Austrians have made their careers in Germany's economy and culture (and substantially fewer Germans have done so in Austria's), there has been no interchange of people in politics. No Austrian "made it" in the Federal Republic's political establishment, nor have Germans played any role in Austrian politics. Such strict separation was not the case until 1945—Hitler was merely the most successful Austrian in German politics.

The strict separation of Austria and the Federal Republic assumed a crucial legitimating role for the postwar identity and the state-building process in both countries. It was, in fact, an essential requirement for the rebuilding of both polities. Whereas the Federal Republic's postwar identity became inextricably tied to the country's central role in two key alliances, NATO and the EEC, later EU, Austria's very existence became identified with political neutrality in a world divided into two distinct blocs. Germany's absolution from its National Socialist past depended on the country's complete political, cultural, economic, and social immersion in the West. Austria's absolution—if indeed it was an issue for this lucky country—was much more simple: It had to remain completely separate from Germany lest anything remotely resembling *Anschluss* incur the wrath of the Allied powers, particularly the Soviet Union. If the Federal Republic's *West-bindung* (ties with the West) served to create *Verfassungspatriotismus*, Austria's neutrality formed the most important pillar in constructing a viable "Austrian-ness."

Austria's political fortunes lay in its active distancing from Germany, beginning with the Moscow Declaration of 1943 in which the Allied powers decreed Austria Hitler's first victim and continuing with the emergence of the Cold War. The process was reinforced by the Austrian State Treaty of 1955 and concretized by the departure of the four Allied powers in that same year. Everything that Germany attained in international politics, culminating in unification, was thanks to its integral part in the Western Alliance; Austria's postwar identity derived from precisely the opposite constellation: not a member of NATO and neutral regarding the Western Alliance. Germany anchored its well-being and its security policy in a closely knit web of multilateral pacts, whereas Austria's security was based on the country's belonging to nothing. Indeed, it was neutrality coupled with smallness that the country—especially under the leadership of Bruno Kreisky throughout the 1970s and the early 1980s—parlayed into diplomatic prominence. Like the three other small neutrals on the European continent—Switzerland, Sweden, and Finland, Austria gained immense domestic and international mileage from being small. In the course of the Second Republic, neutrality has attained a mythical dimension in the eyes of the Austrian people. It continues to be seen as an integral parts of what it means to be Austrian.[9]

The data clearly suggest that whereas nearly 30 percent of Austrians saw themselves as somehow *politically* related to Germany as late as the early 1960s, this sense of affinity has declined to fringelike proportions in the past thirty years. Even among FPÖ voters, only a minority questions the validity of the Austrian state by claiming that Austria's fate belongs in some kind of unity with Germany. Indeed, the opponents of Austria's joining the European Union, among whom the FPÖ leader Jörg Haider assumed the most outspoken position, buttressed their argument by claiming that Austria's independence will be compromised by having to follow the *diktats* of the Eurocracy in Brussels and by becoming even more dependent on Germany. The Second Republic's greatest success has been to relegate *Anschluss* sentiments to the dustbin of history. Not only is *Anschluss* now completely irrelevant to Austrian politics (it was never really relevant to German politics except in the Nazi period), but the Second Republic, buttressed by political neutrality and economic prosperity, created a sense of pride among Austrians in their country. Though still substantially behind comparable figures for the United States, survey data register national pride as somewhat ahead of that expressed by the French (which seems unbelievable to us) and way ahead of that articulated by the Germans (which is most definitely believable).[10] Austrians have developed a deep sense of pride about their country which, if anything, borders on provincial self-satisfaction. Certainly, they are devoid of the deep self-doubt and self-criticism characteristic of the Germans during much of the postwar period. Whitewash worked for the Austrians. Armed with the Moscow Declaration, Austrians could escape confronting their past, let alone having to assume responsibility for it, by blaming everything on the Germans. If ever there were high dividends for a country's exit from its history, Austria cashed them in.

Successful political separation from Germany does not mean that Austrians have turned indifferent toward Germans. All opinion polls consistently show that Austrians like Germans much more than their other neighbors, indeed more than any other nation in the world. According to 1993 data, 60 percent of the Austrian public still feel a strong affinity with Germany, as opposed to 22 percent who did so with Hungary, the runner-up. Surprisingly, only 6 percent of Austrian respondents perceived such an affinity with Switzerland, which despite many objective similarities has never attained the affection enjoyed by Germans in Austrian public opinion.[11] To an overwhelming majority of Austrians, German unification was completely unproblematic. Almost 90 percent welcomed it, and virtually nobody perceived it as posing dangers to Austria or Germany's other neighbors. At the same time, 92 percent of the Austrians categorically rejected any *Anschluss*-like maneuvers that would have brought Austria into some political condominium with Germany. Austrians view Germans as related, but politically distinct. In short, the political boundaries between Austria and Germany are well defined. Whether Austria's joining the EU on January 1, 1995, will change this dimension of its long-term relationship with Germany, it is too early to tell.

Austrian-German relations have had a lengthy history of extreme closeness and interdependence, to the point where—until 1806 to be sure, arguably until 1866, and quite possibly until 1945—it was unclear whether the relationship properly belonged to domestic or to foreign affairs. It is perhaps safe to say that it belonged to both.

After the defeat of the Nazi Reich, which a substantial number of Austrians actively supported, there ensued a fascinating split in this relationship.[12] On the level of the economy and culture, interdependence has become if anything stronger than ever, with Germany clearly the superordinate and Austria the subordinate. In politics, however, there developed a clear separation of the two entities: both countries are completely secure in their political sovereignty, enjoy their unquestioned autonomy, and have absolutely no desire to enter into any kind of political condominium. At least for the time being, any kind of irredentism or *Anschluss*-like movement is nonexistent.

This arrangement worked superbly for both countries between 1945/49 and

1989. Will it continue in its benign ways and in its beneficent manner? The answer depends on three interrelated developments: Germany's newly enhanced role in Europe; Austria's changed role in Europe; and developments in Europe apart from and in reaction to Germany and Austria. Will some EU members continue to harbor silent but no less real fears concerning the possible development of a German-speaking bloc of nearly 90 million people? What effect will conflict in the Balkans have on the EU? When will Hungary, Poland, the Czech Republic, and Slovakia join this exclusive club, at what cost, and to whom? How will these new members alter the axes and constellations of current alliances and arrangements in the EU? All these developments will have effects on Austrian-German relations. For the time being, however, the relationship is enjoying the most stable, wealthy and mutually beneficial era in its long history.

CHAPTER EIGHT

The World of Post-Communism:
Poland, the Czech Republic, and Hungary

with Manik Hinchey

> BMW is building an automobile plant in South Carolina. They say that they will produce all-terrain, all-purpose four-wheel drive vehicles there. Boy, we better be worried. Last time the Germans built these kind of machines you know quite well what they did with them: they drove them straight to Poland.
> —David Letterman, *The Late Show*

Reactions to German unification on the part of Germany's eastern neighbors were varied and heavily influenced by each country's historical experience. The response of the Hungarians was extremely positive, but the Poles and Czechs were decidedly more ambivalent. Fifty years after the end of World War II, there is strong evidence that, at least, in Poland and the Czech Republic, the memories of Nazi brutality are still alive. Indeed, they have been passed on to younger generations.

Poland

In the *New York Times*/CSA survey 2 out of 3 Polish respondents expressed overt opposition to German unification; a survey conducted by the *Economist* in collaboration with the *Los Angeles Times* found that Poland was the only country in which German unification evoked "distinct fear" as opposed to "unease" or "concern." It is evident that of all Europeans the Poles have been the most concerned about the changing nature of German power in Europe. This finding is hardly surprising; the troubled history of relations between Poles and Germans over the past seven hundred years made us expect nothing less.

The violence began with the Teutonic Order's subjugation of Poland during the thirteenth and fourteenth centuries and ended with Polish victory at the Battle of Tannenberg in 1410. The partition of Poland by Russia and two German states, Prussia and Austria, in the late eighteenth century destroyed Poland as a nation until the end of World War I. Not surprisingly, one result has been a wealth of mutual stereotypes. The Polish word for German (*niemiec*) derives from the word for "mute" (*niemy*), that is, someone who cannot speak Polish. The Poles also saw the Germans as brutal, powerful, cold, and ruthless. The term

Kryzak, etymologically related to the German *Kreuzritter* (Knight of the Teutonic Order), conjures up images of brutality. Similarly, the Polish word *Prusak* means both "Prussian" and "cockroach."[1] For their part, the Germans viewed the Poles with distaste and often contempt. Wilhelmine Germany's 1913 citizenship law (which prevails to this day) was designed in large part to keep Polish inhabitants of the German Reich from becoming German citizens, and *polnische Wirtschaft* (Polish economy) in German came to mean political immaturity, lack of culture, and generally shoddy conditions.[2]

The Poles have long had a negative view of Germans, but it took the extreme brutality of the Nazi occupation, a brutality unmatched anywhere in western Europe and only equaled in the Soviet Union, to criminalize the image of Germany in Poland. The enslavement and murder of millions of Polish Jews, and hundreds of thousands of non-Jewish Poles, left the Poles with an intensely negative image of Germans.

The beginning of the postwar era was fraught with difficulties, too. As a result of the agreements at Yalta and Potsdam, Poland's borders were shifted to the west. Ethnically mixed eastern territories in western Ukraine, western Byelorussia, and southern Lithuania were annexed by the Soviet Union, but Poland gained most of East Prussia and German territories south of the Oder and east of the Neisse rivers.[3] Massive population transfers—now better known by the heinous term "ethnic cleansing"—were approved by the Allied powers as the only way to avoid future ethnic problems. As a result, an estimated 3 million Germans were removed from these territories.[4] To replace them, 2–3 million Poles were transferred from the former Polish provinces annexed by the Soviet Union. As a result of border changes and population transfers—as well as the annihilation of Polish Jewry—Poland became, for the first time in history, a united political entity that was ethnically homogeneous. A bare 500,000 minorities became all but negligible in a Polish population of 39 million.

The postwar expulsion of 3 million Germans, most of whom settled in what would become the Federal Republic, was a contentious issue between Poles and Germans. Many of these expellees became politically active on the right of the Federal Republic's political spectrum, and so Polish fears of German revanchism (which the Communist government of Poland used to gain domestic legitimation)[5] were a self-fulfilling prophecy. Such fears were not reduced by the refusal of the German government to recognize the Oder-Neisse border. The German position throughout the 1950s and 1960s remained basically what Konrad Adenauer articulated in 1949: "We can under no circumstances come to terms with the annexation of these territories, which was unilaterally undertaken by Soviet Russia and Poland."[6] Not until the signing of the German-Polish friendship treaty on June 17, 1971, one of the main pillars of Willy Brandt's *Ostpolitik*, did fear of German revanchism abate in Poland. It did not disappear.

Poland and the GDR feigned cordial relations as part of the fraternal bond between all so-called socialist countries. There were, however, frequent tensions between the two regimes. Whenever the Polish government attempted even the slightest internal liberalization or tried to gain a little distance from the Soviet Union (for example, in 1956, 1968, 1970, and 1976), the rulers of the GDR reacted critically and emphasized their own closeness to the Soviets. In particular, Erich Honecker's regime reacted strongly to any attempt by the Polish government to reach an accommodation with the "antisocialist forces" represented by Solidarity.[7]

On the level of civil society, relations were even worse. As they traveled west in the 1980s, Poles were acutely aware of the blatant racism and contempt with which they were received by the East German population. Accusations by the East Germans that Poles were engaged in unlawful commercial activities that hurt the indigenous population were reminiscent of traditional German prejudices, which held that Poles were shifty, unreliable cheats. Graffiti demanding *Polen raus* and signs that proclaimed that shops were *Nur für Deutsche* (only for Germans) did not endear the GDR to the Poles. Socialist brotherhood was absent when Polish tourists were physically intimidated, sometimes even assaulted, in the GDR's provincial towns. To the Poles, the East Germans exhibited all of the Germans' traditional bad qualities with an additional drawback: they were also poor, drab, and like the Poles themselves part of the socialist system. A survey conducted in February 1990 asked Poles to rank more than twenty countries on a scale of −50 to +50 in terms of their attraction, and the GDR came in dead last with a score of −11 followed by the Federal Republic with a score of −6. As expected, the United States attained first place with a score of +28.[8]

The Poles differentiated between the poor East and the rich West. In a survey carried out in 1991, the Poles rated the East Germans −0.8 on a scale of −5 to +5 (−5 was absolutely negative, +5 absolutely positive), whereas the West Germans scored a +0.9.[9] West Germans, albeit saddled with negative connotations common to all Germans, were at least glitzy instead of drab, and Polish antipathies were somewhat mitigated by the attractiveness of cars, video cassette recorders, and other consumer goods abundant in the Bundesrepublik.

Nonetheless, the Bundesrepublik's political discourse remained deeply troubling, and not just the vocal revanchism of various expellee associations operating on the fringes of the CDU and CSU. *Ostpolitik* notwithstanding, for example, the much-respected Constitutional Court in Karlsruhe decided on July 31, 1973, that the 1937 borders of the German Reich remained the sole constitutionally recognized borders of Germany. This decision, repeatedly confirmed, holds that even currently unified Germany is not constitutionally coterminous with the Germany recognized by the court. One of the Federal Republic's most trusted institutions has not accepted the political realities of 1945 and claims, at least in theory, that a large part of present-day Poland is still (perhaps will be again?) part of Germany.

It was hardly surprising that the prospect of German unification was not popular with the Polish public. When questioned in late October and early November 1990, around the time of formal unification, Poles expressed deep mistrust of the Germans. When asked how much trust they placed in people from different countries, 4 percent of those questioned said they had a lot of trust in the Germans, 13 percent had some, 21 percent answered "not much," and 49 percent answered "no trust at all"; 13 percent did not know. (In comparison, 18 percent placed a lot of trust in Americans, 41 percent some, 22 percent not much, and only 5 percent no trust at all.)[10]

Polish elites had no choice but to accept German unification, although the speed of the process seems to have caught them by surprise. Indeed, the new non-Communist government of Poland, established in the summer of 1989, adopted a highly pragmatic attitude toward the German Question. The new foreign minister, Krzysztof Skubiszewski, declared that the two Germanys had the right to unify. He also made it clear that for Poles, the border question was no longer open. Other leading figures from the Solidarity movement, such as Bronislaw Geremek and Adam Michnik, voiced similar sentiments. In September 1989, Prime Minister Tadeusz Mazowiecki expressed his wish for a breakthrough in German-Polish relations.[11]

The Communists, still strong in the Polish parliament, opposed such efforts to change the direction of Polish-German politics and insinuated that the Solidarity-led government's attempts to improve relations between the two countries were naive, indeed represented a selling-out of Polish interests. Domestic pressures on the Polish government were exacerbated by the rapidity of developments in Germany. Reactions in Poland to Chancellor Kohl's Ten Point Plan of November 28, 1989, were mostly negative, for he did not guarantee the Oder-Neisse border.[12] Kohl refused to make a direct statement about the border largely to appease his party's Right, but he thereby exacerbated Polish fears that Germany wanted to change the border. Prime Minister Mazowiecki's appeal to Soviet troops to stay in Poland as a defense against a potentially expansionist Germany becomes understandable in such a context.

The Ottawa Declaration of February 13, 1990, established the framework for talks on German unification and led to a reorientation of Poland's policy on the German Question. The new Polish policy involved slowing German unification and linking it to a host of pan-European issues, but it met with little support among the four Allied powers. The Poles then demanded participation in the "2 + 4" talks and insisted that the border question be settled before unification. Ultimately, Poland simply had to accept that the border question would be settled simultaneously with unification.[13] The German-Polish border treaty was signed in Warsaw on November 14, 1990, followed by a second treaty on "good neighborliness and peaceful cooperation" on June 17, 1991.

The treaty did not seem to allay Polish anxieties. A major *Spiegel*/EMNID survey done in summer 1991 revealed the ambivalent feelings of the Poles. When asked whether Polish-German reconciliation was likely, 9 percent of the Poles questioned replied that it was very likely, 59 percent that it was likely, 18 percent that it was hardly likely, and 6 percent that it was unlikely, where 8 percent replied that it was "difficult to say." Sixty-two percent of Poles said that the burden of World War II had a very or somewhat strong influence on Polish views of the Germans, whereas 32 percent stated that it had a negligible influence and 6 percent that it did not exist at all.[14]

A slight majority of Poles felt that the Oder-Neisse border was still not secure. Forty-two percent answered that it was "rather insecure" and 9 percent that it was "very insecure," while only 4 percent answered that it was "very secure" and 45 percent that it was relatively secure. Fifty-one percent thus did not believe in the good intentions of the Germans despite the signing of the border treaty. When asked "How certain is it that united Germany will remain a democratic country and that there will not be some kind of dictatorship?" 48 percent replied that it was either rather uncertain (42 percent) or completely uncertain (6 percent). Only 7 percent were completely sure Germany would remain a democracy, and 44 percent were quite sure.[15]

Questioned about the popularity of Germans in Poland, 2 percent of Poles replied that the Germans were very well-liked, 46 percent relatively well-liked, 42 percent rather disliked, and 10 percent greatly disliked. Again, a slight majority of Poles (52 percent) expressed negative feelings toward the Germans. These figures were mirrored by the Germans themselves. When asked a similar question about the Poles, 55 percent of West Germans replied that Poles were either rather disliked or greatly disliked.[16]

The negative vision of Germany continued to dominate. In a survey done by a leading Polish newspaper in November 1992, two years after German unification, Poles were asked to name the countries they found most attractive. The United States topped the list at 58 percent, the Germans did not even make the list. Instead, they came in fourth on a list of most *disliked* peoples, behind Gypsies, Ukrainians, and Romanians.[17] A survey by the Polish public opinion research institute CBOS at the end of May 1995 had similar results. Poles then found the French most appealing (67 points), followed by Americans (63), Hungarians (56), Swedes (53), British (51), Slovaks (44), and Czechs (43). The Germans tied the Lithuanians with 35 points. Only Israelis, Byelorussians, Russians, Serbians, Ukrainians, Romanians, and Gypsies were less popular than the Germans.[18]

However much they continue to dislike the Germans, the Poles seem to have decided that the development of Poland as a viable modern capitalist society depends completely on Germany—thus continuing patterns established even before the fall of communism. The dependence is made clear by statistics on trade. From 1989 to 1994 the Federal Republic's share of total Polish exports grew from 12.9 percent to 39.1 percent, and its share of total Polish imports grew from 13.8 percent to 27.7 percent.[19]

The Poles love Americans and dislike Germans, but they wholeheartedly believe that their only chance to avoid the miseries of the past is to hook up to the

German economic locomotive. Asked in the spring of 1994 where their country's future lay, 12 percent replied that it lay with the United States, 36 percent with the European Community, and 5 percent with the Federal Republic even though Germany was not one of the possible answers.[20] In the spring of 1995, 13 percent of Poles questioned said their future lay with the United States, 37 percent with the European Union, and 7 percent spontaneously named Germany. This was the third-highest spontaneous nomination of Germany for any of the central and eastern European countries surveyed, following closely behind Hungary and Albania.[21]

The Poles' ambition seems to be a Dutch or Danish level of integration with Germany. The inevitable outcome would be the creation of an unequal relationship between rich leader and poor follower. Thus, in addition to the immense burdens of history, German-Polish relations have entered a phase of crypto-colonialism and neo-imperialism. This is nobody's fault. It is a functional reality of the new Europe. More Polish openness means more exposure to Germany, and hence greater Polish dependence on Germany. The problem is that increasing economic dependence will not render the political relationship any easier. Though not as acerbic as in the past, German-Polish relations remain subject to underlying tensions. The case of Poland, like that of the Netherlands and Denmark, suggests that greater economic integration and even relatively smooth political cooperation do not necessarily go hand in hand with affect and enthusiasm when the dominant partner happens to be Germany. The Poles, Dutch, and Danes have a high degree of economic integration with Germany and considerable political linkages, but no emotional affinities.

The Czech Republic

The collective memories of war, occupation, and ethnic cleansing still shape Czech-German relations today.[22] Nineteenth-century Czech views of Germany were marked by ambivalence. Although Czech sympathies were almost completely with the French in the Franco-Prussian War of 1870, the Czechs respected German industrial prowess, technology, and know-how—indeed, far more than they did that of Austria, their imperial ruler.[23] After centuries of Habsburg rule, an independent Czechoslovakia was created at the end of World War I. Czechoslovakia's borders included a large minority of Germans, most of whom lived in areas near the borders with Germany and Austria. Tensions between the German minority and Czech nationalists ran high during the interwar years.

The Nazi seizure of power in Germany emboldened some of the more radical ethnic Germans, and in October 1933 Konrad Henlein founded the Sudetendeutsche Heimatfront. In 1935 the Heimatfront became the Sudetendeutsche Partei, which with two-thirds of the German vote soon developed into a powerful opposition party. When Hitler annexed the Sudetenland in 1938, he did so with the support of most (though not all) Sudeten Germans, and the Nazis occupied the rest of Czechoslovakia in March 1939. The German occupation lasted six years and inflicted untold suffering upon the Czechs. At least 80,000 Jews were murdered, and non-Jewish Czechs were subjected to fearsome reprisals for any acts of resistance.[24]

After the war the Czechs were not especially careful to distinguish those Germans who had actually collaborated with the Nazis from those who were assumed guilty for merely being German. On May 19, 1945, Edvard Benes, first president of postwar Czechoslovakia, issued a decree that declared "all persons of German nationality" unreliable and placed their possessions under supervision. Article 13 of the Potsdam Agreement of August 2, 1945, put the seal of Allied approval on the Benes decree, and on the ethnic cleansing of eastern Europe in general, by calling it the "transfer of the German population to Germany." Over two million ethnic Germans were driven out of Czechoslovakia, and tens of thousands (no-one knows how many) died along the way or were killed in acts of reprisal.[25] Many Sudeten Germans settled in Bavaria, where they have played a considerable role in the domestic politics of the Bundesrepublik to this very day.

After the takeover in 1948, the Communist regime in Prague used anti-German propaganda as a basis for popular legitimation throughout the 1950s. Like the Polish regime, the Czech government used the division of Germany to distinguish the good Germans of the GDR from the bad Germans of the Bundesrepublik, who were seen as revanchism incarnate.[26]

The Prague Spring in 1968 began a brief thaw in relations between Czechs and Germans, but Soviet invasion and the subsequent clamp-down ended discussions of the German Question. Official Czech relations with Bonn improved during the era of Ostpolitik, culminating with the Prague Treaty on December 11, 1973, but still permitted no discussion of the postwar expulsion of the Germans and expropriation of their property.

A few dissidents tried to take a more measured stance toward the expulsion, and indeed the 1985 "Peace Manifesto of Charter 77" even expressed unequivocal agreement with German unification.[27] The Velvet Revolution of 1989 brought one of the most prominent dissidents, Vaclav Havel, to power. In December 1989, as newly designated president, he apologized for the expulsion of the Germans.[28] His first foreign trip as head of state was to East and West Germany, where he said that Europe had no reason to fear unification. A united Germany could be "as large as it wants," although "democratic awareness and a democratic system in Germany are more important than the possibility that it might become one nation of 60 or 80 million people."[29]

The Czech public, however, was harder to convince. Havel's apology for expulsion met with a considerable amount of domestic protest, and opinion polls in 1989 and 1990 showed public unhappiness. In answer to a Eurobarometer poll from the spring of 1990, 37 percent of the Czechs surveyed said they were in favor of German unification, 22 percent were against, 22 percent had no reply, and 19 percent were indifferent. The percentage favorable to German unification was smaller than in any other country, including the European USSR, where 49 percent favored unification.[30] In the fall of 1990, the Eurobarometer polled people in Czechoslovakia about how much trust they had in people from various countries. Twelve percent of the Czechoslovaks polled had a lot of trust in the Germans, 36 percent some trust, 28 percent not much trust, and 16 percent no trust at all, while 8 percent did not know. These numbers, while not as unfavorable as the Polish results, still indicate that a sizable minority of the citizens of Czechoslovakia were highly suspicious of Germany and its motives.[31]

Czech suspicions were not helped by the activities of the Sudetendeutsche Landsmannschaft, the main organ of Sudeten Germans living in Germany, which has close connections to the ruling CSU in Bavaria. Representatives of the Landsmannschaft traveled to Prague in 1990 to meet with representatives of the Czechoslovak government, but their insistence on a right of return and the right to self-determination exacerbated Czech fears that Germany would try to regain formerly German territories on the Czech Republic's western border.[32]

Despite the signing of a German-Czech treaty in October 1991, followed shortly thereafter by the dissolution of Czechoslovakia, Czech-German relations remained frosty during the early 1990s. The activities of the Sudetendeutsche Landsmannschaft were heavily reported in the Czech press and hurt the image of Germans in the Czech Republic. In a survey from early 1992, three-quarters of the Czechs surveyed agreed with the statement that the "Germans have a superior attitude towards the Czechs." Distrust of Germans was highest among those over 55 and those between 18 and 25 years old, among people with less education, and among those who identified themselves as left-oriented.[33] Another survey from the summer of 1995 revealed that Czechs were still ambivalent about the Germans five years after unification. When asked what feelings they associated with Germany, 53 percent answered "apprehension," 51 percent "uncertainty," and 46 percent "admiration" (multiple answers were possible). Sixty-nine percent of those questioned thought there was still a danger that Germany would revert to National Socialism—this percentage was constant across age groups. Sixty-eight percent thought that the expulsion of the Sudeten Germans was justified because of what the Czechs had suffered under the Nazis. However, 79 percent saw Czech-German relations as "good on the whole," and 56 percent hoped they would continue to evolve.[34]

On the elite level, relations faced continued difficulty. Germany's asylum law changed in 1993, and leading Czechs saw the change as an unfair shifting of the burden of policing the borders and caring for asylum seekers onto the poor, small Czech Republic.[35] A German press report that Foreign Minister Klaus Kinkel had said that the Potsdam agreements could not be considered binding because they had legitimated the expulsion of Germans from eastern Europe caused a furor in early 1996. In the eyes of many Czechs, and particularly the opposition, any questioning of Potsdam was tantamount to questioning the legitimacy of the Czech state.[36] Even German encouragement of Czech membership in NATO was viewed with suspicion. Some Czechs suspected that the Germans were trying to create a buffer zone to the east, just as the USSR had formerly done on its western borders. Leading members of the ruling coalition privately feared that the Czech Republic would once again be sacrificed to the geopolitical goals of its powerful neighbors, and particularly Germany.[37] When the Germans, led by Finance Minister and leading CSU politician Theo Waigel, linked the fate of the Czech Republic's application for EU membership to its issuing an official declaration of contrition for its expelling Germans in 1945, Czech suspicions and dislikes of Germans reached new heights in the spring of 1996.

Hungary

Unlike the Czechs and the Poles, the Hungarians display no animosity toward the Germans. Indeed, Germany is as popular among Hungarians as among Finns. The Hungarians, like the Finns, share many positive associations with things German, particularly with West Germany. Only Austria, with 93 out of a possible 100 points, surpassed the Bundesrepublik's 89 score in Hungary on a scale measuring affect, friendship, and hopes for close ties.[38] No other country came close to the figures attained by Austria and the Federal Republic.

Hungarian sympathies for Germany emanate from the distant past and from the postwar period. Both are characterized by Hungary's deep yearning to be part of the West. For the Hungarians, the West (*nyugat*) has always meant liberation from the oppressive East (*kelet*). The former was associated with periods of enlightened absolutism, the modern nation state, bourgeois liberalism, democracy, individual freedom, human rights, capitalism, and of course a consumption-driven welfare system. In contrast, the East has represented darkness, backwardness, primitivism, authoritarian paternalism, and repressive collectivism of one kind or another. Asked in the fall of 1990 whether they ever thought of themselves not only as Hungarians but also as Europeans, 68 percent of Hungarians replied that they often (23 percent) or sometimes (43 percent) thought of themselves as Europeans. In comparison, only 13 percent of the Czechs and 9 percent of the Poles often thought of themselves as European.[39]

To Hungarians, the East means political and military repression at the hands of systems and peoples whom they regard as both hostile and inferior: the Slavs, particularly the Russians, and the Turks. In short, the West—and this for all intents and purposes meant Germany—signifies much-revered Europe. Even though the Hungarians never forgave the Austrian Habsburgs, and young Kaiser Franz Josef in particular, for allying with the reactionary Russians in 1848 to crush the Hungarian independence movement, the *Ausgleich* (Equalization of

Sovereignty) of 1867 mollified them, and they were loyal to the Dual Monarchy until its demise in 1918.[40]

Even though certain antipathies toward the Austrians remained intact, none was transferred onto the Germans. As the Hungarians came to rule over certain "lesser" peoples to the east, south, and north, so they deemed themselves the Germans' and Austrians' equals in central Europe. The Hungarians' respect for the Germans emanated in part from the superiority that the Hungarians exhibited vis-à-vis other peoples.

To Hungary's immensely creative and impressive intellectual elite, German was more than a second language. Perhaps because of their Jewish origins, great thinkers such as Karl Mannheim, George Lukacs, Theodor Herzl, and many others became German-language authors. Hungarian antisemitism later vilified these great contributors to Hungarian culture, but their links to the world of German *Geist*, *Bildung*, and *Kultur* were profound.

A German minority has lived in Hungary for over eight centuries. The first German settlers arrived in the twelfth century from the Rhineland, and another wave came during the reign of Maria Theresa in the eighteenth century. This group settled in the south around the Danube, an area devastated in the wars between the Habsburgs and the Ottomans. Making the town of Pécs their center, the Germans remain to this day a cultural and political presence in this part of Hungary. These *Donauschwaben*—all Germans, regardless of their regional origins, are called Swabians in Hungarian—comprised some 370,000 people in 1945. About 170,000 were expelled by the new Communist rulers, and most of these expellees settled in the Federal Republic, but they never formed the political constituency opposing accommodation with Hungary that the Sudeten German organizations became. Ties between the remaining 200,000 Swabians and West Germany were never severed, even at the height of the Cold War. With the fall of communism and German unification, contacts have intensified significantly.

After World War II, the communist regime of Hungary differentiated between the "fascist" West Germans and the "socialist brother nation" of the German Democratic Republic. But with the beginning of "goulash Communism" in the late 1960s and the concomitant opening to the West, ordinary Hungarians were allowed to travel as tourists to the West every three years. Many took advantage and traveled to the Federal Republic, where they saw "real existing capitalism."[41] The Hungarians heaped all their hopes and accolades on the good Federal Republic and reserved their anger and contempt for the bad East Germans. The West Germans were democratic, free, rich, and colorful, and they arrived at Lake Balaton with D-Marks and BMWs. Their East German cousins were repressive, authoritarian, poor, and drab, and if anything they drove a Trabant, which had become for the Hungarians the hated symbol of socialism's shortcomings. The Hungarians certainly did not share the East Germans' subsequent identification of the "Trabi" as a cute little anti-auto symbolizing the lost independence of the east.

By the mid-1970s *Ostpolitik* and the CSCE had led to further openings on the part of the Hungarian regime. In particular, there were strong, albeit state-controlled, economic ties between Hungary and the Bundesrepublik, especially the southwestern states of Bavaria and Baden-Württemberg. Newspaper and magazine articles began to present a nonideological picture of the Federal Republic, and by the mid-1980s were engaged in a sharp critique of the socialist brother GDR's economic failures.[42]

In early May 1989 the Hungarian government dismantled the barbed wire defenses on its border with Austria, and this little-noticed move ultimately led to German unification. To quote the late Jozsef Antall, the first conservative prime minister of post-Communist Hungary and a deep admirer of Germany's Christian Democracy: "I was always an unconditional supporter of German unification. . . . I would like to quote the famous Hungarian politician Baron Jozsef Eötvös. He said in the middle of the nineteenth century: 'Hungary's independence depends on German unity.' I am proud to be able to say today that German unity depended on Hungarian independence."[43]

Hungarians displayed no ambivalence on the issue of German unification. In June 1990 Antall said that Hungary unconditionally supported unification and the NATO membership of a unified Germany. His foreign minister, Géza Jeszenszky, said in October of that year that "Hungary has always honored the right to self-determination of nations. Thus, it is natural that we always wished in our hearts for German reunification and now we greet it with pleasure."[44]

A survey conducted in May 1990 of five hundred members of the Budapest intelligentsia asked: "Would the unification of the two German states be economically and politically advantageous or disadvantageous for Hungary, and in general for Europe?" The overwhelming majority saw unification as advantageous for both. Fifty-eight percent expected German unification to have positive political and economic effects for Hungary, and 75 percent answered that unification would help the integration of Europe. The Hungarian press clearly recognized that unified Germany would be a major power in Europe, but Hungarians did not see this as a worrying development. In Hungary, Germany was seen as a mediator between eastern and western Europe and a spokesman for central European interests.[45]

The Hungarian public, too, saw Hungary's interests tied to Germany. When asked in the spring of 1995 where their country's future lay, 11 percent replied that Hungary's future lay with the United States, 22 percent with the European Union, and 9 percent spontaneously replied with the Federal Republic (the last answer was not one of the choices offered).[46] The result for Germany was higher in Hungary than in any of the other central and eastern European countries in which the survey was carried out. It is safe to say that in few if any European countries are Germany and the Germans as liked and admired as in Hungary. The feeling is mutual. Chancellor Kohl has repeatedly acknowledged Hungary's audacious opening up of the Iron Curtain in May 1989, which Kohl has gratefully identified as the beginning of German unification.

CHAPTER NINE

The Big States:

Italy, France, Great Britain

On the morning of an important soccer match between England and Germany, one conservative minister expressed fear that England would inevitably lose to Germany at its very own national sport. Margaret Thatcher responded, "Well, we've beaten them at their national game twice this century."

—*Economist*, 8 June 1996

Italy

The Italian reaction to German unification was moderately positive, with little enthusiasm but with no major fears. In terms of popular approval, Italians overwhelmingly viewed German unification as legitimate. In the Eurobarometer poll of November 1989, 80 percent of Italians questioned were favorable to the unification of the two German states, 10 percent were opposed, and 10 percent had no reply. By the spring of 1990, the numbers of Italians who were "personally in favor of . . . the unification of the two German states" had dropped slightly to 77 percent, while 11 percent were opposed, and 12 percent had no reply.[1]

Nevertheless, there existed a clear difference between the "legal" (public) opinions expressed in these surveys and the "real" (private) ones articulated informally and—only in part, of course—reported by the Italian press. Generally, Italians did not exhibit anywhere near the dislike for Germans of the Poles and Danish and Dutch elites. Nor did Italians convey any of the imperial envy vis-à-vis the Germans which we encounter in the French and British cases. But apprehensions had not disappeared. There still existed worries about the Germans' inability to handle power, even if fears about their Prussian militarism had abated. Concerns remained, especially on the Left and in liberal circles, that the Germans might have difficulties reconciling power with democracy.

Some Italians felt that democracy had been easy for the Bundesrepublik, which had abdicated power to the Americans on the global scene and to the French and Americans in Europe. But what about Germany's role in the new Europe and the new world order? The tenor of Italian views was of caution informed by history rather than hysteria. On the mass level, most Italians seemed to think that German unification would benefit Italy. Asked in the spring of 1991 whether a unified Germany made them hopeful about their own country's future, 26 percent of Italians replied that they were very hopeful, 44 percent rather hopeful,

11 percent rather fearful, and 2 percent very fearful, while 17 percent did not know.[2] Nonetheless, worries about "king D-Mark" as Europe's new dictator were repeatedly voiced. For good reason: after all, barely a decade earlier a German Social Democrat, in the person of Chancellor Helmut Schmidt, openly coerced the Italian government to pursue strict austerity. Indeed, the Exchange Rate Mechanism crisis of September 1992, precipitated by the Bundesbank's monetary policy in the face of a widening budget deficit, had a catastrophic effect on the value of the Italian Lira and, subsequently, the Italian economy.[3] Adding insult to injury, Italians had to submit to lectures from German finance minister Theo Waigel in the fall of 1995, reprimanding them because they had failed yet again to "bring their financial house in order."[4]

The Italian business class never had anything but the highest respect for Modell Deutschland and continues to envy its successes. The Italian Left, however, has dreaded German capitalism, whose social democratic packaging in its view merely obfuscates its truly repressive nature. To parts of the Left, particularly the intellectuals, modern Germany is associated not only with economic streamlining, austerity, and imperialist expansion but also with aspects of a *Sicherheitsstaat* or security state, which the Italian Left views with great suspicion.

In Italian apprehension vis-à-vis Germany, the present prevails overwhelmingly over the past. Of course, Italians are not oblivious to their recent past, in which Germans played a rather ignominious role. After all, the national holiday, April 25, commemorates Italy's liberation from German occupation. Place names such as Fosse Ardeatine and Marzabotto still conjure up horrible images of Germans massacring Italian civilians. When the German war criminal Herbert Kappler escaped under mysterious circumstances from his minimum security prison in Gaeta and fled to Germany, all Italian parties (except the neofascists) protested loudly. The trial of Erich Priebke, one of Kappler's most brutal assistants, an unrepentant Nazi and a self-confessed killer, captured Italy's attention for months. Forty-three percent of Italian respondents agreed when questioned whether the image of contemporary German was still substantially influenced by the Holocaust. This contrasts to 20 percent in France, 24 percent in Sweden, 29 percent in Britain, and 35 percent in the Netherlands.[5] In general, however, fear of German economic might, the Bundesbank's dictatorial powers, and the unknown of how Germans will handle their newly won importance prevailed decisively over historically anchored concerns.

Stereotypes of Germans which exist everywhere in Europe are also found in Italy: Germans are efficient, hard-working, diligent, and accomplished. They are also humorless, cold, arrogant, and selfish. Most Italians do not actively dislike Germans, but they do not like them either. Germany ranks among the last European countries that Italians like to visit. In 1989, only 9 percent of Italian respondents had been to Germany at least once in their lifetime, compared to 84 percent of the Dutch, 68 percent of the Swedes, 33 percent of the French, and 31 percent of the British.[6]

The Italian press provided a more intricate and sophisticated picture of the complex interrelationships surrounding the German Question than we encountered in the Greek, Spanish, or Portuguese press. We were impressed by the range and depth of Italian journalists, who paid close attention to virtually every player on the new European scene, analyzed the fluid situation with care and alacrity, and offered the Italian reading public an in-depth picture of a complex new world.

Briefly, Italians seemed not to have been frightened by the sudden emergence of a strong Germany. Certainly one could detect no "historical" fear that equated today's Germany with the Nazi era. Nevertheless, there was discomfort and worry regarding global uncertainties and the Italians also worried that they would not be treated as equals by the big boys of the new game. Nowhere has this inferiority complex been more clearly reinforced than reactions to Italy's omission from the "contact group" of the Big Five (the United States, Russia, Germany, France, and Britain) that became the arbiter in the Bosnian tragedy. Italy shared a border with the former Yugoslavia, continues to do so with Croatia and Slovenia, and has historically been involved in conflicts with Croatia over the port city of Rijeka (Fiume in Italian). Despite its greater immediate interest than any member of the contact group, Italy was deemed insufficiently important to join this exclusive club.

According to data published in *Corriere della Sera* on December 17, 1989, 70 percent of Italians were in favor of German unification. Eighty-four percent of Italians questioned by the Belgian newspaper *Le Soir* in its pan-European survey favored unification. In the *Corriere* survey, 16.6 percent opposed German unification which, though low, was still relatively high compared to, for example, the 9 percent of Belgians who had adverse reactions.

Italians had not shed all their worries about recent German developments. Thus, 40.5 percent of respondents believed that German unification might destabilize Europe, 27.4 percent thought it would mean an economic threat to other European countries, and 20.2 percent believed that German unification would render European integration more problematic. However, in the Eurobarometer survey of spring 1991, the Italians saw unification as a relatively hopeful development for Italy's future.

Age and geography closely correlated with respondents' attitudes toward unification. The older generation (64 and above), whose members retain active memories of World War II, was least favorably disposed, though 59 percent of this category still expressed positive views toward it. Eighty percent of respondents between the ages of 20 and 24, by comparison, supported unification. As to geography, the closer to Germany, the less favorably disposed were Italians toward unification. Only 54 percent of northerners were "optimistic" about unification (the exact nature of "optimistic" was never specified) compared with 63 percent of southerners. *Corriere della Sera*'s survey makes it amply clear that a substantial majority of Italians were afraid not of Germany and Germans but of the consequences of recent German developments and of economic competition.

A significant dose of anti-Germanism existed in some Italian commentary. "We are now entering Germany, we are now among the animals," wrote one *Corriere* correspondent on entering the Federal Republic. Indeed, she was surprised to find Germans and Germany so pleasant. Italians inside Germany were apprehensive: said one, "If this thing comes about, we must leave, and so must the Spaniards and the Turks."[7] This comment proved prescient. The early years after German unification saw a rise of neo-Nazi violence against foreigners, as well as the Federal Republic's tightening of its asylum law, formerly the most liberal and magnanimous in Europe. The Italian government found itself in a delicate position, between domestic apprehension and its duties as a major partner in the European Union and NATO. Italian Socialists claimed that Prime Minister Giulio Andreotti should have been more cautious in voicing his negative views about unification. Indeed, the Bundestag's CDU floor leader Alfred Dregger expressed displeasure over Andreotti's opinions, which called unification "utopian" and "a political hypothesis."

Debates in the Italian parliament indicated that the Italian government wanted to accelerate European integration, transform NATO from a military to a political alliance, and, most important, prevent Italy's exclusion from decisions about the future of Europe. Specifically, Foreign Minister Gianni De Michelis reiterated that Italy opposed any border changes in Europe and wanted to ensure that unification did not hamper European integration. Needless to say, every commentator and politician called the Germans' desire to unify completely understandable and highly legitimate—provided unification occurred within the larger context of European integration.

Cartoons, as usual, were often more revealing than lengthy newspaper articles. One cartoon, in *Unita* for December 13, 1989, showed a person saying to another, "Kohl gave Baker guarantees that when the two Germanies unite they will not question Poland's borders." The other responds, "No, they will take what's inside." Another cartoon, also from *Unita* (February 15, 1990), shows two clerics. One says, "The Pope will visit Poland next year." Response: "Please ask him to say hi to Kohl for me."

As in Spain, so in Italy much of the assessment of Germany's role in the world bordered on awe. *Corriere* argued that Germany could become another Japan. Germany had traditionally been preeminent in machine building, engineering, automation, chemicals, metallurgy, automobiles, and pharmaceuticals. Its main problems, high cost and an insufficient labor pool, might be alleviated through unification. To put the Federal Republic's economic prowess in perspective, *Corriere* noted that with roughly equivalent populations, West Germany had 53 companies on the Fortune 500 list, Italy only 6. Since eastern Europe badly needed those products which Germany produces in abundance, German products would find a new export market to the east, stimulating the German economy to even greater heights.[8]

The assessment of Kohl was fairly neutral. He was depicted in a whirl of activity, trying to bring the two Germanies together. Evidently, Kohl wanted German unification before European integration. Indeed, the Bundesrepublik postponed an accord with France and the Benelux countries—the so-called Schengen agreement—which was to open their borders because the West Germans did not want the East Germans excluded. A few months later we read in the Italian press that Kohl definitely wants a united Germany firmly anchored in the European Union. To Kohl, "his" victory in the GDR's March 1990 elections means a victory for Europe.[9] A number of Italian commentators praised Kohl's deeply held commitment to Europe.

Although Kohl in the view of some Italian commentators hurried from victory to victory, German intellectuals and the Left came across as politically irrelevant. Ridiculing the Social Democrats' complete misgauging of the situation in the GDR, one article reported that West Berlin mayor Walter Momper, a leading member of the SPD, accused Kohl of "having understood nothing about what is happening in the GDR. He [Kohl] continues to think in terms of the day before yesterday. . . . It is not unification that the citizens of the GDR want. Kohl may not like their new GDR identity but it is a reality."[10] The press ridiculed many Leftists, including Daniel Cohn-Bendit and playwright Heiner Müller, none of whom wanted unification and most of whom predicted that it would not happen. Kohl was portrayed as a savvy politician, but the SPD and the German Left were characterized by the Italian high-brow press as hopelessly misguided dreamers. German intellectuals such as Joachim Fest, Günter Grass, and Juergen Kocka, even Ernst Nolte, were extensively quoted, interviewed, or published.

Other topics frequently discussed in the Italian press were the comeback of *Mitteleuropa*; Oskar Lafontaine's opposition to the transfer of Germany's political center from the Rhine to the Elbe and from Bonn to Berlin; and Bonn's victory in establishing the 2+4 formula as the primary means to attain German unification. Hans Modrow, the last Communist leader of the GDR, came across as particularly inept: " 'We can offer you culture,' he said to the FRG, as if the FRG did not have any."[11]

Many articles on France, Britain, the United States, and Poland and other East European countries typically assessed the ramifications created by the momentous changes of 1989. They suggested overall that German unification would alter the playing field for each contestant without, however, generating a situation dominated by danger and fear. Not only did the Italians offer surprisingly insightful accounts of the German Question, but they seemed convinced that—to use an old Habsburg adage—the situation was critical but not serious. Optimistic voices clearly prevailed over pessimistic ones.

France

German unification certainly struck a deep chord in the French psyche, provoking intense public debate. Even the silences and omissions were telling. Succinctly stated, the sudden reappearance of the German Question in a new guise caught the French by surprise and caused them much worry mingled with a good dose of introspection.

Perhaps nowhere in Europe was the difference between the political class and the mass public more pronounced than in France. The French view of Germany and the Germans had experienced a metamorphosis since the 1950s, with elite and mass opinions reversing sometime in the 1970s.

During the 1950s the masses viewed Germany with unmitigated hostility. Ever since the 1870s, the Germans—until then seen in a favorable light by the French—had assumed the role of most prominent enemy. The Germans were an intrusive nation (*une nation envahissante*) of militarists and national fanatics whose romanticism—once extolled by segments of the French intelligentsia—was yet another cause for suspicion. Opinion polls showed that the French chose the Americans, the Italians, the Spaniards, even the British, over the Germans when asked whom they trusted and viewed as France's friend. Elites were less rabid in their dislike. Indeed, in the active collaboration between the two countries in forming what was then called the European Economic Community, French elites developed a certain acceptance, even appreciation, of the new Germany.

By the late 1970s and early 1980s, opinion polls showed the French listing the Germans and the Federal Republic as France's most reliable friend, far ahead of everybody else. This positive change was interrupted on occasion. In a memorable semifinal game during the 1982 World Cup, for instance, the French player Battiston's career was ended by a vicious foul by German goalie Tony Schumacher, provoking images of German militarism and Nazi brutality in the French popular press. On the whole, however, if the French public did not love the Germans, it certainly stopped hating them.

The trajectory was different for the Parisian *classe politique*. Its change in the course of the 1970s and early 1980s had much to do with its metamorphosis from a fundamental adherence to Marxism to an extolling of liberalism. Left-wing intellectuals enjoyed real political importance during the events of 1968 and subsequently transformed the moribund SFIO into the trendy, New Leftist, Mitterrand-led Parti Socialiste. Parisian intellectual discourse came to focus on the values of radical politics and its transformatory potential in Europe and the Third World. As a result, the United States and the Federal Republic became bogeymen: both capitalist to the core, they engaged in repressive politics at home as well as abroad. The ugly German for French intellectuals was not so much the old Nazi as it was the new carrier of the much-despised (and much-envied) Modell Deutschland, the efficient manager and the moderate, technocratic union leader. This was, after all, an era when for virtually all European Lefts, the Bundesrepublik was little more than a slightly milder version of the Third Reich.[12] The French Left had nothing but contempt for the SPD.

By the early 1980s two other crossings altered the situation considerably. The first was in France where, just as the French Left attained political power in 1981, it shed its Marxism as an intellectual and cultural discourse, embracing liberalism and various forms of poststructuralism instead. The second was in Germany, for whereas the French discovered liberalism, the Germans turned radical. By the early 1980s the French intellectual elite looked with horror across the Rhine, where it saw a rebirth of German romanticism, irrationalism, green activism, defeatism, pro-Sovietism, nationalism (albeit in a pacifist guise) and above all anti-Westernism. If the French political class and Parisian intellectuals criticized the Germans for excessive pragmatism during the 1970s, it was German idealism that these intellectuals distrusted in the 1980s.

The French continue to be self-absorbed and concentrate reportage almost exclusively on their own country. In contrast to the Italian press, avidly interested in the opinion of others and writing about the world for interest's sake, the French discussed foreign affairs only to the extent that they affected France. Also, France's imperial legacy clearly influenced the way its intellectuals commented on the new world order.

Oddly, we did not come across one single French opinion poll concerning attitudes on German unification proper. French papers published the results of Italian and Belgian polls, as well as those of the large international poll conducted by eleven European newspapers and radio stations.[13] Questions on Germany in French polls were always part of a larger preoccupation with the changing nature of Europe, never an issue *sui generis*.

This absence is all the more puzzling since there is plenty of evidence that the German Question was much on the mind of the French. *Canard Enchaîné* noted that "it [the German Question] is a fashionable topic. One can hardly meet anyone in the office, in a bar, at table or at any turn of conversation without someone popping the fuse: 'Is Germany to be feared?' "[14] It bemoaned the pettiness of French politics, preoccupied with domestic squabbles that paled in comparison with the cataclysmic developments in the USSR and South Africa. The piece concluded that one should be afraid not so much of Germany but of France, which cannot gain Germany's respect however desperately it tries. This article combined two prevalent French reactions to unification: suspicion of Germany, and a profound lack of faith in France's abilities.

According to the Eurobarometer, the French public on the whole supported German unification. Questioned in November 1989, 80 percent of the French polled were in favor of unification, 9 percent against, and 10 percent had no reply. The number of those in favor slipped by the spring of 1990: 66 percent of the French then replied that they were in favor, 15 percent were against, and 19 percent had no reply.[15] By a very small margin, the public also said that unification would be, on the whole, a positive development for France. In the spring of 1991, 7 percent of the French said that unification made them personally feel very hopeful about the future of France, 39 percent were rather hopeful, 37 percent (the highest percentage in any EC country) were rather fearful, and 5 percent were very fearful, while 12 percent did not know.[16]

The elite level featured different views on the German Question, depending on political persuasion. On the far Right, Jean-Marie Le Pen supported "historic" Germany, which he suggested must get back the power and sovereignty that it justly deserved. Le Pen also called for the dissolution of NATO and the Warsaw Pact. In their stead he advocated a close pact between Germany and France (Vichy style?), which other European countries would be welcome to join.[17] On the Left, George Marchais and the French Communists reacted in the most nationalistic of tones on the German matter. To wit, "a unified Germany means a crushed (overwhelmed) France."[18] Also, the French Communist party published a declaration that millions of Frenchmen fear Greater Germany, that the tragic past "is deeply inscribed in the conscience of the people . . . that Greater Germany is full of dangers for our country . . . [and that] France must reconquer her rightful place which she should not have lost, in Europe and in the world."[19] Interestingly, though not surprisingly, given its unrepentantly Stalinist nature, the communist Left had become more narrowly nationalistic than the extreme Right (except, of course, regarding immigration).

In the center of the political spectrum, too, there was considerable difference of opinion. Some, like Serge-Christophe Kolm, director of the School of Social Sciences in Paris, tried to deny the validity of German unification. Such voices claimed that the entire project was the result of confusion about the nature of Germany, the right of people to self-determination, and the rationality of the choice.[20] Kolm even suggested that all countries occupied by Germany during World War II should hold plebiscites on whether to allow unification. Kolm denied the political nationhood of the German people and forgot that rationality and popular will rarely coincide.

An interesting analogy was drawn in *Le Monde*, which saw parallels between resurgent anti-Germanism and the traditional anti-Americanism of the post-1945 period. Both "antis" tried to protect the French from being colonized; in the case of the United States the fear was of a colonization of the mind, whereas in the case of Germany, the apprehension was more political and economic. Both fears were linked to desire for the status quo, or as the French say, "give the times a little time." On the other hand, the French bemoaned the fact that history accelerates while France waits. "This damned fatalism," wrote *Le Monde* on February 28, 1990, stating that "beneath the surface tensions are growing. There is a fear of social explosion, conflict of generations, crisis of national identity— all of which encourage nationalist populism represented by Le Pen and Pasqua [later French interior minister]."

Clearly not everybody was hostile to German unification. "Vichy lasted 4 years, German Vichy 40 years," wrote *Le Monde* on March 2, 1990 in an attempt to explain to a skeptical French public the Germans' understandable yearning for a unified Germany. "Our head says yes [to unification], but our belly contracts [with fear] . . . we should build a united Europe because in the world of 'real' empires such as the U.S., USSR, China and India only a united Europe can be a first-class power."

Thus, some French saw the unification of Europe not only as a means of survival among giants but also as a defense against Germany. If some people still remain skeptical, wrote *Le Monde* on March 7, 1990, just remember the negative reaction from the British, the Scandinavians, and the Soviets to creation of the European Economic Community. Once the EEC became a reality, its opponents had no choice but to deal with it. Now a gradualist approach was needed, a step-by-step inclusion of everybody which would give less developed countries ample time to prepare.

A similar idea of European unification *faute de mieux* was developed by the Socialist deputy Michel Vauzelle in the same issue of *Le Monde*. France, so Vauzelle suggests, simply had no choice but to learn to live with a unified Germany. Alone France could never compete with the United States and Japan. Only a united Europe could. André Giraud, former French defense minister, had the same sentiment in different words: "Should we support [German] unification? Not to do so will destroy European integration . . . we must show our solidarity with Germany."[21] Such commentary sounded forced, defensive, resigned.

The discomfort was unmistakable. Some people on the Quai d'Orsay said, "We should not even talk about it [German unification], it's a catastrophe!" And at the Elysée, there was much attention given to the consternation among the British and the Dutch."[22] This was strikingly reminiscent of the French reaction to the loss of Alsace Lorraine, whence developed the popular slogan *Y penser toujours, en parler jamais* ("Always think of it, never speak of it"). The Boche was recalled in the French imagination.

To make matters worse, France appeared to be trapped. There was no alternative, no exit, no substitutes for the Franco-German axis. Margaret Thatcher was good only as an anti-German cheerleader, but she offered no alternative to France's ties with Germany. The Mediterranean countries were much too weak to offer a viable option. France, for better or worse, was stuck with Germany as an equal, perhaps even superior, partner. *Quelle horreur*!

Such fears brought nostalgia for the good old days, when Germany was safely divided. It also led to a surge of self-recrimination: "We are always afraid of something: pacifism, Americans, German competition. . . . Are we really so weak? What about our economic strength, our force, our power?"[23]

So François Mitterrand, in his televised appearance on March 25, 1990, appealed to the French to have confidence in themselves.[24] Furthermore, the uncertainties explain the French attraction to a strong, prosperous, and unified Europe that would allow France a modest but respectable place in the world.

But was the faith in Europe an illusion? *Figaro* bemoaned the notions that "unification is not a problem," that "neither West nor East Germans want it," and that "the FRG does not want 17 million mouths to feed and GDR citizens are not attracted by a consumer society."[25] The French might find the pill bitter, wrote *Figaro* on March 23, 1990 in its analysis of the elections in the GDR, but it was time to face the truth. Instead, the French preferred to close their eyes and make a "cascade of errors."

French worry of Germany reached such a pitch that Richard von Weizsaecker, Germany's official confidence-inspiring "good guy," had to assure France that it had nothing to fear. "We are still friends," he said, "and our mutual dependence is vital for both of us. . . . We don't want the French people to think that they are losing something through our unification."[26] Kohl, too, felt obliged to reassure his nervous allies. He did so at Strasbourg and in a speech on French television on March 29, 1990, specifically addressing the sensitive topic of unification. "French-German friendship," he insisted, "is at the center of European evolution."[27]

Still, fears abounded. Father Serge Bonnet expressed them with humor. He wrote sarcastically that the construction of Europe required sacrifices. German unification was all but inescapable, so France should not wait but offer Alsace-Lorraine now, giving the Germans what they otherwise will exact by force: "Do not wait, save yourself another invasion." Former prime minister, the late Michel Debré decried French inaction vis-à-vis a newly hegemonic Germany and insisted that there was no alternative to a strong France.[28]

Repeatedly, newspapers commented on French inaction. French conservatives perceived France as besieged by Germany from the east, by Muslim immigrants from the south.[29] Among calls for action were practical proposals: do not allow Brussels to levy additional taxes in order to help West Germany absorb East Germany; abandon a Greater Europe, which many French conservatives continue to see as a trap; keep the Franc independent of the Deutsche Mark (*Figaro*, March 20, 1990). Some commentators waxed philosophical: the problem is that the French psyche never accepted the transition from colonial empire and world power status to a regional force of limited means.[30]

In brief, the French were confused. Like everyone else, they had precious little time to prepare for the new Europe. When they realized that changes were real and lasting, they seemed paralyzed by uncertainty. Insecurity coupled with resentment. Added to this was a sense of being trapped. Germany over the years had developed into France's most important trading partner, and France had built its future on an integrated Europe, so France seemed locked into a European solution. But before November 1989 Europe clearly saw France assume the political role of *primus inter pares*; now the option of political grandeur became increasingly remote. Germany seemed to have stolen Europe, but France simply could not do without either Germany or Europe. At the end of the day, German unification catapulted the French into serious self-doubt. The Germans may continue to have problems with their identity, but unification caused the French difficulties in a new European order where France is no longer *la grande nation*.

The French remain profoundly ambivalent about the Germans as the 1990s progress. On the one hand, they are immensely proud that they, with Germany, form Europe's core. It flatters them to occupy a position of such importance. At the same time, however, this position creates obligations. Above all, it forces the French to keep up with the Germans, which in turn nourishes French anxiety about France's perceived inferiority. It grates that Germany, now Europe's unquestioned power, has accorded the French the privilege of helping decide Europe's future. " 'The French-German relationship is skin deep, there is real animosity there,' said one French economist who insisted on anonymity. 'French businessmen often blame their problems on the Germans.' "[31]

France has certainly paid a heavy price for becoming Germany's partner. Germany's demand that France reduce its budget deficit by $59.3 billion in 1995 led to massive strikes in December which paralyzed the country and forced President Jacques Chirac to desist from harsh reductions in France's generous social benefit system. Strikers succeeded in saving the core of the system, but cuts will nevertheless occur. More important, the Chirac government resorted to a hitherto unimaginable reduction in France's most cherished symbol of national power: the armed forces. Hitching France's fate to Germany has made Germany an integral part of France's political life.

Nowhere was this change more evident than in France's referendum ratifying the Maastricht Treaty in autumn of 1992. Both sides, those in favor of ratification and those opposed, argued their case with reference to Germany. The pro-Maastricht forces, exhorting the French to join Germany to build a more prosperous France, presented partnership with Germany as a boon to France. Anti-Maastricht voices, almost half of those participating, saw this partnership as detrimental to France. The Left worried about Germany's economic domination of France, the Right feared Germany's political might. Both expressed apprehensions.

Great Britain

Britain, like France, witnessed the disappearance of its empire in the postwar era, leading it to become a middle-level power alongside its special partner, the United States. Culture is a good deal stickier than structure, and the end of empire was not accompanied by the disappearance of imperial culture. If anything, this imperial "lag" has made the British relationship with Germany more fraught with jealousies. Difficulties are greater because part of this imperial grandeur consisted in defeating Germany twice during the twentieth century.

Yet at the end these victories seem to have been for naught. While Britain was losing its empire, the Bundesrepublik was experiencing its *Wirtschaftswunder* (economic miracle), which placed it well ahead of Britain as an economic power by the late 1950s. Unification made it certain that it was only a matter of time until Germany superseded Britain as a political power as well (if indeed it had not already done so). British elites, with the possible exception of the most fanatical Euroskeptics in the Conservative party, seem somewhat less obsessed with

Germany than their French counterparts, but they are certainly uneasy about German ambitions. Britain's relationship to Germany remains substantially colored by experiences that occurred in the first half of the twentieth century. It would not be too exaggerated to characterize the British as well as the French as living the trauma of the once-powerful.

In notable contrast to small countries, where antipathy results from a history of German domination, Britain views German power as that of a restless rival which has repeatedly challenged Britain in all aspects of interstate relations, militarily, politically, and economically. Defeated twice, Germany has, phoenix-like, reemerged to confront Britain precisely when Britain's might is on the wane. Britain, like France, has yet to come to terms with living in the shadow of the Germans.

Antipathy still colors the response of British schoolchildren. A survey published by the Goethe Institute in London showed that one-third of six- to nine-year-olds believed that Germany will start another war.[32] In a meeting between German and British youths designed to promote better understanding, the Germans were asked why they were always so bitter and humorless.[33] At the elite level, a telling example of British agitation about Germany occurred in the "Chequers Affair." Prime Minister Margaret Thatcher extended an invitation to six independent experts on Germany to offer their thoughts on Germany's future. Four British scholars of varying ideological persuasions—Lord Dacre (Hugh Trevor-Roper), Norman Stone, George Urban, and Timothy Garton Ash were joined by two eminent American historians, Gordon Craig and Fritz Stern. The meeting, held at Chequers on March 24, 1990, was a free-for-all in which many things were said that were never meant for publication.

Nevertheless, a document was leaked to the *Independent on Sunday* and published on July 15, 1990. Only the negative comments were circulated, and one sentence attained special notoriety: "Some even less flattering attributes were also mentioned [at the meeting] as an abiding part of the German character: in alphabetical order, angst, aggressiveness, assertiveness, bullying, egotism, inferiority complex, sentimentality."[34] Many positive things were also said about the Bundesrepublik, but it was this assortment of negative characteristics which stuck as the British elite's perception. What is interesting here is not the list of attributes but that such a meeting occurred in the first place, at the behest of a prime minister. We are not so sure about German angst, but there seems to have been at least some in British ruling circles. The fear of Germany persists after unification. In 1995 Lord Tebbit, former chairman of the Conservative party, commented that "Great Britain does not want to be ruled by fax from Frankfurt."[35]

Britain is a country where little stigma attaches to such pejoratives as "Frogs," "Krauts," and "Huns." One piece of information speaks volumes about the British public's attitude: when the Germans played the Argentinians in the World Cup Final in the summer of 1986, a survey asked the English public which contestant it supported. The answer was 75 percent the Argentinians, 15 percent the Germans, the rest undecided—and this barely three years after war over the Falkland Islands (Malvinas), and just a few days after the English team had been defeated by the Argentinians (The decisive Argentinian goal was scored illegitimately by Maradonna's infamous "hand of God," in which he fooled the referee by illegally punching the ball into the English net.) At least on some emotional level, the memories of two world wars still have a formidable effect in crowding out more recent enmities. Crudely, the British have much deeper and negative feelings about the Germans, their allies for the past fifty years, than they do about the Argentinians with whom they waged a short but serious war only three years prior to the contest and who had cheated the England team only a few days earlier.

An alternative interpretation exists. *Le Soir*'s survey of January 6/7, 1990, measuring European popular opinion concerning unification, places British public support at 82 percent approval, near the top. The CSA survey published in the *New York Times* on February 20, 1990, shows over 60 percent of British respondents favorably disposed toward German unity, 20 percent supporting it very strongly. The Eurobarometer survey of November 1989 showed that 71 percent of the British surveyed were in favor of German unification, 17 percent were opposed, and 12 percent had no reply. In spring 1990, 64 percent of the British were in favor, 18 percent opposed, and 17 percent had no reply.[36] These decidedly positive figures resembled the French results.[37]

What distinguished the British from the French case was the measured, decidedly positive tone of the British press toward unification. In stark contrast to the French, the British papers of record (the *Times*, the *Independent*, and the *Guardian*) gave not only an immensely thorough account of events but ran balanced editorials that were anything but Germanophobe. If anything, we compare British reactions on the German Question to those of the Italians not the French.

There were some notable exceptions. Most significant was Conor Cruise O'Brien's infamous piece "Beware, the Reich Is Reviving," published in the *Times* on October 31, 1989. O'Brien paints a bellicose and expansionist German monster which, as the Fourth Reich, will pick up where its ill-fated predecessor left off. This article met severe criticisms not only in letters to the *Times* but in other newspapers, as for example Hella Pick's "Laying the Ghosts" in the *Manchester Guardian Weekly* of November 26, 1989. One of the most decisive rebuttals came the very next day from Bernard Levin, also writing in the *Times*.

Then, of course, there was the Ridley Affair. Published in the form of an interview given to Dominic Lawson, son of former chancellor of the exchequer Nigel Lawson and editor of the respectable conservative journal the *Spectator*, Nicholas Ridley, minister of industry and commerce, accused the Germans of engaging in a racket which, among many devious things, was primarily "designed to take over the whole of Europe."[38] Ridley was particularly bitter about Germany's economic prowess which, in his interpretation, it used to bully others to accommodate Germany's needs. Ridley also feared losing sovereignty to a new

European bureaucracy, which would rule the British from Brussels. Such concerns, always pronounced in Britain, subsequently became general across Europe in the wake of the Maastricht Treaty concluded in December 1991. Fear of an all-powerful and unaccountable Europe has, perhaps not by chance, accompanied the growth of German power on the continent.

Ridley coupled these two events in outrageous terms by stating that if Britain was prepared to cede sovereignty to the Commission of the European Communities, "You might just as well give it to Adolf Hitler, frankly."[39] His opinions were so blatantly anti-German that Margaret Thatcher, known to share them in private, dismissed the minister from her Cabinet. Nevertheless, Ridley did express at least a kernel of the concerns felt by parts of the British elites and mass public.[40]

The fall of the Berlin Wall was greeted with much joy in virtually all quarters. In editorials on November 10 and 11—entitled "Blast of Trumpets" and "Victory for Democracy," respectively—the *Times* welcomed the lifting of the Iron Curtain which, in true conservative fashion it dated from the Bolshevik Revolution not the end of World War II (which merely shifted it westward a couple of hundred miles). The editorials were explicitly hopeful about German changes, provided they occurred slowly and were implemented cautiously with European and Western consensus.

The editorial tenor differed a good deal regarding Margaret Thatcher's role. The *Times* was virtually never critical of the prime minister, whereas both the *Independent* and the *Guardian* were. The *Times* reserved its harshest tone for U.S. Secretary of State James Baker, whom it accused of "brutal diplomacy" in pulling off the "2 + 4" deal in Ottawa. Baker, according to the *Times*, "battered" his way past the British, French, and Soviets, railroading through an agreement that only Hans-Dietrich Genscher found to his complete liking. The *Times* was anything but pleased by a Baker-Genscher axis setting the framework for a post-Yalta rearrangement of Europe. Yet only a few days later, the *Times* paid much attention to Mrs. Thatcher's appeal for U.S. troops to stay in Europe. It also stressed that the prime minister delivered this particular speech to the British Board of Deputies, the most important leadership group for Britain's 300,000 Jews. It also paid attention to the rift between Downing Street and the Foreign Office, with the latter accepting German unification much earlier and much less resentfully. In an excellent editorial, "Obituary for a State," the *Times* argued that most people in the West overestimated the staying power of the GDR because they relied for information on an articulate but unrepresentative elite. The *Times* also opposed the neutralist tendencies of the German Left as well as Kohl's flirtations with an "incorrigible minority" on the Right.

In a perceptive article in the *Independent*, Edward Steen pondered whether "selfish and tedious consumerism" in Germany might some day "give way to a powerful new strain of German nationalism, for long suppressed by a war guilt now only felt, if at all, by old men." Roger Berthoud, also in the *Independent*, provided a fascinating critique of Thatcher's appeal to nationalism and anti-Europeanism, which he saw as not too distant from dangerous appeals to various forms of neonationalism in eastern Europe and in Germany itself.

In conclusion, the British reaction seemed just as contradictory as the French. There were voices of genuine joy and positive reactions from a substantial segment of the British public as measured by opinion surveys. However, there also emerged fears and resentments which we attribute to the trauma of the once-powerful: Britain, like France, had been a major imperial player and did not take kindly to losing its privileged status. Both countries resented a former enemy and constant rival emerging as a more important actor on the European, perhaps even the global, scene.

Yet, in notable contrast to the French, the British were much less self-obsessed and self-doubting about their own position in the world and, most important, their abilities. Thus, even the most negative British reactions—though snide, hostile, and angry—lacked the urgency that stems from insecurity. Whereas British critics of the new Germany had a "to hell with them" attitude, their French equivalents worried "how can we keep up with them" and "let's make sure that we tame them." In both cases, however, German unification had a seriously unsettling effect.

Part Three

THE THREE FACES OF POWER

CHAPTER TEN

The Deployment of German Soldiers Abroad

The strangest thing happened the other day: The Germans and the French decided to form a joint military unit. I guess this entity will now bring extra rudeness to the countries which it will occupy.

—Jay Leno, *Tonight Show*

If our argument that the Germans wish to remain small is correct, then it should be reflected in any debate about commitment of German troops. Conventionally, great powers do not impose unconditional restraints on troop deployments or announce to the world that their commitments are only for narrowly defensive or humanitarian purposes. It is reflective of the changed nature of Germany's position since 1989 that the Bundeswehr's role has developed into one of the most contentious debates in contemporary German politics. The controversy began with German unification and was exacerbated by the Gulf War.

Unification, in principle, made Germany a normal country. One of the defining characteristics of any normal country is the conventional use of its armed forces. Normal states have normal armies, which they use for normal purposes—such as defense in the case of an unprovoked attack that clearly threatens the national interest. Few if any other items (owning a national airline, perhaps) are a more definitive assertion of national sovereignty. As of the official date of unification, October 3, 1990 (or March 15, 1991, with formal recognition from the USSR), Germany therefore became just like its neighbors.

Only a few weeks later, the Gulf War broke out, and the United States led a multinational force into battle against Iraq. This was the true test of German normalcy. Clearly, German national interest was threatened—its access to vital oil supplies would be severed by Iraqi control of Kuwait. Yet Germany did not respond as a normal country.

The United States was less directly threatened than Germany but commited forces to battle. It was assisted by several countries, notably its trusted allies Great Britain and France. Conspicuously absent was the newly sovereign and rich Germany, whose interests were defended by American, British, and French troops. The controversy about the Gulf War inside Germany led to the most acrimonious debate anywhere in the advanced industrialized world. Central to this debate was the issue of German power, and at this time the deployment of German troops became a major matter in German politics.[1]

The debate concerning the Bundeswehr's creation in the early-to-mid-1950s featured much more than pragmatic disagreements about policy options and strategies. So now the acrimony suggested there was much more at stake than budgetary considerations and the usual disagreements characteristic of democracies. The reasons for acrimony were clear: at the heart of the matter was whether and how to redefine Germany's power and—more important—the proper projection and deployment of this power. The debate entailed a full reconsideration of Germany's identity in relation to those of previous Germanys. In short, beneath the controversy about the new role of the German army lurked larger topics— German power, history, identity, and collective memory, the essence of the modern German Question.

The problem is simple: What should the role of the Bundeswehr be? Should it be deployed anywhere in the world? If the answers are affirmative, then under whose command is this to happen and for what purposes? Is deployment to occur for any reason or only defense and peacekeeping? Such questions engendered a huge constitutional and political debate in Germany, a debate that bespeaks Germany's new role in Europe and the world. It also testified to the maturity of the Federal Republic's democratic institutions.

Until the late 1980s virtually no public opinion data attempted to gauge German views concerning defense and German military engagements. (Opinion research is not interested in nonissues.) Until the end of the 1980s, the Federal Republic's foreign and security policy rested on three main pillars, which formed the normative basis for consensual policy. The first pillar, peace and security, subordinated German military policy and strategy to the leadership of the United States and the NATO alliance. The second pillar, economic prosperity, also necessitated a security and defense policy that was subordinated to the logic of (West) European integration. The third pillar was German national unity.

Before unification, Bonn pursued versions of rapprochement, better known as détente and *Ostpolitik*. Despite the rhetorical differences between conservative parties and their liberal and social democratic counterparts, *Ostpolitik* and détente enjoyed the overwhelming support of the entire German political class as well as the public. Terms such as "out of area," "blue helmets," AWACS, now part of the German vernacular, were unknown to all but a handful of defense specialists. Out of area deployment first entered the public discourse in the late 1970s.

Beginning with President Jimmy Carter's partial revision of American military strategy, which emphasized the deployment of mobile units anywhere through Rapid Deployment Forces (RDF), the United States pressed its European allies to participate. Chancellor Helmut Schmidt, well known for his personal dislike of Carter, remained cool to this idea and invoked a constitutional restriction allegedly prohibiting German participation outside NATO's area.[2] But potential German involvement under the aegis of NATO had in fact started. The issue remained confined to policy makers and specialists, even though the huge peace demonstrations that engulfed Germany politicized the whole matter of military involvement in the 1980s (particularly between 1982, the first massive peace march in Bonn, and the deployment of Pershing II and Cruise missiles in late 1983).[3]

Not until 1987/88 did out of area involvement become a concrete issue in Germany. Toward the end of the Iraq-Iran war, the United States became engaged, leading to the tragedy of the frigate *Stark*, which was hit by a French-made Iraqi rocket, killing 37 American sailors. The United States raised its presence in the Gulf to forty warships in 1987. In the wake of this engagement the Americans began to pressure the Europeans to share the financial and military burden. Only Britain and France supported the Americans. However, on August 20, 1987 at a meeting of the West European Union (WEU) in The Hague, the decision was made that Belgium, the Netherlands, and Italy would also deploy ships to the Gulf region.[4] Although a limited operation, which did not lead to joint command or even multilateral coordination of strategies, this decision involved military involvement outside NATO's immediate area.

The Germans remained completely uninvolved. They were not interested, nor were they expected to participate. A completely consensual discourse characterized the political *Zeitgeist* of the old Bonn Republic. The fall of the Berlin Wall and unification changed attitudes precipitously, and the problems of normalcy emerged for the new Germany. (This is not to say that German troops had never participated out of area before 1990. They had—as we briefly describe.)

The Bundeswehr's Engagements

German soldiers, military, and police personnel have been engaged in Europe and elsewhere since the 1960s, attracting little attention or controversy either in Germany or abroad. Indeed, German military personnel have participated in approximately 125 actions in 50 countries with no fanfare. To be sure, most of these activities were humanitarian.[5] Notable engagements abroad began in 1960, following the earthquake in Agadir, Morocco. The most controversial, in the wake of the Gulf War, was the largest deployment of German troops since the formation of the Bundeswehr, on behalf of Kurdish and Shiite refugees from Saddam Hussein's terror regime. From April to June 1991, 2,000 German soldiers airlifted relief supplies to Turkey and Iran for distribution to Kurdish refugees. In addition, German medical personnel set up and ran a general hospital.

The Bundeswehr has also provided occasional military support, especially in the Third World and with a preference for Africa. In such cases, Bundeswehr technicians and soldiers, officially "peace and skilled workers in uniform," serviced technical equipment and taught local soldiers the proper usage of the matériel.[6]

The Bundeswehr was reluctant to engage in UN missions between the Federal Republic's finally joining the organization in 1973 and 1990. It limited its involvement to a shuttle service, flying airplanes filled with UN troops from other countries to various areas of engagement. After unification, German soldiers were for the first time deployed under UN command. Their numbers have been tiny and their activities severely circumscribed, but there can be no doubt that a hitherto unthinkable threshold was crossed.

A new Bundeswehr mission after unification began with deployment under the official slogan "humanitarian aid for the affected region." In one early case, the German navy had five mine sweepers and two supply ships participate in mine clearing in the Persian Gulf between March 11 and July 15, 1991. These German ships were deployed pursuant to a direct request by the UN Security Council, but they remained legally under German command. Their activities were coordinated with other forces belonging to the West European Union. In the same region, two German air force transport aircraft and three army helicopters have been assisting the UN Special Commission for disarming Iraq since August 1991.

Other UN commitments followed. Since spring 1992, over 150 German soldiers, thirty doctors among them, have been manning a field hospital for the United Nations in Cambodia. The "angels of Phnom Penh" constituted the largest German force engaged on behalf of the United Nations. German military personnel served as civil police and helped with preparations for and monitoring of elections in Cambodia. As of July 1992, German Bundeswehr troops were actively engaged in UNPROFOR in the Bosnian conflict. German ships helped enforce the UN embargo against Serbia, and AWACS with German crews surveyed Bosnian and Yugoslav airspace. Since March 1993, German air force planes have dropped supplies over eastern Bosnia. As of August 1995, German military personnel were actively engaged in assisting the UN Rapid Reaction Force, with 1,500 troops, fourteen Tornado jets, twelve transport aircraft, and a military hospital.[7] On December 17, 1992, the German government announced, unexpectedly, that "in support of UNOSOM II within pacified areas of Somalia a reinforcement of supply and transport troops up to 1,500 men was to be deployed for humanitarian purposes." Only professional soldiers were obligated to go; draftees could refuse assignment under the "principle of voluntarism" (*Freiwilligkeitsprinzip*).[8]

February 19, 1992 is a watershed in postwar Germany's military policy. On that day the cabinet approved a working paper entitled "Military and Strategic Bases and Conceptual Re-formulation of the Bundeswehr," which provided for amendment of the Federal Republic's constitution along the lines of Chapter VII of the UN Charter to permit German forces to participate in UN missions. Germany clearly was willing to contribute to military operations under the aegis of the UN beyond the strict limitations of peace keeping. In May of that year a special working group dealing exclusively with matters related to UN military operations (the Arbeitsgruppe Vereinte Nationen) was installed in the defense ministry in Bonn. One month later a staff was assembled to work out "guidelines for further concretization of deployment in crisis situations." On November 26, 1992, Minister of Defense Volker Rühe announced the government's new defense guidelines, which redefined the tasks of the Bundeswehr.[9] On December 15, 1992 the government announced its readiness to commit two battalions to UN military missions. A new era in Germany's foreign and security policy had begun. And with it also began a passionate and complicated debate.

The Legal-Constitutional Debate

As in every important issue in the history of the Federal Republic, whether abortion or codetermination, electoral reform or freedom of speech, so here the constitutional angle assumed a central role. When the Basic Law became the new country's provisional constitution in May 1949, the Federal Republic had no army. Telling of the Federal Republic's attempt to construct a new German identity in opposition to that of the Third Reich, only two passages in the Basic Law dealt with defense-related matters: the constitutionally sanctioned right of conscientious objection (Article 4 Paragraph 3) and the constitutional prohibition against engaging in wars of aggression (Article 26, Paragraph 1). Not until 1954, the year of the establishment of the Bundeswehr, did issues such as the sovereignty of the Federal Republic and its protection, as well as compulsory military service, become part of the Basic Law.

Central to the debate of the 1980s and 1990s was a cryptic statement found in Article 87a, Paragraph 2 of the Basic Law: "Apart from defense, the Armed Forces may only be used to the extent explicitly permitted by this Basic Law." Three questions shaped the debate: What is the exact meaning of "defense"? What precisely does "may only be used" denote? And what does the Basic Law "explicitly permit"?[10] On all three issues there was an abundance of interpretations, but even the most expansive version, which eventually was adopted, does not approach the definition of use of the military common in other countries.

Narrow interpretations of "defense" held that only an attack on the sovereign territory of the Federal Republic of Germany could justify deployment of the Bundeswehr for belligerent purposes. Moderates held that deployment was permissible within the defensive alliances of NATO and WEU. Most argued that the Federal Republic had clear obligations to such collective security arrangements, though they did not extend to the United Nations. The expansive interpretation held that Germany could come to the aid of any third country even if it was not contiguous with the Federal Republic. In other words, the Bundeswehr could be deployed anywhere in the defense of the Federal Republic—although such arguments still stopped short of a broad definition of "defense."

Equally diverse interpretations occurred over what "may only be used" means, as well as what actions the Basic Law "explicitly permits." Four articles of the Basic Law delineate conditions of the Bundeswehr's deployment within the Federal Republic of Germany, but none do so outside. Debate centered on the following constitutional passage: "For the maintenance of peace, the Federation may enter a system of mutual collective security; in doing so it will consent to such limitations upon its rights of sovereignty as will bring about and secure a peaceful and lasting order in Europe and among the nations of the world" (Article 24, Paragraph 2). The narrow interpretation held that language under no circumstances permitted deployment of German troops under the aegis of the United Nations. Those adhering to an expansive interpretation argued that by belonging to an international organization such as the United Nations, the Federal Republic assumed all duties and responsibilities which such a membership entailed.

The constitutional side of the debate was ultimately decided by the Constitutional Court in Karlsruhe, one of the Federal Republic's most significant pillars and the country's ultimate arbiter of all weighty issues. On July 12, 1994, the Court ruled that no changes were needed in the Basic Law to permit deployment of German troops outside NATO's defense area.

The court also ruled on October 12, 1993, that Germany's signing of the Maastricht Treaty on European Union did not violate the German constitution. These two decisions are landmark adjudications concerning foreign affairs.[11] But in notable contrast to the Maastricht ruling, the decision on out-of-area deployment had no precedent in the court's history. The court confronted a novel situation, which in itself suggests how considerations related to military force had atrophied in the Bonn Republic. Until events in Somalia and the former Yugoslavia, governments and political parties had uniformly agreed that German troops were to be deployed only in defense of Germany proper. Deployed abroad, they could engage only in purely defensive activities, in the framework of a multinational mission. Under no circumstances could German troops ever participate in combat. Few issues enjoyed a more solid and widely accepted consensus.

According to the court, only the consent of a parliamentary majority was needed, provided that German military action occurred in the context of a UN mandate. The reasoning of the court is revealing. On the one hand the justices held that member states of systems of collective security had to help safeguard and restore peace, even by military means. Moreover, the court opined, membership in any collective entails acceptance of that collective's rules and regulations, provided one has joined voluntarily. Since Germany had joined NATO, the WEU, and the United Nations voluntarily, it was incumbent upon Germany to abide by collective rules. Nevertheless, membership in a system of collective security did not constitute a transfer of sovereignty rights to such a system.

By this verdict the Constitutional Court confirmed completion of the new Germany's unincumbered sovereignty. In constitutional terms, the country was now fully empowered to support its foreign policy with military force. The court had constitutionally sanctioned the beginning of a new era in German politics. But did its sanction pertain to the country's political arena?

The Political Debate

Some constitutional scholars and technocrats would probably have preferred that issues of such weight be decided by pure constitutional reasoning devoid of passion, but clearly the ultimate arbiter of the debate was going to be the political process.

That debate happened at all bespeaks three interrelated developments. The first, backed by public opinion research, conveys one of the unsung success stories of the Bundesrepublik. Better known for its successful economy and stable polity, the Federal Republic typically claimed little by way of evolution of its political culture. There had developed an unmistakable affinity with Western values as manifested in the salience of personal freedom, parliamentarism, and rational discourse in politics. Moreover, the Federal Republic's indigenous and purely republican development—the New Left's generation of '68—bequeathed an ongoing pacifism to the country. The deep skepticism of any adventures in foreign policy continues, a staple of the Bundesrepublik's cultural legacy to the new Germany.

The second development represents the clear beginnings of a challenge to this ideological reluctance. Immense changes altered Germany and its environment after 1989, and this voluntary pacifism may not be as acceptable to the country's political class now as it was in the smaller Bundesrepublik. The battle over the Bundeswehr's role established a new culture alongside the dominant values of reticence and pacifism. Far from being bellicose or expansionist, however, this new position—founded on a collective memory forged in the Bonn Republic— is overtly pragmatist. Germans may no longer be ashamed of power as a concept, a tool, and possibly even an end. They do, however, remain extremely wary of any kind of military commitment or engagement.

The third development simply affirms the strength of German democracy. In the struggle between pacifism and pragmatism, the new Germany again affirmed the democratic politics which it inherited from the old Bundesrepublik. The military is not a complex apart from or engaged in debate with the democratic polity. It is subject to the decisions of that polity.

The Party of Democratic Socialists (PDS) has consistently had the narrowest interpretation among German parties of the Bundeswehr's role outside Germany's borders. The party strictly opposes "militarization of foreign policy."[12] Germany is not to deploy troops abroad under any circumstances. It is not to participate in any military action under any auspices and in any alliance, whether NATO, WEU, the United Nations, or the Conference of Security and Cooperation in Europe (CSCE). German soldiers are never to appear outside Germany's borders in any capacity, including civilian and humanitarian.

Many of the members and activists of the Alliance '90/The Greens harbor views virtually identical to those favored by the PDS, but elements in this motley political grouping hold a slightly more moderate view. Some of the party's realists and liberals, as opposed to the heirs of its Marxist and fundamentalist tradition, believe that under certain limited conditions German soldiers can participate in peace-keeping missions under the command of the United Nations. Such actions can occur only as a matter of last resort. Moreover, German participation has to be confined to professional soldiers; draftees must be able to abstain.

The Social Democratic party (SPD) was so disturbed by the government's deploying of a German destroyer to the Adriatic Sea, in the context of NATO's blockade of Serbia and Montenegro, that it brought the case to the Constitutional Court in mid-1992. With virtual unanimity, the Social Democrats believed that (as originally constituted) the Federal Republic's constitutional framework does not permit participation of German troops in the international arena. Major disagreements within the party concerned a revision of the Basic Law which would make possible German participation in multinational operations. Even then, the Social Democrats wanted to limit German participation to peace-keeping missions under UN command, in which German troops are to carry light arms for purposes of self defense only. The Social Democrats maintained that any involvement by German soldiers outside the territorial limits of the Federal Republic requires parliamentary approval of a simple majority in the Bundestag.

The Free Democrats (FDP), just like the SPD, believed that a change in Article 24 of the Basic Law was necessary to allow German troops to operate out of area. For that purpose the party submitted a proposal in August 1992 to change the Basic Law so that German soldiers could participate in UN operations, of both the peace-keeping and the peace-enforcing varieties. All such operations had to be sanctioned by the UN Security Council. German participation was to require a simple majority vote in the Bundestag. The FDP also envisioned the possibility of German troops participating in CSCE operations. In addition, the FDP proposed that all matters related to German military involvement abroad be codified in a new federal law.

The Christian Democratic Union (CDU) and Christian Social Union (CSU) represented the expansive end of the spectrum. Voices within Germany's conservative establishment argued that the Federal Republic should assume a military and political responsibility commensurate with its economic might. Volker Rühe, arguably the CDU's most eminent spokesperson on defense and security, had long maintained such a position.[13] The CSU in particular held that no changes in the Basic Law were necessary to permit the deployment of German troops under any aegis anywhere in the world. Part of state sovereignty, so the argument goes, lay in the freedom to deploy troops at any time and in any place deemed in the national interest. The CDU held much the same expansive view as its Bavarian sister party, though it was willing to allow minor corrections to the Basic Law as long as they entailed only matters of clarification. The CDU's pragmatism also brought the party to emphasize the importance of a parliamentary majority for any military operation by German troops outside the Federal Republic.

It was essentially the CDU's view that informed the bill submitted to the Bundestag in January 1993. The verdict of the Constitutional Court had all but confirmed the CDU's interpretation, giving it the aura of constitutional legitimacy and, more important, the full scope of political power.

Despite the decision of the Constitutional Court, however, actual commitment of German troops in the former Yugoslavia provoked heated debates in 1995. The first controversy arose over German Tornado aircraft in Bosnia in the summer. The CDU/CSU believed that Germany had to fulfill its commitments to its allies by sending the aircraft. Indeed, some CDU deputies, such as Klaus Rose, the chairman of the defense committee (Verteidigungsauschuss), even argued that deployment in Bosnia finally gave Germany the opportunity "to discuss openly our interests as a sovereign state." The foreign policy speaker of the CDU parliamentary group, Karl Lamers, insisted that a precondition for German influence abroad was willingness to participate in international military actions.[14] Foreign Minister Klaus Kinkel claimed that common European policies, and Germany's credibility, depended on its willingness to commit troops to the resolution of conflict in Bosnia.[15]

The majority of the opposition, however, refused to support sending the Tornados to Bosnia. To them, the issue was whether Germany would give up its traditional reluctance and become embroiled in military adventures. Joschka Fischer of the Greens spoke of a caesura in German foreign policy and the potential for Germany to become involved in a military debacle. Rudolf Scharping, parliamentary leader of the SPD, argued that German aircraft in the air was no guarantee of peace on the ground. Nonetheless, on June 30, 1995, the Bundestag voted to have German Tornado aircraft participate in the UN mission in Bosnia. Of 655 parliamentarians present, 386 voted in favor, 258 against, and 11 abstained. Forty-five deputies of the SPD and four from the Greens voted with the ruling coalition.

The Srebrenica massacre of thousands of Bosnian Muslim men in July 1995 at the hands of Bosnian Serbs added urgency to the German debate. Particularly among the German Left and Alliance '90/The Greens, a six-month controversy ensued. This fascinating intra-Left and intra-Green debate was, we believe, vicariously representative of German society as a whole as it continues to confront its various collective memories and their relevance for contemporary German politics.

Nowhere have the clashes and conflicts of history, collective memory, guilt, responsibility, the exigencies of power, the relationship to other countries—in short, the key issues of contemporary Germany—been articulated more acutely or with greater urgency than in the intra-Green debates between August and December 1995. At issue was nothing short of a fundamental redefinition of twenty years of Green identity and a fifty-year consensus about German society. Tellingly, for all the immense importance of this debate, there were no real winners. It is true that Joschka Fischer carried the day, and a solid majority of

Green voters agreed in that they, too, now want German troops to participate in internationally sanctioned emergency campaigns. Yet a majority of party delegates to the Greens' Bremen convention voted against this policy. It is safe to say that a majority of Green party activists continue to oppose the policy and remain unmitigated rejectionists concerning the deployment of German troops.

Two fundamentally different interpretations of the epoch of National Socialism confronted each other. The first holds that ultimately thuggery understands only force (after all, National Socialism was defeated with weapons and not with appeasement) and that Germans have a particular responsibility after Auschwitz to stand up to thuggery. Diametrically opposed to this interpretation is the idea that force is never an acceptable means of legitimate politics, particularly for Germans, whose militarism unleashed the forces that made Auschwitz possible.

The first round of the debate ended in an uneasy stalemate, which has left the conflict unresolved. We are certain that the Berlin Republic will offer plenty of opportunities to continue this identity-forming and identity-defining debate within the Greens as a party and movement, the Left as a milieu, and the country as a whole.

The first rumblings of this transformatory development began during the Gulf War. Most Greens vehemently opposed the Allied campaign against Iraq (having uttered few words about Iraq's invasion of Kuwait in August 1990), but some key individuals—notably Joschka Fischer, Waltraud Schoppe, and Hubert Kleinert, as well as other members of the Realist wing of the party—advocated deployment of Bundeswehr-owned Patriot missiles to Israel. This position became Green party policy in Hesse, traditionally one of the most Realist in the Federal Republic.

The second step entailed Green advocacy of independence for Slovenia and Croatia in late June and early July of 1991. The Greens adopted a neo-Wilsonian support for any people's aspirations for self-determination and political independence; hailing from the former East German civil rights movement, Alliance '90 members evinced a particular distaste for the Stalinist regime of Slobodan Milosevic.[16] To be sure, some Greens advocated caution on this immensely volatile issue, worrying that the break-up of Yugoslavia might not bode well for the area. Moreover, even the majoritarian Green voice, which clearly supported the independence of Slovenia and Croatia, did so for reasons very different from those advocated by the German Right, notably the CSU and the influential editorial page of the *Frankfurter Allgemeine Zeitung*.

The third step ensued in the passionate intra-German debate about deployment of German troops out of area. Whereas the Greens remained by and large true to their rejectionist principles on this matter, there were certain discernible cracks in a previously iron-clad position. The PDS continued unequivocally to hold that German troops were never to be deployed anywhere outside Germany, but the Greens recognized that, under certain particularly compelling circumstances and with very specific limitations, German military personnel might participate in activities outside of Germany's borders.[17] The PDS outflanked the Greens on this matter from the Left.

The fourth step began on August 2, 1995, with the publication of Joschka Fischer's letter imploring his party colleagues to rethink the Greens' sacrosanct tenet of *Gewaltfreiheit* (nonviolence) in light of the massacres in Bosnia.[18] Precipitated by the butchery at Srebrenica in July, his letter asked the Greens to consider several existential dilemmas: Will the German Left lose its soul if it shirks its duty (whatever the pretext) to intervene into what amounts to genocide? How is one to deal with a new fascism that mocks reason, spurns appeals for clemency, refuses to negotiate in good faith, and seems to understand only force? Might it be that human life and liberty, two fundamental Green principles, are irreconcilably opposed to pacifism and nonviolence, two equally central Green principles?

Fischer asked 'What is to be done?' His answer, though devoid of specifics, was nevertheless crystal clear. Genocide made it the Greens' political and moral duty to support military intervention by a multilateral force that included German military personnel.

One of the taboos of the Greens and the German Left had finally been broken. Fischer's written words brought to a head an issue that had quietly divided the Greens, and the German Left, for quite some time. Criticisms of Fischer were vocal and relentless. He was accused of everything: he was guilty of Eurocentrism, since it was war in Bosnia not Rwanda or Afghanistan that led him to write; he had become a stooge of NATO and the Americans; he had taken sides in a murky civil war in which all combatants have been guilty of war crimes; he had forsaken the special burdens of German history that, in the opinion of many, automatically preclude Germany's ever taking part in an armed conflict again.

Many party members reminded Fischer that a special Green party convention in October 1993 had by a vast majority urged abstention from military engagement in Bosnia regardless of circumstances. That this sentiment still represented the wish of a majority of activists became evident at a special foreign policy meeting convened on September 30, 1995, in Bonn. Fischer delivered the main theses of his letter again, to often vehement objections and criticisms. Still, some important party members and sympathizers rallied to Fischer's side. They argued that it was precisely the burden of German history which should make Leftists particularly sensitive to any renewal of fascism, especially on such a murderous scale as in Bosnia. They also suggested that it was simply hypocritical—and profoundly ahistorical—for Greens to hide behind absolute pacifism when some of the party's most vocal anti-interventionists had ardently advocated various Third World liberation struggles, which were anything but nonviolent.

The debate among the Greens continued throughout the fall of 1995. Fischer and his "Realo" colleagues were attacked for violating the most sacrosanct Green principle, that of nonviolence. In a particularly brilliant response, Fischer accused his critics of violating an equally sacrosanct Green principle with their uncompromising pacifism: that of human life, dignity, and freedom.[19] Fischer rejected the accusation that German participation in a multinational force would for all intents and purposes bind the Greens to the government's position. Bosnia, he urged, was a unique situation where some form of military intervention on behalf of the victims had become indispensable. He rejected his critics' worries that once the taboo was broken, Germany would find itself on the slippery slope toward militarism and Nazi bestiality.

The entire debate over Bosnia featured the collective memory of Auschwitz. Its inescapable shadow loomed over the conflict. Whatever the road to normalcy involved, it was sure to feature many obstacles from the country's ignominious past, a past that remains alive and well in the collective memories of Germans and Germany's neighbors.

Inching toward Normalcy

Ironically, it was in the debating and eventually shifting toward a more normal definition of defense policy that Germans demonstrated how their country differs from other major powers.[20] Only Japan rivals Germany in ambivalence about the issue of troop deployment. And like their German counterparts, Japanese policy makers have long hidden behind constitutional limits.

The political Right eventually won on expanding troop deployments, but the debate clarified two broader points about contemporary Germany. First, the primary limitations on military activity have always been ideological rather than institutional. Germans could always have chosen to expand the operations of their troops; they chose not to. Once challenged, the Constitutional Court affirmed this fact. Second, Germans still maintain tremendous reservations about the use of force. That major parties had to debate the issue strenuously in the face of such a direct challenge to humanitarian principles or the national interest is a sign of the limited nature of German options. By comparison, Americans, as in Grenada, Kuwait, Somalia, and Haiti, commit forces in the absence of any threat to U.S. military security and often with an invocation of the broadest definition of humanitarianism. Thus, Germans reject the use of force even where their interest is patently threatened, whereas Americans invoke its use even where the threat to their national interest is not readily apparent.

The German public's reservations about foreign engagement and the narrow German definition of appropriate commitment are likely to inhibit any thoughts of adventurism on the part of German governments. Germany's "ideology of reluctance" in all military matters remains deeply imbedded and legitimate, as indicated by a multiyear study of German public opinion conducted by RAND. Results for 1994 indicate that 92 percent of those queried supported German involvement in humanitarian missions, but only 57 percent favored military participation in UN peace-keeping operations. About 32 percent backed German military participation in NATO operations outside Germany, and 22 percent supported involvement in UN-sanctioned operations like the Gulf War. To quote the *Financial Times*, the Germans have become, and will continue to be for the foreseeable future, "peaceable, fearful—and Green."[21]

The major limitations on German expansion, we argue, are self-imposed and ideological rather than externally or institutionally constructed. In the case of troop deployment, it was domestic ideology founded on an acute collective memory which served as a critical constraint. If the highest tranche of German law is open to dramatic reinterpretation over the most sensitive of subjects, as when the Constitutional Court approved Germany's potential use of force out of area, then it is fair to assume that issues of lower sensitivity and status can be similarly reinterpreted. Domestic institutions have not tamed the German state. Rather, an evolving ideology emanating from the salience of a particular collective memory has done the trick.

CHAPTER ELEVEN

Germany's Economic Power in Europe

with Frank Westermann

Ralf Dahrendorf: They [the Germans] push for a European integration under German conditions. They are not pushing for a European integration which genuinely accepts the totally different conditions of other countries.

Die Zeit: If, however, the German proposals had the advantage of reason on their side [would the Germans' eagerness for a European integration still be ill perceived by other Europeans?]

Dahrendorf: Why is it more reasonable to push inflation to one percent, or perhaps to zero, instead of accepting an occasional three, four and five percent? Why is it more reasonable to chain one's own currency in an unchanged manner to other currencies instead of countering international imbalances via occasional devaluations? It is clearly a German concept of economy and order which is being implemented [in Europe] and which is seen as natural and reasonable in Germany. Elsewhere, other things are seen as natural and reasonable.
—Interview with Ralf Dahrendorf, *Die Zeit*, 31 May 1996

In the opening chapters, we suggested that the primary constraints on German regional hegemony have been twofold: the reluctance of the Germans to develop an ideological framework consistent with their structural power; and the inability of Germany to export its culture. We have illustrated German reluctance, what Hans-Peter Schwarz has called a shift from an "obsession with power" to the "forgetting of power," and we then contrasted it with the acceptance of German engagement by foreigners.[1] Although it is desirable that Germany not develop the aggrandizing nationalism of its past, a key problem remains: the gap between German structural power and Germany's unwillingness to engage in responsible behavior consistent with that power. This chapter illustrates German structural power in Europe, which, we suggest, is primarily economic.

Liberals (whether old-fashioned or neo) have consistently suggested that the Germans benefit from the institutional arrangements of the EU, but others benefit just as much or more. Intra-EU trade balances that favor the Germans can, they suggest, be offset by exports beyond the EU. In other words, goods and services that the Germans sell to their EU partners result in third-party exports to non-EU members. This claim may be true, but liberals have not been quick to offer an input-output model that would validate it.

150

Realists, in contrast, assume a zero-sum relationship between states. They stress German structural power and assume that a necessary concomitant is German regional influence. Currency fluctuations exemplified by the EMU crisis epitomize, for realists, how the Germans wield such power.

We differ from both the liberal assumption of mutual benefit and the Realist assumption of conflict. We replace such assumptions with largely empirical questions: Does everybody clearly benefit? If not, who benefits most and who loses? Our overriding concern is to demonstrate that Germany is not only the largest economy in Europe but also the dominant one—the pivot around which other economies, east and west, rotate. We do not assume this situation is necessarily good or bad. Our response is a theoretically cautious and empirically skeptical one, and we seek to provide illustrative data where presently there are only assumptions.

This chapter focuses on who does best in the present structure of European relations—and the degree to which the distribution of benefits is lopsided. Our findings are only suggestive, but we nevertheless conclude that the Germans do indeed enjoy a high degree of structural economic power, what Susan Strange defines as

> The power to shape and determine the structures of the global political economy within which other states, their political institutions, their economic enterprises and (not least) their scientists and other professional people have to operate . . . Structural power, in short, confers the power to decide how things shall be done, the power to shape frameworks within which states relate to each other, relate to people, or relate to corporate enterprises. The relative power of each party in a relationship is more, or less, if one party is also determining the surrounding structure of the relationship.[2]

If we are correct, then Germany wields the structural power that behooves at least a regional hegemon. A *Washington Post* headline may be correct in describing German intent when it suggested "Germans Invest in East Europe but Curb Image of Empire," but it may not adequately capture the effects of the German investment as seen from the Czech Republic, Hungary and Poland.[3]

Structural power manifests itself in differing ways in eastern and western Europe, largely as a consequence of differing historical relationships between Germany and the major European economies and of the contrasting supra-institutional arrangements that have developed between East and West in the postwar period. The East, long isolated from engagement with the world's economy, enjoyed limited, conditional, and largely bilateral economic contacts with Germany between 1945 and 1989. The West, in contrast, built political bridges based on increased economic integration through the EEC, the subsequent EC, and the EU.

Western Europe

To assess Germany's economic influence in Europe, we analyze trade flows and the international role of the Deutsche Mark as a benchmark currency to evaluate how much Germany benefits, in both absolute and relative terms, from the EU. This assessment indicates the benefit Germany enjoys from present arrangements relative to other Western European states.

But we must also examine costs. We look at the most transparent and institutionalized indicator: each country's contributions to and receipts from the EU budget. This analysis addresses how much Germany is willing to pay to maintain the rules. We can assess, at least partially, whether Germany is a free-rider or plays the hegemon by paying a disproportionate share of costs. Together, trade flows, currency strength, and net budget contributions should establish whether Germany's position in the EU broadly conforms to what we expect of a country with hegemonic, structural power.

We place two limits on the data to simplify matters. First, we confine ourselves to EU members at the time of unification. Second, we examined data among EU states only since 1972, when Britain joined the European Community (data older than 1992 we call "EC data," data thereafter are "EU data").

If the EU is a relatively integrated market structure, then data for EU members provide a way to examine Germany's regional role and relationship with other members. By examining statistical trade (i.e., comparative export share of GDP) and currency data from the EU, we can evaluate the degree to which Germany underwrites the EU system and benefits from its operations—in both relative and absolute terms. These data will furnish evidence as to whether the pessimists' fears about German economic domination are justified. If Germany does indeed dominate western Europe in economic terms, then its dominance should be reflected in patterns of trade and currency flows. Such information will provide insights into Germany's future role in western Europe.

Trade Flows

Countries come to occupy hegemonic positions because they enjoy comparative advantages over their major rivals as a result of uneven growth. They seek to create an interdependent global economy predicated on free trade, so that they can use trade to stimulate their GDP and thus exploit comparative advantages and generate profits by exporting high value-added products. Historically, freer trade accompanies hegemony.[4]

It is common knowledge that the German economy thrives on exports. West Germany attained the title of "world export champions" for the first time in 1988. A newly united Germany repeated the feat in 1990 and nearly replicated it every year since despite enormous difficulties with unification, recessions, and lagging European demand.

How does Germany fare on a regional basis? To examine market penetration within the EU, we looked at the relationship between exports and GDP among EU member states from the 1970s to the mid-1990s. Clearly, German export penetration of global markets outstripped that of its major European rivals—Italy, France, and the United Kingdom—over these twenty-five years. West German exports as a percentage of GDP grew from 20 percent in the 1970s to more than 36 percent in 1993, whereas the French and Italian economies started from a much lower base and expanded at a slower rate. Britain started with a higher percentage (albeit a smaller base in real terms) than West Germany but grew at a significantly slower rate.[5] Although not in itself a sufficient indicator of economic hegemony, this pattern is consistent with the expectations of a growing economic power. We note in passing that other, small EU member states—notably the Netherlands, Belgium, Luxembourg, Ireland, and Greece—have also enlarged their global market penetration. This evidence supports the view that the German economy has pulled along its regional trading partners.

How much of Germany's export base has rested on increased market penetration of other EU member states rather than on trade outside the EU? And how did Germany fare on this score relative to its major economic competitors? To answer these questions we compared data from 1958, when the EC free trade zone was not established, to figures from 1992. The relevant data on exports to EU states reveal two tendencies. First, the smaller states greatly benefited from membership in the EU as measured by growing exports to member states. Access to the EU's free trade zone raised their sales in EU countries—albeit at a cost to traditional markets. For example, the Benelux states all increased their exports to the EU, from roughly 55 percent in 1958 to 75 percent in 1992.[6]

Second, Germany was the primary beneficiary from free trade relations as measured by increased exports. In general, exports accounted for over 30 percent of GNP prior to unification, the highest ratio of any major country.[7] And despite the expansion of the EU, French and Italian exports to EU states as a percentage of total exports stagnated or fell slightly, whereas the German percentage grew by over 15 percent.

This German increase had two dimensions. Not only were German global exports growing at almost twice the French and Italian rate (in the 1970s to the early 1990s), but Germany also increased exports to the EU while its respective rivals' exports stagnated. It is true that British exports to the EU doubled in the decade after Britain joined. But placed in context, this achievement is not as impressive as it first appears—especially when compared to German gains. After all, it was reasonable to expect that Britain's new membership would stimulate significant growth in exports as it refocused from traditional Commonwealth markets to long-neglected European ones. The doubling of Britain's exports to EU members started from a much smaller export base than that of the Germans, and exports were still significantly smaller than German exports (in absolute and percentage terms) at the end. Furthermore, Britain's growing percentage of EU exports is less impressive when one bears in mind that in most cases the German increases occurred in fairly mature markets.

In sum, Germany's performance in EU export growth over twenty-five years is extremely impressive. Whether facing established or new rivals, the Germans outsold their rivals globally and regionally, in both absolute and relative terms. The Germans were doing so at the start of the 1970s, and they have significantly increased their advantage on every dimension since. As countries joined the EU, they found themselves importing predominantly German goods, and Germany extended its regional export base. By the mid-1980s Germany's export domination within the EU became evident.

As a case of Germany's economic prowess by virtue of the EU's expansion in 1995, we note Germany's economic relations with Austria. By *any* economic indicators, Austria's dependence on the German economy is overwhelming. And Germany's dominance of Austria's economic life continues to grow from a formidable base line. What makes this dominance truly hegemonic in the agenda-setting sense is the fact that the Austrian government has abdicated its sovereignty in certain key aspects of economic policy making, preferring to follow German guidelines. Georg Winckler argues persuasively that Germany's dominance is not so much a result of German ownership of Austrian firms or property, nor a function of German direct investment in or trade with Austria. Rather, "the direct economic linkages between the FRG and Austria play a less significant role in moving the Austrian macroeconomy along the West German path than do the policy decisions of the Austrian government or of the social partners. Austrian economic policy, in a pragmatic way, follows West German policy decisions. Those political decisions transmit the impact of the economy of the FRG to the Austrian economy. The justification for this policy is usually the concern about Austria's competitive position in West German markets."[8] Austria constantly invokes the exigencies of the world market (*Sachzwang Weltmarkt*) to justify its economic policy but for all intents and purposes appeals to exigencies delineated solely by the German market, the German economy, and German economic policy.[9] For the Austrian economy, the world and Europe are really tantamount to Germany.

Crucial data corroborate this finding. Even though Canadian dependence on the United States for trade and investment is more than twice as great as Austrian dependence on Germany, on significant indicators of economic behavior the Austrian economy correlates more closely with the German than does the Canadian economy with the U.S.[10] Winckler demonstrates that over decades West Germany's GNP correlated much closer with Austria's than it did with those of Belgium and Denmark, countries similar to Austria in size of economies. Most important, Belgium and Denmark had been members of the EEC/EC/EU with Germany since 1957 whereas Austria did not join until January 1, 1995. The strength of correlation of GNP between Austria and Germany shows the particular closeness of the German and Austrian economies, whose ties on this important indicator defied the fact that these two countries formally belonged to different trading groups.[11]

Nowhere is Germany's dominance of the Austrian economy more pronounced than in monetary policy. It would not be an exaggeration to argue, and many Austrian economists do, that Austria's monetary policy has been consistently made in Frankfurt. Winckler's comparison with Belgium's and Denmark's economic relations with Germany again highlights the particular intensity of Austrian-German relations. He demonstrates that after 1973 monetary cooperation between the three small countries' central banks and the Bundesbank increased steadily. Once again, however, Austria's closeness was consistently more pronounced than that of Belgium and Denmark. German hegemony is exercised not so much by outright control as by setting the agenda for Austrian policy, by providing the arena for Austrian decision making, by defining Austrian options.

This relationship was not necessarily to Austria's detriment. *Der Standard* aptly stated "that the monetary 'Anschluss' . . . brought the country substantially more advantages than disadvantages."[12] Austria's Bundesbank-led monetary policy helped the country pursue a "hard currency" strategy, which kept Austria's level of inflation almost as low as the Federal Republic's, and it made the Schilling (dubbed the "Alpine dollar") "harder" than any of the currencies in the EMS—thereby making Austria attractive as a candidate for EU membership. As early as 1989 Chancellor Helmut Kohl and Bundesbank president Karl-Otto Pöhl were repeatedly emphasizing Austria's importance in a new Europe. Austria's successes in maintaining a strong currency, low inflation, and closeness to the preferences of German economic policy were major assets for Germany's agenda in Europe.[13] What renders the Austrian success story truly remarkable is the fact that the constraints placed on it by the Bundesbank's stringent monetary requirements did not prevent Austria from achieving the second-lowest unemployment figure among advanced industrial democracies. Known as "Austro-Keynesianism," this policy combined high budget deficits, major financial support for publicly held industries, export subsidies by the state, and aggressive public investment, particularly in the construction industry. Austro-Keynesianism's heyday was under the venerable Bruno Kreisky, and it weakened with the changing nature of recent coalition politics and, more important, the Westernization of Austria.[14]

Export/import data further underline Austria's economic dependence. Only in four years between 1955 and 1990 did Austria's annual imports from the Bundesrepublik decline to under 40 percent of the country's total imports. The trend has been a small but gradual growth, which reached 44.5 percent in 1988 and 46 percent in 1990.[15] A whopping 66 percent of Austria's imports from all EU countries come from Germany. While export figures are of a lesser order of magnitude, they still convey an overwhelming German presence in Austria's daily life. Austria's exports to the Federal Republic were between 20 and 35 percent of total exports in 1955 to 1990, with the higher figures clustered in the 1980s and 1990. The trend has been unmistakably upward. Even before Austria joined the EU, its imports from Germany were four times greater than those from all EFTA (the European Free Trade Association, to which Austria belonged) countries combined; Austria's exports to the Federal Republic were "only" three times its exports to its EFTA partners.

Concerning foreign direct investment in Austria, the Federal Republic—as might be expected—leads other countries by a wide margin. As late as 1961, the United States was the leading investor in Austria, with 27.9 percent of total foreign direct investment. [16] Germany was in fifth place, with a mere 9.5 percent. By the end of the decade things had changed decidedly: Germany catapulted to 27.7 percent of all foreign direct investment, thereby assuming a leadership it has never relinquished. In the early 1990s German investors officially hold management equity in 2,737 Austrian companies, followed by 950 with American direct investment and 738 from Switzerland and Liechtenstein; 938 Austrian companies had direct investment from other countries.[17] In fact, many German companies use Swiss or Liechtenstein affiliates to invest in Austria, for tax reasons, further reflecting German dominance. German investment tends to cluster in key areas of the Austrian economy: metal processing, automobiles, the electrical and electronics industry, and chemicals. Only 7 percent of Austrians working in manufacturing and industry, and only 1–2 percent of the entire work force earns its livelihood in companies under German control. But German influence increased considerably in the 1980s, because this decade witnessed Austria's first concerted effort to privatize key components of a formidable state sector.[18] German investors were ready and able to capture these new investment opportunities.

The evidence is overwhelming: in virtually every aspect of economic life and on most commonly used indicators of economic relationships, Germany is "number one" for Austria. In direct investment, exports, imports, ownership of equity or real estate, and tourism (still the largest generator of foreign income for the Austrian economy), Germany leads all other countries.

Austria is nowhere near as important to the Germans. It is a significant economic partner, and often appears among the top ten countries with which Germany interacts, but it is virtually never number one. Even in tourism, more Germans visit Italy and France than go to Austria. The verdict is obvious: Germany's dominance of the Austrian economy cannot be overemphasized. But the results are not entirely one-sided. The great success story of the Austrian economy over the past fifty years suggests that complete dependence on Germany was by and large to Austria's benefit.

A Nominal Test

Our analysis of trade flows can be supplemented by an econometric approach. We assess whether German export growth yields a spillover effect on other members of the European Union. Concretely, we are interested in whether an increase in German export growth is "causing" a subsequent increase in the growth rates of other EU countries.[19]

Our results support a finding that an increase in German export growth does have a positive spillover effect on the Benelux countries, three to six years after the initial increase of exports from Germany. We did not find an analogous effect on the export growth rates in Great Britain.[20] Such results verify key ingredients of our argument. They show that smaller countries do in fact benefit from trade relations with Germany inside the European Union. They also demonstrate that large countries, especially Britain, do not benefit from Germany's increasing export performance.[21]

Market Share

The data so far reflect only the growth in each country's export trade relative to its own earlier performance. We compare each country's individual development over time. But to say that Germany's export base is growing faster compared to that of its major trading partners is not significant in understanding Germany's influence in the EU. We need to supplement that discussion with a cross-national comparison on how much of the total EU market is dominated by German exports. Table 1 outlines the structure of EU exports. Here the extent of German influence on markets becomes apparent.

With a market share in excess of 25 percent, Germany is Europe's biggest exporter to other members of the EU; it dominates such trade. Europe is Germany's primary trading domain. To put this in perspective: after 1989 Germany's imports from the rest of Europe surged by 30 percent, and its exports to the EU declined from a staggering DM 94 billion, yet Germany *still* had a DM 21 billion *surplus* with the EU in 1991.[22] For the Germans, "bad times" in trading with their EU partners has a different meaning than it holds for other countries.

Table 1 demonstrates that Germany continues to account for over a quarter of all intra-EU exports. Table 2, which reflects export dependence on the EU of member states, says much about the power of Germany within this context. Table 2 indicates that Germany's major European trading partners and rivals have a growing and sustained dependence on EU markets as integration deepens and broadens, but it also reveals that Germany's dependence has shrunk in the 1990s even as Germany continues to dominate exports. These data are reminiscent of the analysis offered by Albert O. Hirschman: Germany's reliance on the markets of Western Europe (as it directs trade eastward) lessens, while that of other Western European countries grows, giving Germany ever greater leverage over those countries as a provider of investment goods.[23]

In sum, the EU remains Germany's trading domain, but it is becoming less important to the Germans while it has grown in importance to all other members of the EU. The Dutch exemplify this tendency. They generate huge surpluses

Table 1. National market shares of EU member states in the EU (country's exports to other member states as a percentage of total intra-EU exports)

	1980	1985	1989	1992[a]
Germany	25.6	29.1	27.8	26.2
France	16.0	15.3	15.6	16.3
Italy	10.4	8.2	11.7	11.5
Netherlands	14.1	13.5	11.9	11.8
Belgium/Luxembourg	13.2	10.0	10.8	10.3
United Kingdom	13.3	14.2	11.4	11.9
Ireland	1.7	1.9	2.3	2.4
Denmark	2.3	2.9	2.1	2.4
Greece	0.6	0.1	0.7	0.7
Spain	2.8	3.2	4.4	5.1
Portugal	0.7	1.0	1.3	1.5

Sources: 1980 and 1989 data from David Cameron, "The 1992 Initiative: Causes and Consequences" in Alberta Sbragia, ed., *Euro-Politics: Politics and Policymaking in the "New" European Community* (Washington, D.C.: Brookings, 1993). For 1985 data see *IMF Direction of Trade Statistics: Yearbook 1990* (Washington D.C.: IMF, 1990). For 1992 data, *OECD Monthly Statistics of Foreign Trade*, Series A, November 1994.

[a]1992 statistics are for united Germany

from EU trade and remain heavily dependent on the EU (nearly 75 percent of all sales) for those surpluses. The value of the Guilder is tied to that of the D-Mark, and Germany remains a provider of essential products and investment capital to the Netherlands. The Dutch economy is so heavily integrated with that of its German neighbor that Germany has enormous influence over its neighbor.

Do these figures indicate hegemony? We believe they do indeed constitute a sign of German regional domination, especially in a liberalized trading system in which German export power will not be constrained by either protection or war. Germany's economic predominance is a basis from which it can enhance its structural economic power.

Historically, hegemons like Britain and the Netherlands have exported in huge volume. Still, export prowess might render Germany dependent on and vulnerable to its EU partners. These other two countries, after all, had the instruments of both *Machtstaat* and *Handelsstaat* at the same time. Germany by contrast, has the army and economy to be a *Machtstaat* but has thus far adhered to the ideology of a *Handelstaat*.

Who would hurt more if Germany stopped exporting, Germany or the other countries of the EU? At first glance, it looks as though Germany has been rendered dependent by its reliance on exports. But German dependence is falling as it turns eastward. Furthermore, consider the makeup of German exports. In

Table 2. Export dependence on the EU of the member states of the Union (exports to EU members as a percentage of all exports)

	1960	1965	1972	1979	1984	1989	1991	1992	1993	1994
Germany	29.5	35.2	46.9	49.4	50.0	55.1	50.3	50.1	41.5	41.0
France	29.7	42.3	55.3	52.4	50.7	59.1	61.9	61.5	59.6	59.4
Italy	29.6	40.2	50.3	53.5	47.4	56.4	59.2	58.0	53.3	53.5
Netherlands	45.9	55.7	52.5	73.2	73.3	75.4	76.7	76.3	72.3	72.6
Belgium/Luxembourg	50.5	62.0	73.8	73.4	70.2	73.6	75.3	75.1	72.8	67.3
United Kingdom	15.3	20.0	30.1	49.2	53.3	50.7	58.7	56.0	48.0	49.0
Ireland	17.1	12.8	—ᵃ	77.9	70.1	74.0	74.6	74.8	68.3	67.5
Denmark	27.7	25.9	41.8	49.3	44.7	50.6	54.3	54.8	51.8	49.4
Greece	32.9	37.2	52.5	49.1	55.0	64.2	63.7	64.8	59.7	54.8
Spain	38.5	36.5	45.3	48.7	51.5	66.9	70.6	71.4	68.2	68.6
Portugal	21.7	20.8	46.9	57.3	61.8	71.8	72.7	73.5	75.4	75.2

Sources: 1960 statistics: IMF *Direction of Trade Annual, 1958–62* (Washington, D.C., 1962); 1965 statistics: IMF *Direction of Trade Annual, 1964–68*; 1972 statistics: IMF *Direction of Trade Statistics Yearbook, 1969–75*; 1979 statistics: IMF *Direction of Trade Statistics Yearbook, 1974–80*; 1984 and 1989 statistics: IMF *Direction of Trade Statistics Yearbook, 1990*; 1991–94 statistics: IMF *Direction of Trade Statistics Yearbook, 1995.*
ᵃNo data for Ireland's trade with the EC were given in 1972.

1994, approximately 20 percent were investment goods. With such goods Germany does not engage in price competition, as it does with consumer goods. European countries have to purchase these investment goods from Germany and so are less likely to boycott German products.[24] German goods have become an essential ingredient in European well-being and prosperity.

The export of ideas is perhaps of equal importance to that of goods and services. We argue that Germany influences the governing EU principles on social management, economic exchange, and open markets. Despite some scurrilous revisionist claims by British policy makers that Britain's great contribution to the Maastricht Treaty was the adoption of these principles, it is clear that Germany's long-standing advocacy of free trade and open markets triumphed in the end, especially in opposition to the more protectionist French.

In the debate within the EU after unification, it is not surprising that the Germans favor the broadening of the EU rather than its deepening (especially in the eastern European countries, where Germany enjoys strategic, historical, and economic advantages over its major European partners). Broadening to include more markets enhances prospects for German exports in a way that deepening (greater economic integration) might not. Nor is it surprising that the Germans have won the debate. The outcome reflects the capacity of the Germans to influence priorities among decision makers in Brussels.

The broadening of the EU to include countries in northern, central, and eastern Europe expands the domain for German exports. If the data of the last twenty-five years are any guide for future developments, these countries may well export more in the coming years. At the same time, they will primarily import German products.

German Financial Power and the ERM

German economic might clearly rests on two legs: the relative power both of its currency, the Deutsche Mark, whose position has shifted both globally and regionally in the context of America's gradual decline, and of its central bank as a determinant of interest rates.[25] As an international reserve currency and an anchor against inflation, the Deutsche Mark's centrality has grown from an 8.8 percent share of world currency reserves in 1975 to 19.3 percent in 1989. It was then second only to the U.S. Dollar with 60.2 percent and ahead of the Japanese Yen with only 7.9 percent.[26] The precipitous decline of the dollar's value in 1994 and 1995 against both the D-Mark and the Yen adds support to the claim that there are now three global reserve currencies rather than a single benchmark.[27]

The Bundesbank has meanwhile become the main institutional determinant of European interest rates. It has also created what some observers now term a "Deutsche Mark bloc," for the D-Mark functions as Europe's reserve currency.[28] Pessimists believe the bank has actively sought this role—at worst, without any concern for its effects on Germany's neighbors, at best, heeding only its domestic mandates to maintain price stability and a steady money supply.[29] The latter view has received corroboration from occasional comments on the part of leading Bundesbank officials.[30] The Bundesbank, pessimists fear, might simply extend German economic power if left in charge as Europe's central bank. Some commentators have suggested that German officials all but conspired to bring about European Monetary Union for the purpose of greater German control over Europe.[31]

Bundesbank officials demonstrated both the bank's centrality and their disregard for their neighbors' welfare, according to critics, when bank officials raised interest rates in December 1991. This measure was described by the *New York Times* as "meant to stem rising domestic inflation and reaffirm German hegemony over European monetary policy." One senior German banking official concluded that "this is the Bundesbank's way of showing that they will use their power and independence without regard to the economic conditions in the rest of Europe."[32]

Optimists suggest that Economic Monetary Union is the key to controlling German economic domination by embedding the German economy in a broader European construct.[33] They also offer alternative motives for the Bundesbank's preoccupation with low inflation and stable interest rates. It is the optimists who invoke the specter of history. As one analyst commented in the *New York Times*:

there still exists in Germany a powerful consensus that a sound currency is the basis not only for sound economic growth but also for sound politics. Debasement of the money supply leads to debased politics, they believe; the Nazis came to power after a catastrophic bout of inflation destroyed the German currency in 1923. Ever since they began rebuilding the country after World War II, German leaders have been determined to prevent a repetition of this disastrous sequence. The Bundesbank is the vehicle for accomplishing this.[34]

Whether motivated by narrow self-interest or by enlightened self-preservation, the German financial system appears to optimists to have attained in the European economy a structural centrality that is stabilizing and reassuring.

Perhaps no more vivid illustration of the structural power of the German economy can be found than in Germany's role in the ERM.[35] Consider, for example, the following characterization of entry of the British Pound into the ERM:

> Like an older sibling, the Deutsche Mark may rough up its new little brother, the British pound, occasionally but will make sure no one else does now that Britain has entered the Exchange Rate Mechanism (ERM) of the European Monetary System.[36]

A broader, comprehensive analysis that is consistent with this view of the role of the D-Mark in the ERM is offered by C. Randall Henning:

> Frankfurt's monetary policy has generally dominated the ERM. Monetary policies of the participating countries have converged towards the Bundesbank's monetary standard, rather than towards a European average. To the surprise of many observers, during the 1980s Germany's partners accepted the Deutsche Mark as the "nominal anchor" of the system. Because countries such as France and Italy were strongly committed to existing parities, the ERM became, effectively, a Deutsche Mark zone. The area of this zone was extended to Switzerland, Austria and the Nordic countries, which, with varying degrees of commitment, linked their currencies to the Deutsche Mark, or to the ECU, by shadowing the Bundesbank's monetary policies. The dominance of the Deutsche Mark persisted even after the unraveling of the ERM during 1992–1993, as most partner countries continued to match German monetary policy despite the shift to wide bands. From the German standpoint, the ability to pursue German monetary preferences was and remains the fundamental difference between EMS and the old Bretton Woods regime.[37]

Henning characterizes the Bundesbank's response to the idea of monetary union, entailing a single central bank and single European currency, as "publicly cool and privately hostile." As he notes:

The project would, if carried to its ultimate end, fully replace the power and dominance of the Bundesbank and the Deutsche Mark within the EMS with a European monetary institution and currency that the Bundesbank would have only a small and indirect role in managing. Frankfurt recognized from the outset, however, that EMU was first and foremost a political decision for the government.[38]

It is remarkable that Germany would even contemplate fulfilling the terms of the Maastricht Treaty, by which Germany is supposed to surrender the power of the Bundesbank and jeopardize the strength of its currency by having the Deutsche Mark join a pool of currencies, the European Currency Unit, which is to become the Euro by the end of this millennium. Many Germans see this idea as "a recipe for inflation rather than a guarantee of economic stability," according to one *Wall Street Journal* report.[39] To optimists, Germany's willingness to abandon the security of the D-Mark for the vagaries of an ill-defined Euro is further evidence for the country's continued commitment to the common European project.

What did EMU mean in practice? Karl Otto Pöhl, head of the German central bank, stressed the need for other countries to conform to what he considered acceptable terms for the institution of EMU and a single European central bank. To the surprise of many at the Bundesbank, leaders throughout Europe seemed willing to contemplate such stringent conditions. The bank delineated the necessary conditions that would ensure monetary stability: low inflation, low government deficits, comparable long-term interest rates, and a lasting period of exchange rate stability within EMS.

And what of the rules and institutional structure of the proposed central bank? According to Henning, "the Bundesbank recommended not simply itself as a model for the European Central Bank—frequent references to the 'Eurofed' not withstanding—but its own legal structure plus the amendments that it would have made to its own law."[40]

A much-publicized domestic debate about European monetary integration followed between the German government and the Bundesbank. Bundesbank officials feared that integration would destroy the Bundesbank's independence from the political process, but the views of Helmut Kohl and the German government on the structure of pan-European financial integration eventually carried the day.[41] Despite Pöhl's subsequent criticisms, the proposals that went forward for discussion at Maastricht more closely approximated the government's recommendations than those of the Bundesbank.[42] The results of these Maastricht negotiations were, according to Henning, startling:

The concessions made by the other European governments in the design of monetary union leading to Maastricht were extraordinary. The French government in particular proved to be flexible, for example, in accepting unconditional central bank independence, underscoring the depth of historical change in the French political economy. The German government and Bundesbank received virtually every important negotiating item for which they had asked in the monetary area.[43]

Again, the German response was to up the ante, first by stressing "stability-policy performance," then by Bundesbank decisions to raise interest rates by 0.5 percent to 8 percent immediately after Maastricht, and subsequently by a 0.75 increase the following July. These increases precipitated conflicts among German groups, and between them and their central bank, that cumulated in the ERM crisis. Currencies fluctuated violently in value: the British Pound, Portuguese Escudo, Spanish Peseta, and Italian Lira all were formally or informally devalued against the D-Mark.[44] In a final act of assertiveness, after the crisis, Bundesbank officials suggested a two-step process of EMU—dividing an inner core of countries centered on Germany, whose economies were considered sound, from those whose currencies had been devalued due to the precarious performance of their economies. Officials also reiterated an earlier demand that any future European central bank be located in Frankfurt.[45]

These events illustrate several contradictory tendencies. The first reflects the power of Germany's currency—and, by extension, its financial institutions—to get others to adapt to German demands. The proposed entity would have replicated the principles of the German central bank, not those of counterparts such as the Bank of England. Every time the Germans (bankers and politicians) made demands, everybody else jumped, even though some demands made little economic sense locally, precipitated the ERM crisis, and ultimately postponed European economic recovery.[46]

The second tendency demonstrates German reticence about engaging in great-power activities. Parts of the German political class as well as the public pleaded for continuation of the D-Mark. They did not want to surrender this great symbol of the Federal Republic's success for a technocratically designed European currency. For the first time in the history of the Federal Republic, a considerable anti-European mood developed in passionate defense of the D-Mark. German stability and prosperity (as well as German postwar pride) were not to be sacrificed on the altar of European integration.[47] This "D-Mark nationalism" created, at least temporarily, some strange bedfellows, from the mass-circulation daily *Bild-Zeitung* on the right to two prominent leaders of the Social Democratic party, Rudolf Scharping and Gerhard Schröder, on the left[48]; from stability-oriented, pro-European bankers to populist, anti-European nationalists. This issue provoked the first considerable kink of the postwar era in Germany's hitherto impeccably pro-European sentiment.

Finally, the decision to raise interest rates, and ultimately to precipitate a series of ERM crises, tells us much about the gap between diffident ideology and extensive structural power.[49] Optimists embrace control by the German central bank over European interest rates as an instrument of necessary discipline and an expression of commitment by the Germans on behalf of European unity. Pessimists worry about the Bundesbank's track record of focusing on domestic considerations at a cost to Germany's neighbors.[50] These pessimists fear, in effect, the gap between what the Bundesbank can do and what it chooses to do—its refusal to demonstrate leadership—when broader European interests are at stake.[51] We share this concern.

Profits and Losses

Finally, we have to address what the benefits of free trade arrangements were to various EU members in the 1980s, and how this distribution was affected by unification. Who wins and who loses in the EU's free trade arrangements? Are these gains and losses significant? Are they lop-sided, as Table 1 suggests? The degree of maldistribution is important because limited losses might be recouped through other means (e.g., net receipts from the budget); or they might be compensated through noneconomic benefits (e.g., enhanced security or solidarity on political matters). The data in Tables 3 and 4 address these questions.

Liberals often decry the balance of trade as an indicator because they consider it a zero-sum measure. After all, in a limited, integrated set of economies like the EU, one country's import balance can increase only when another's decreases. But these figures retain some utility. They clearly demonstrate, in the absence of an input-output model that can calculate offsetting exports to countries outside the EU, who benefits from the present set of trading relationships.

As the 1980s developed, Germany consistently ran by far the largest trade surplus within the EU (see Table 3). After a brief dip following unification, this position was restored in the mid 1990s. Table 4 demonstrates the linear growth in Germany's trade and current account balances—enviable figures by the standards of other European countries (with the possible exception of the Netherlands).

After impressive increases in the 1980s, Germany's overall trade balance declined from $77.87 billion in 1989 to $23.82 billion in 1991 (see table 4). The current account balance declined even more drastically, from $57.51 billion in 1989 to minus $22.02 billion in 1992. More recent data show a change in trend for the trade balance, which has been steadily increasing since 1992, but Germany's current accounts balance continues to be negative.

Three main factors appear to be important for these recent developments. First, the global recession of 1991 reduced the demand for German export goods in countries that had previously been Germany's most important trading partners, especially Britain and the United States. Second, the D-Mark was revalued in 1992 during the reformation of the European currency system. German export goods became more expensive and thus less competitive in international markets. The final reason is that part of the current accounts balance, services, has been negative: reduced net return to capital abroad has contributed to, and German tourist expenditures abroad are accounted for as imports of services.[53]

The amount Germans spend as tourists abroad increased from 1988 to 1993

Table 3. Balance of trade of EC member states with other EC members (exports minus imports in billions of $U.S.)

	1980	1981	1982	1983	1984	1985	1986	1987	1988	1989	1990	1991	1992	1993	1994
Germany	7.5	6.4	11.7	7.4	9.2	10.9	23.9	34.8	46.3	50.3	39.1	15.4	21.4	22.9	33.0
France	-5.0	-5.4	-10.1	-8.4	-7.0	-7.7	-7.8	-9.6	-7.1	-8.4	-7.3	0.17	3.2	5.7	5.3
Italy	-5.7	-4.1	-1.9	-0.4	-3.2	-4.8	-3.1	-5.5	-6.2	-7.3	-4.8	-5.2	-7.8	8.1	7.0
Netherlands	10.8	13.5	13.0	13.1	13.8	12.6	12.0	10.9	13.2	15.1	22.9	21.5	20.2	27.5	29.5
Belgium/Luxembourg	1.2	0.9	0.5	-0.2	-1.4	-1.5	0.7	1.5	1.0	3.2	0.7	1.0	0.5	6.6	-21.8
United Kingdom	0.8	-1.0	-3.7	-5.6	-5.9	-4.3	-14.0	-16.6	-26.6	-26.9	-18.9	-3.7	-9.3	-6.5	-6.0
Ireland	-1.6	-2.1	-1.1	-0.2	0.3	0.5	1.3	2.8	3.6	4.0	3.9	4.5	6.1	7.7	6.2
Denmark	-0.9	-0.8	-0.7	-0.2	-0.8	-1.4	-2.0	-0.9	0.1	0.9	0.9	1.3	3.6	3.2	2.4
Greece	-1.8	-2.6	-2.7	-2.4	-2.0	-2.4	-3.0	-3.6	-4.2	-5.4	-7.5	-7.5	-8.4	-6.6	-9.4
Spain	0.2	-0.1	0	0.3	2.3	1.6	-1.2	-5.0	-7.9	-11.1	-13.6	-15.9	-15.6	-7.5	-5.8
Portugal	-1.5	-2.1	-1.9	-0.8	-0.2	0.1	-0.7	-2.6	-3.7	-3.7	-5.2	-6.4	-8.5	-5.7	-5.7

Sources: 1980–89 data: David Cameron, "The 1992 Initiative," in Alberta M. Sbragia, ed., *Euro–Politics: Institutions and Policymaking in the "New" European Community* (Washington D.C.: Brookings Institution, 1992), p. 69; 1990–94 data: IMF *Direction of Trade Statistics Yearbook*, 1995.

Note: The notation "EC" is used since at the time of much of the data collection the entity was still the European Community, not the European Union.

Table 4. Trade and Current Accounts Balance of Germany, 1980–1994 (in billion $U.S.)

	Trade Balance	Current Accounts Balance
1980	+10.15	-13.83
1981	+17.44	-3.55
1982	+26.10	+5.11
1983	+22.34	+5.30
1984	+23.10	+9.81
1985	+28.77	+16.42
1986	+56.14	+39.50
1987	+70.53	+45.88
1988	+79.92	+50.64
1989	+77.87	+57.51
1990	+72.38	+46.85
1991	+23.82	-19.44
1992	+32.01	-22.02
1993	+43.40	-20.10
1994	+50.80	-20.60

Sources: Sachverständigenrat, *Jahresgutachten* 1994/95, p. 326, and 1995/96.

from $24 billion to over $37 billion while Germany's receipts from tourism were stagnating (see Table 5). Remarkably, the deficit Germany runs in tourism, approximately $27 billion, is bigger than the country's entire current accounts deficit. Also, Germany spends more on tourism than the next two countries, Britain and Italy, combined. Indeed, between unification and 1994, Germans spent more than $1 billion on goods and services just in visiting Poland.[54]

The strong Deutsche Mark accords the Germans inordinate opportunities to travel, and even though money allegedly cannot buy love, German "sex tourism" to Hungary, Poland, the Czech Republic, and to faraway Thailand is booming.

The negative current accounts balance also underlines Germany's weight in the European Union. After Germany moved to a negative current accounts balance in 1991, the aggregate EU balance turned negative as well. As the German balance began to recover, the EU current accounts balance turned positive again in 1993.[55] Germany appears poised to resume sustained growth. We assume that the trajectory of the 1980s will continue in the near future, particularly as transformation of the GDR is completed and that formerly desolate area attains the advanced levels of production and efficiency characteristic of the Bundesrepublik. It is, we believe, only a question of when this will happen.

We noted earlier that small states seem to benefit from the present system. Between 1980 and 1992, a further pattern emerges for larger countries: Germany consistently makes enormous gains while its major trading rivals (Britain, France, and Italy) lose. Whereas small states are likely to have economies that complement Germany's, its larger neighbors, with less specialized economies, are more likely

Table 5. Tourist receipts and expenditures, 1988–1993 (in million $U.S.)

	Receipts						Expenditures					
	1988	1989	1990	1991	1992	1993	1988	1989	1990	1991	1992	1993
Austria	10,090	10,717	13,410	13,800	14,526	13,566	6,307	6,266	7,723	7,392	8,393	8,180
Belgium	3,416	3,057	3,718	3,606	4,053	4,071	4,577	4,254	5,471	5,528	6,603	6,363
Denmark	2,423	2,313	3,322	3,475	3,784	3,052	3,087	2,932	3,676	3,377	3,779	3,214
Finland	983	1,017	1,170	1,247	1,360	1,239	1,842	2,040	2,740	2,742	2,449	1,617
France	13,786	16,245	20,185	21,375	25,051	23,410	9,715	10,031	12,424	12,321	13,914	12,805
Germany[a]	8,449	8,658	10,493	10,424	11,055	10,509	24,564	23,411	29,509	31,027	36,626	37,514
Greece	2,396	1,976	2,587	2,567	3,255	3,293	735	816	1,090	1,015	1,186	1,003
Ireland	997	1,070	1,447	1,511	1,620	1,639	961	989	1,159	1,125	1,361	1,256
Italy	12,255	11,938	20,016	18,421	21,450	20,521	5,929	6,774	14,045	11,648	16,530	13,053
Netherlands	2,888	3,049	3,636	4,246	5,237	4,690	6,701	6,461	7,376	8,149	9,330	8,974
Portugal	2,402	2,685	3,555	3,710	3,721	4,176	533	583	867	1,024	1,165	1,846
Spain	16,686	16,174	18,593	19,004	21,181	19,425	2,440	3,080	4,254	4,530	5,542	4,706
Sweden	2,334	2,536	2,916	2,704	3,055	2,650	4,545	4,961	6,134	6,291	6,969	4,464
United Kingdom	10,938	11,293	14,003	13,070	13,932	13,451	14,510	15,344	19,063	17,609	19,850	17,431

Sources: 1988 figures, and 1989 figures for Germany; *Market Research Europe*, December 1994, p. xx; 1989–1993 figures: *Market Research Europe*, December 1995; p. xx.

[a]1988 and 1989 figures refer to West Germany only.

to be rivals. The French, Italians, British, and Germans all have significant automobile, chemical, steel, and pharmaceutical industries. Small states rarely produce such products, or if they do, they generally specialize in niche markets. The Swiss make watches, the Belgians lace, and the Germans cars. Germany's three major EU competitors lose in this free trading arrangement, and Britain loses most heavily of all. Germany has consistently proved to be the sole beneficiary from free trade among large EU members.

Some large EU members have continued to resist more liberal trade arrangements with Japanese and American producers. The figures suggest they should be more concerned about internal competition from German exports rather than external competitive threats. Indeed, the only threat to Germany's regional trade dominance, apart from unilateral decisions by German producers to divert exports to alternative markets (e.g., eastern Europe), comes from foreign direct investment by Japanese and American firms. German governments have not vocally opposed Japanese investment in Europe, but they have benefited from strenuous French attempts to proscribe Japanese investment. The Germans have played the role of tactful bystander, corroborating their image as sturdy proponents of free markets and letting the French assume the role of the protectionist bully.

The auto industry provides one example. The eight-year limits on the sale of Japanese cars in Europe (agreed in 1991 and begun in 1993) was advocated most aggressively by French producers and their government, opposed most vehemently by the British. The Germans had the opportunity to adjudicate, but while they continually professed support for free trade, Japanese producers never garnered more than 15 percent of the German market. No evidence of formal barriers to trade exist, but Simon Reich was repeatedly told in interviews that an informal understanding exists between the German government and Japanese producers. In one meeting described to him, representatives of the Japanese auto industry volunteered to come and tell German officials about their sales plans for the next five years. We do not know if the story is true or apocryphal, but it certainly is instructive and suggests a sophisticated reciprocal understanding between the two countries.

Why do Germany's trading partners in the EU, with the exception of the Dutch, the Irish, and the Danes, willingly adhere to these arrangements when they so adversely affect these countries' balances of trade? There are at least two possible answers. The first is consistent with neoliberal arguments in that it emphasizes the preeminence of interests as a determinant of behavior, and looks for an alternative financial basis for membership beyond trade statistics.[56] The second is consistent with sociological and cultural arguments in that it emphasizes ideological consensus in explaining the continuity of trading relations. The next section critically considers the interest-based argument by looking at intra-EU trade relations in the context of broader EU fiscal understandings.

Underwriting the Rules or Paying the Bills

We believe that we can get a sense of whether and to what degree Germany underwrites the EU system simply by looking at the annual balance of payments of the member-states with the EU, which reflects budgetary contributions. Table 6 presents figures for EU member contributions to and receipts for the late 1980s and early 1990s. As these figures clearly indicate, the Federal Republic was by far the largest contributor to the EU budget.

Other analysts have substantiated three further claims. The first is that the Germans contributed so much to the EU budget that they clearly have under-written the rules in the 1980s, although they often complained about doing so, especially in regard to subsidizing (as they see it) some of their larger European partners.[57] The Germans have taken a more benign view of the treatment of the poorer, southern EU states, supporting moves, for example, to untie aid and thus weaken national procurement restrictions within the EU.[58] The smaller countries were the primary direct and indirect beneficiaries from the budget. Second, the indirect effects of EU programs, most notably the Common Agricultural Policy, mitigated the effects of trade deficits for the French and the Italians. But when all factors are considered, the figures on trade and budget suggest that the French and the Italians were still net losers. Third, the British claimed that Britain did not benefit from EU membership from the mid-1980s onward, and they were most certainly correct. Britain's trade deficit with EU partners was not offset by direct or indirect subsidies from the EU budget. Britain was the largest loser, and generally the second largest budgetary contributor behind the Germans.

The pattern is clear. The Germans are the primary beneficiaries of the EU system of trade. They partially offset their tremendous gains through extensive budgetary contributions. But the Germans enjoy a market dominance which is growing over time. Their dominance increased over the 1980s and will continue to grow after the immediate cost of unification is completed by the late 1990s. In both absolute and relative terms, the EU system enhances Germany's wealth and power, and reduces that of its major trading partners.

Eastern Europe

Germany enjoys much closer historical, political, and economic relations to the countries of eastern Europe than does any other major state in central and western Europe. Furthermore, Germany has historically been a more dominant actor in the affairs of eastern Europe than it has in the west. East European politics has centered on the often delicate navigation between the Scylla of German power and the Charybdis of Russian and/or Ottoman might. Events since 1989 mark,

Table 6. Balance of payments of the member states of the European Union, 1987–1992 (current account balance in million ECU)

	1987			1988			1989		
	Credit	Debit	Net	Credit	Debit	Net	Credit	Debit	Net
Belgium	2488.3	2616.2	−127.9	2815.1	2919.4	−104.4	2685.9	2967.0	−281.0
Luxembourg	207.1	515.6	−308.6	310.8	540.5	−229.6	223.0	604.6	−381.6
Denmark	1044.9	1148.3	−103.4	1209.7	1363.2	−153.4	1208.4	1224.1	−15.7
Germany^a	10558.1	6018.4	4539.7	13122.1	7617.1	5505.0	12856.2	7166.2	5689.5
Greece	576.8	1761.6	−1184.9	708.3	1844.8	−1136.5	851.8	2435.8	−1584.1
Spain	1840.5	2239.3	−398.8	2936.9	4208.4	−1271.5	4165.4	5204.9	−1039.5
France	8724.8	7628.6	1096.2	10972.0	8797.2	2174.9	10762.5	7508.8	3253.7
Ireland	628.9	1393.0	−764.1	644.7	1534.4	−889.6	644.9	1824.0	−1179.1
Italy	7085.9	5878.0	1207.9	7613.8	6406.4	1207.3	9976.8	7282.8	2694.0
Netherlands	2876.7	3586.9	−710.3	3481.8	4899.0	−1417.2	3469.5	5117.6	−1648.1
Portugal	416.5	898.9	−482.4	512.1	1026.9	−514.8	667.6	1248.1	−580.5
United Kingdom	7123.6	3907.5	3216.1	6901.1	4334.1	2567.1	8155.8	4439.1	3716.7

	1990			1991			1992		
	Credit	Debit	Net	Credit	Debit	Net	Credit	Debit	Net
Belgium	2694.1	3451.5	-757.4	3257.8	4416.3	-1158.5	3379.0	4875.9	-1496.9
Luxembourg	252.8	705.2	-452.3	238.5	731.9	-493.4	285.2	795.9	-510.7
Denmark	1120.7	1325.1	-204.4	1474.4	1543.0	-68.6	1584.9	1460.3	124.6
Germany	11966.9	7063.6	4903.3	17092.8	8886.2	8206.6	19025.7	9953.5	9072.2
Greece	814.7	3141.3	-2326.6	1176.2	3646.0	-2469.8	1155.2	4482.2	-3327.0
Spain	4359.9	5772.3	-1412.4	5572.9	7469.6	-1896.7	6048.2	8055.0	-2006.9
France	9945.5	7838.7	2106.8	12816.6	9945.1	2871.5	12860.7	10842.3	2018.4
Ireland	633.2	2383.9	-1750.7	747.6	2868.5	-2120.9	759.0	2655.5	-1896.5
Italy	8737.6	6840.7	1896.9	11772.3	8728.6	3043.7	11441.2	9266.1	2175.1
Netherlands	3174.2	3969.8	-795.6	4034.3	3905.9	128.4	4037.5	3481.2	556.3
Portugal	743.7	1369.3	-625.6	1046.4	2315.2	-1268.8	1272.9	3094.5	-1821.6
United Kingdom	8194.9	4590.9	3604.0	6590.4	5609.1	981.3	8616.0	5945.8	2670.2

Sources: 1987–1990 data: Eurostat, *Balance of Payments of the Community Institutions from 1987–1990* (Luxembourg: Statistical Office of the European Communities, 1993), pp. 108–159; 1991–1992 data: Eurostat, *Balance of Payments of the Community Institutions from 1991–1992* (Luxembourg: Statistical Office of the European Communities, 1993), pp. 106–131.

[a]Data 1987–1990 refer to West Germany.

of course, a period of weakened though potentially troublesome Russian influence.

Germany's unconditional surrender in 1945 and the subsequent Yalta world seemed to establish Russia as the sole political actor of importance in that part of the world. But Germany was not to be dismissed so easily. German influence in Eastern Europe was to revive in economic cooperation and conflict reduction instead of political bullying and military occupation. The two pillars of the Bundesrepublik's influence in Eastern Europe have been *Osthandel* (pertaining to the economy and commerce) and *Ostpolitik* (its counterpart in politics and ideology).

As to *Osthandel*, it is extremely difficult to identify *any* category of commerce and trade in which the Federal Republic has not consistently been the most important western presence in eastern Europe.[59] Germany is the most important trading partner to the aggregate of former Soviet republics and to each of the Visegrad countries (Hungary, the Czech Republic, Slovakia, and Poland), as well as the "in-between-states" of Bulgaria, Romania, Albania, Slovenia, Croatia, Bosnia-Herzegovina, Macedonia, and Yugoslavia (Serbia and Montenegro). Perhaps more impressive than this aggregate dominance is the fact that Germany has been leading partner to each of these countries in virtually every conceivable category, ranging from cars, electronics, and chemical products to textiles, agricultural goods, and artwork.

German dominance is, if anything, even more pronounced at the level of individual firms. Data on company investments and joint ventures in eastern Europe show Federal Republic firms way ahead of the competition (mainly Austrian, Italian, and to a much lesser extent American). Some contacts make headlines, like Volkswagen's purchase of the Skoda works in Czechoslovakia; others do not, like the more than three hundred joint ventures begun by German and Hungarian firms in Hungary in 1989. *Osthandel* is changing every facet of the eastern European economies.

Ostpolitik initially improved and subsequently institutionalized East-West relations in the post-1945 world, and it served as the intellectual and structural precursor to detente. *Ostpolitik* certainly gave the Germans a running start in eastern Europe after the Cold War era.

Ostpolitik aimed to secure peaceful relations between East and West. Its successor in the new Europe places the highest priority on maintaining stability within each eastern country while encouraging economic reform.[60] This concern can, of course, be traced to self-interest on the part of the Germans, but some commentators have reasonably suggested that it is, at least in part, motivated by a sense of guilt. Craig Whitney sees "a wish to atone for the sins of the Nazis, by extending a helping hand now. Some of it is relief: They are so grateful for the [former] Soviet Union's agreement last year [1990] to let two parts of their country reunite within the NATO alliance that it sometimes seems there is little they won't do."[61] The German definition of security has been broadened in the context of changing European conditions.

By the *annus mirabilis* of 1989, the German model was the most cherished option for all the countries of eastern Europe. East Europeans wanted to emulate the *Wirtschaftswunder* as the best agent of transition to a democratic polity and as its most reliable guarantor. With most aspects of the postwar German order enjoying great respect in eastern Europe, it is no surprise that some countries have actively sought to copy German institutions in the establishment of their new polities. The Hungarians, Poles, and Romanians have adopted key elements of the German electoral system; the Czech Republic's constitution closely resembles certain passages of the Federal Republic's Basic Law.

Such factors combine to give Germany a strategic advantage over its main western European competitors in trading with the countries of eastern Europe. The advantage is augmented by a familiarity on the part of the Germans with the contours of culture and the terrain of business in eastern Europe. As one journalist suggested, "the race to the East is going to the holders of German marks."[62]

Much of the traditional economic structure in these East European countries has, of course, disappeared. Furthermore, no institutional arrangement like the EU promises to integrate these countries' economies, as well as their politics and culture. We therefore divide our analysis of Germany's economic relations with eastern Europe into three subgroups: the Visegrad countries, the "in between states," and the successor countries of the former Soviet Union. We also divide our analysis into an examination of trade, investment (through joint ventures), and loan and aid—the last being a way of underwriting the rules of the system. First, however, we look at data concerning Germany's relationship with states that comprised the defunct Council for Mutual Economic Assistance (CMEA).

Trade Flows

Germany shares a long history with many of the countries of central and eastern Europe, often regarding itself as the bridge between east and west in Mitteleuropa. Pessimists often fear that the German tendency to seek domination will now reassert itself, albeit in a milder and nonviolent form. Germans clearly recognize that they walk a fine line between the normal processes of trade and the appearance of laying the foundations for domination. Such fears are echoed in newspaper articles that either question the motives for German activities or offer reassurances about such motives.[63]

German attempts to reassure are consistent with our view of the Germans as favoring a *Handelstaat* rather than a *Machtstaat*. The purpose of economics is to gain wealth, without an ulterior motive. Indeed, Chancellor Kohl has repeatedly claimed that Germany's mission in eastern Europe is to provide political stability and economic prosperity.[64]

Germany has avidly pursued enlarged trade. Imports to the EU from the major markets of eastern Europe increased from DM27.248 billion in 1990 to DM

Table 7. Export sales to central and eastern European countries (in million $U.S.)

	1989	1992	1993	1994
Germany[a]	6882.0	15430.8	16710.0	22262.4
France	1156.8	2748.0	2625.6	3516.0
Italy	1542.0	3684.0	4227.6	7028.4
United Kingdom	933.6	1965.6	2163.6	2692.8
Austria	1624.3	3576.2	3547.1	4852.0
Finland	263.4	841.9	1058.9	1913.4
Switzerland	829.0	1030.9	1026.4	1779.7
United States	926.4	1872.0	2323.2	2008.8
Japan	577.2	726.0	632.4	613.2

Sources: 1989 data: OECD *Monthly Statistics of Foreign Trade*, Series A, January 1991; 1992 and 1993 data: OECD *Monthly Statistics of Foreign Trade*, Series A, October 1994; 1994 data: OECD *Monthly Statistics of Foreign Trade*, Series A, February 1996.

Note: 1989 figures are for sales to COMECON Europe minus sales to the USSR. 1992–1994 figures refer to sales to Poland, the former Czechoslovokia, Hungary, Romania, Bulgaria, and the Baltic States.

[a]1989 data refer to West Germany only.

38.622 billion by 1992. Germany alone accounted for 46 percent of that total in 1990 (DM12.633 billion) and over 57 percent (DM22.091 billion) by 1992.

German exports to central and eastern European markets grew faster still, in both absolute and relative terms. EU exports to these markets totaled DM27.726 in 1990, of which German exports were valued at DM13.038 billion (47 percent of the EU total); by 1992 EU exports grew to DM43.867 billion, of which the German share was over 53 percent, at DM23.360 billion. German exports to the east totaled about the same as to Austria in 1992, making the present cost seem enormous, but the German focus is on market potential not present volume of sales.[65] With a combined population of 400 million in eastern Europe (comparable to the 430 million in western Europe), the expanded demand in these immature markets could be enormous. Moreover, increases in average incomes in eastern Europe augur well. As a result of the increase in trade between 1990 and 1992, for example, the proportion of German trade with central and eastern Europe as a percentage of total German foreign trade grew from 2.0 to 3.5 percent. Growth was particularly high in the Baltic states.[66]

The evidence of Germany's competitive edge in eastern Europe is overwhelming. Germany—and Austria—are the big winners with the opening of EU–eastern European trade.[67] And the erection of trade barriers and domestic content requirements by East European countries, designed to favor EU products, promises only to consolidate Germany's position as the most prominent supplier of major industrial items for the area.[68] The German position is presented in Table 7. More telling than rank order is the disparity between Germany and all the other countries. Indeed, German export sales exceed the combined total attained by the next four countries in every year calculated.

Table 8. Export sales to the Soviet Union and NIS (in million $U.S.)

	1989	1992	1993	1994
Germany[a]	6146.4	8505.6	9016.8	9271.2
France	2874.0	2078.4	1860.0	1608.0
Italy	2732.4	2884.8	2107.2	2670.0
United Kingdom	1114.8	799.2	1080.0	1371.6
Austria	867.2	725.9	655.2	800.9
Finland	3385.1	746.0	1135.2	1654.8
Switzerland	583.2	273.5	337.2	465.2
United States	4270.8	3625.2	3780.0	3388.8
Japan	3081.6	1191.6	1662.0	1348.8

Sources: 1989 data: OECD *Monthly Statistics of Foreign Trade*, Series A, January 1991; 1992 and 1993 data: OECD *Monthly Statistics of Foreign Trade*, Series A, October 1994; 1994 data: OECD *Monthly Statistics of Foreign Trade*, Series A, February 1996.
Note: 1989 data refer to sales to the USSR. Data from 1992, 1993 and 1994 refer to the successor states to the Soviet Union (Newly Independent States, NIS).
[a]1989 data refer to West Germany only.

The Soviet Union's successor states, here collectively named Newly Independent States (NIS), have the poorest economic performance, and in the early to mid 1990s economic uncertainty as well as an inflation rate of 300 percent led to a decrease in trade with most western European countries.[69] Germany was one of the few countries to increase its exports to the NIS against the general downward trend. The 40 percent expansion of Germany's exports combined with contraction or stagnation by other countries to produce an enormous increase in Germany's market share. Germany's total exports to the former Soviet Union are bigger than those of the next four countries combined (see Table 8).

Among all the Newly Independent States, Germany dominates, accounting for nearly 80 percent of Russian trade (the remainder is largely accounted for by the Baltic states). In strategic terms, the really important bilateral trade relationship is between Germany and Russia.[70] It is therefore appropriate to recall the *Economist*'s comment that "German and Russian history is not just a tale of appalling wars, but of long periods of trade, cultural contact and inter-migration. . . . On the eve of the first world war, half of Russian exports went to Germany and close to half of Germany's foreign investment was in Russia."[71] History, it might appear, was repeating itself.

The "in between states" reveal no clear trend in their export data, but they share one common feature: Germany is by far their most important trading partner, collectively and individually.

The economically most prosperous part of eastern Europe, the Visegrad States, has the biggest share of Germany's trade with eastern Europe. Germany is also each group member's most important trading partner (excepting the Slovak Republic, for which it still is the Czech Republic). The order of magnitude of Germany's leadership among these economically strong eastern European countries is especially convincing. German exports to the Visegrad countries are between three and five times the size of Italy's, the runner up (see Table 9). Germany accounts, for example, for 65 percent of all EU exports to the Czech Republic, fueling local apprehension about economic domination.[72]

Foreign Direct Investments and Joint Ventures

The Federal Republic's economic dominance in eastern Europe extends to the world of joint ventures (JVs). The Germans moved rapidly to secure attractive investments in the aftermath of the fall of the Berlin Wall, spurred by the East's desperate need for capital. German firms were offered East European assets at attractive rates. The Germans bought them up with an avidity that belies figures offered by German banks, which claimed that their investments in eastern Europe were not as great as generally believed.[73] Why this secrecy? We believe that German investors did not wish to appear to gain advantages from the economic troubles of peoples whose collective memory of the Germans was at best ambivalent.

The Germans have been active. Of the 1,231 JVs registered in Poland during the first quarter of 1990, over 40 percent (506) involved German firms. Sweden followed with 112, and Austria was third with 81.[74] A similar trend pertained in Czechoslovakia. Of 32 joint ventures begun by Czechoslovak and foreign firms in January 1990, 11 belonged to Germany, the unchallenged western leader. The Germans moved early and fast: by the middle of 1991 they had 873 joint ventures with firms in the Czech Republic, compared to 133 by U.S. firms.[75] At that point, Germans accounted for 86 percent of the value of 1991 FDI in the Czech Republic.[76] To give an idea of the differences in scale between U.S. and Germany investments in the Czech Republic, Volkswagen purchased Skoda, while the *New York Times* focused on an entrepreneur from Alabama named Grady Lloyd who had invested $40,000 to open the first self-service laundry in Prague. His goal was to open ten to fifteen more in the city.[77]

In the meantime Germany also accounted for 19.4 percent of Czech exports and supplied 20.1 percent of Czech imports in the early 1990s.[78] As a result of all this activity, Czechs are beginning to fear Germanization of their country. Approximately $800 million was invested through single and joint ventures by German firms in 1994 alone, compared to about $600 million by the United States and $300 million by France, the next largest EU investor. Four German firms are among the largest twenty companies in the Czech Republic (not including Volkswagen's joint venture with Skoda), and one 1992 article claimed that German firms accounted for more than eighty percent of foreign investment in the Czech Republic.[79]

Both Poland and the Czech Republic have tried to balance German investment with greater U.S. investment. By 1993, for example, American firms had already invested $1 billion in Poland, with the immediate promise of a further $500 million as a result of an announced deal by PepsiCo. One Polish official insisted at the time that "there is still too little U.S. investment in this country. This is so because we prefer it to German investment, especially since in the west of Poland German investment raises certain negative historical connotations."[80]

Hungarians register no such concerns. They doubled their exports to the EU and halved them to the CMEA countries between 1989 and 1991. Germany accounted for 27.8 percent of all Hungarian exports, and 23.6 percent of all imports, by the end of that period.[81]

As a consequence of Hungary's liberal approach to business and its pioneer role among former socialist societies in attracting foreign capital, western interest has been especially keen. As of July 1990, approximately 1,800 JVs had registered in Hungary for that calendar year alone. In comparison, 1,100 JVs were established in all of 1989. By the spring of 1992, $3.5 billion had poured into Hungary from foreign investors.[82] By the following fall that figure had reached $5.5 billion.[83] Early and much-publicized foreign investments in Hungary involved the General Electric purchase of Tungsram and the sale of Lehel, the refrigerator maker, to Electrolux of Sweden. But it was Austrian and German companies that were in fact the most active, accounting for over one-third of joint ventures.[84]

In the former Soviet Union, too, Germany was the early leader, well ahead of Finland in quantity of joint ventures. The lead became even more pronounced if one considers the value of direct investment in those joint ventures. Here the Federal Republic (with $110 million) enjoyed a substantial lead over Italy ($80 million) and France ($65 million). These data, though only for April 1989, are representative of a consistent trend.[85] By the end of 1990, Germany accounted for 12 percent of all joint ventures in the NIS, once again leading France and Finland.[86] Despite German efforts, however, Russia still suffered as foreign investors were deterred initially by political instability and later by the crime and corruption that has become endemic to Russia. Even the Germans have, on occasion, appeared resigned to failure in their attempts to assist economic reform.[87]

Underwriting the Rules or Paying the Bills

Germany is running a positive trade balance with all eastern European countries (except Ex-Yugoslavia), and the surplus is increasing over time. Is Germany willing to underwrite the rules in eastern Europe as it does in western Europe (through payments to the EU budget)? The preliminary answer appears to be affirmative; through trade, aid, and investment Germany is paying the costs associated with economic stabilization and liberalization in central and eastern Europe as well as the successor states of the Soviet Union.

Germany underwrites these rules both directly and indirectly. In direct expenditures, Germany spent DM45.42 billion in aid commitments to central and eastern Europe between 1990 and 1994, in addition to exhorting private-sector officials to invest in eastern Europe. Between 1989 and 1994, Germany allocated DM100 billion in financial assistance to the NIS, the majority in credits and

Table 9. Trade patterns of the leading western trading countries and the countries of eastern and central Europe and the former Soviet Union (in million $U.S.)

	Germany			France		
Trade with	Exports	Imports	Balance of Trade	Exports	Imports	Balance of Trade
NIS						
1992	8505.6	7857.6	648.0	2078.4	3470.4	−1392.0
1993	9015.6	7414.8	1600.8	1860.0	3049.2	−1189.2
% change 1992-1993	6.0	−5.6		−10.5	−12.1	
1994	9271.2	9291.6	−20.4	1608.0	3228.0	−1620.0
% change 1993-1994	2.8	25.3		−13.5	5.9	
Poland						
1992	5293.2	5326.8	−33.6	823.2	658.8	164.4
1993	5864.4	5218.8	645.6	823.2	666.0	157.2
% change 1992-1993	10.8	−3.3		0	1.1	
1994	6418.8	6276.0	142.8	957.6	812.4	145.2
% change 1993-1994	9.5	20.3		16.3	22.0	
Former Czechoslovakia						
1992	5304.0	4672.8	631.2	607.2	456.0	151.2
1993	5470.8	4789.2	681.6	565.2	374.4	190.8
% change 1992-1993	3.1	2.5		−6.9	−17.9	
1994	7244.4	6630.0	614.4	812.4	471.6	340.8
% change 1993-1994	32.4	38.4		43.7	26.0	
Hungary						
1992	3007.2	2970.0	37.2	350.4	423.6	−73.2
1993	3116.4	2734.8	381.6	439.2	357.6	81.6
% change 1992-1993	3.6	−7.9		25.3	−15.6	
1994	3950.4	3358.8	591.6	513.6	403.2	110.4
% change 1993-1994	26.8	22.8		16.9	12.8	
Romania						
1992	853.2	806.4	46.8	571.2	276.0	295.2
1993	1090.8	826.8	264.0	464.4	284.4	180.0
% change 1992-1993	27.8	2.5		−18.7	3.0	
1994	1246.8	1134.0	112.8	346.8	332.4	14.4
% change 1993-1994	14.3	37.2		−25.3	16.9	
Bulgaria						
1992	559.2	390.0	169.2	228.0	128.4	99.6
1993	546.0	345.6	200.4	128.4	133.2	−4.8
% change 1992-1993	−2.4	−11.4		−43.6	3.7	
1994	662.4	460.8	201.6	142.8	157.2	−14.4
% change 1993-1994	21.3	33.3		11.2	18.0	
Former Yugoslavia						
1992	3274.8	3718.8	−444.0	740.4	886.8	−146.4
1993	1378.8	1144.8	234.0	183.6	205.2	−21.6
% change 1992-1993	−57.9	−69.2		−75.2	−76.9	
1994	1767.6	1200.0	567.6	187.2	174.0	13.2
% change 1993-1994	28.2	4.8		2.0	−15.2	
Total						
1992	26797.2	25742.4	1054.8	5398.8	6300.0	−901.2
1993	26482.8	22474.8	4008.0	4464.0	5070.0	−606.0
% change 1992-1993	−1.2	−1.3		−17.3	−19.5	
1994	30561.6	28351.2	2210.4	4568.4	5578.8	−1010.4
% change 1993-1994	15.4	2.6		2.3	10.0	

	Italy			United States			Japan		
	Exports	Imports	Balance of Trade	Exports	Imports	Balance of Trade	Exports	Imports	Balance of Trade
	2884.8	4406.4	−1521.6	3624.0	817.0	2807.0	1191.6	2503.2	−1311.6
	2107.2	4374.0	−2266.8	3780.0	2040.0	1740.0	1662.0	2979.6	−1317.6
	−26.9	−0.7		11.0	149.6		39.4	19.0	
	2670.0	5754.0	−3084.0	3388.8	3752.4	−363.6	1348.8	3673.2	−2324.4
	26.7	31.6		−10.3	83.9		−18.8	23.3	
	1144.8	890.4	254.4	637.2	374.4	262.8	237.6	158.4	79.2
	1398.0	771.6	626.4	916.8	453.6	463.2	151.2	96.0	55.2
	22.1	−13.3		43.8	21.1		−36.3	−39.4	
	1741.2	907.2	834.0	625.2	651.6	−26.4	114.0	66.0	48.0
	24.5	17.6		−31.8	43.7		−24.6	−31.3	
	830.4	800.4	30.0	412.8	242.4	170.4	172.8	134.4	38.4
	844.8	666.0	178.8	300.0	342.0	−42.0	126.0	111.6	14.4
	1.7	−16.8		−27.3	41.0		−27.1	−17.0	
	1219.2	1021.2	198.0	339.6	444.0	−104.4	135.6	104.4	31.2
	44.3	53.3		13.2	29.8		7.6	−6.5	
	814.8	962.4	−147.6	295.2	349.2	−54.0	240.0	126.0	114.0
	928.8	712.8	216.0	434.4	400.8	33.6	278.4	115.2	163.2
	13.9	−25.9		47.1	14.7		16.0	−8.5	
	1161.6	952.8	208.8	308.4	469.2	−160.8	264.0	118.8	145.2
	25.1	33.7		−29.0	17.1		−5.2	3.1	
	504.0	363.6	140.4	248.4	87.6	160.8	30.0	79.2	−49.2
	592.8	429.6	163.2	324.0	69.6	254.4	27.6	69.6	−42.0
	17.6	18.1		30.4	−20.5		−8.0	12.1	
	862.8	892.8	−30.0	337.2	194.4	142.8	30.0	61.2	−31.2
	45.5	108.0		4.1	179.0		8.7	−12.1	
	220.8	232.8	−12.0	85.2	79.2	6.0	37.2	43.2	−6.0
	223.2	177.6	45.6	115.2	158.4	−43.2	30.0	24.0	6.0
	1.0	−23.7		35.2	100.0		−19.3	44.4	
	307.2	320.4	−13.2	110.4	212.4	−102.0	19.2	24.0	−4.8
	37.6	80.4		−4.2	34.1		−36.0	0.0	
	1909.2	2086.8	−177.6	312.0	463.2	−151.2	45.6	49.2	−3.6
	939.6	824.4	115.2	130.8	224.4	−93.6	14.4	15.6	−1.2
	−50.8	−60.5		−58.1	−51.6		−68.4	−68.3	
	1671.6	1033.2	638.4	200.4	201.6	−1.2	10.8	13.2	−2.4
	77.9	25.3		53.2	−10.2		−25.0	−15.4	
	8308.8	9742.8	−1434.0	5614.8	2413.0	3201.8	1954.8	3093.6	−1138.8
	7034.4	7956.0	−921.6	6001.2	3688.8	2312.4	2289.6	3411.6	−1122.0
	−15.3	−18.3		6.9	52.9		17.1	10.3	
	9633.6	10881.6	−1248.0	5310.0	5925.6	−615.6	1922.4	4060.8	−2138.4
	36.9	36.8		−11.5	60.6		−16.0	19.0	

export guarantees.[88] Furthermore, the Federal Ministry for Economic Cooperation has earmarked DM290 million in future direct development aid for the area, having already provided DM600 million between 1990 and 1994 for use as low-interest development loans and technical assistance grants.[89]

In terms of humanitarian aid to the NIS, Germany accounted for $3.5 billion between December 1989 and December 1994, an overwhelming proportion of total EU contributions. German requests for comparable U.S. assistance repeatedly fell on deaf ears, first in the Bush and then in the Clinton administration.[90] The fact remains that only the Germans, for whatever reasons, have shown a genuine commitment to helping the peoples of eastern Europe improve their economies in the belief that this will help stabilize their polities. No other major power has come close to this German commitment.

A comparable story exists for loans and loan guarantees, although here the German lead is not so overwhelming ($20.9 billion out of a total $33.9 billion).[91] Total German spending in the NIS to support reform from 1989 to 1994 through bilateral and multilateral institutions (EU, EBRC, IMF), including disbursements and commitments, totaled DM100 billion or $71 billion. The bulk of these monies was offered through credits and export guarantees, and over 15 percent promoted the social and economic integration of troops returning from Germany to the NIS.[92] To put all these figures in perspective, when aggregated the EU was responsible for 75 percent of all assistance to the NIS between 1990 and 1992. Germany accounted for 57 percent of that total.[93] In addition to its unilateral, direct commitments, Germany also contributes multilaterally and indirectly through the European Union. Germany is the EU's biggest contributor, accounting for 28 percent of aid through subsidies, credits, and humanitarian aid.[94] These sums help underwrite the rules of trade through transfer payments and loans.

Structural Power in the 1990s

Power emanates from the barrel of a gun. Force may still be the ultimate form of power, as Realists claim. But thinking about power in military terms is of limited value in understanding the relationships among the major states of Europe in the 1990s.

Germany still has the largest army in Europe, but armed forces are not the basis for Germany's influence and power. Power lies in the prominence of the German economy: the Deutsche Mark's strength as the benchmark European currency; the Bundesbank's role as de facto central bank for all Europe; the volume and profitability of German exports; the size of German foreign investments; and the varied forms of foreign "subsidies," whether budget contributions, export credits, humanitarian aid, or direct loans. One reporter concludes that "already the rise of the mark is creating resentments all over Europe, where Germany's strength is attracting jobs and investment at the expense of Spain,

France and other neighbors. 'What everyone knows is that in financial terms, at least, Germany can now call the tune on the economic integration of Europe' said David DeRosa, who heads currency trading at Swiss Bank Corporation in New York."[95]

Germans may not have a strategic plan to dominate, as pessimists suggest they do. In fact, Germany's twin strategic goals are to assist the economic and political stabilization of central and eastern Europe and to prevent the importation of inflation. The Germans will act—promptly, energetically, decisively—when instability and inflation threaten, for these historical monsters have created uncertainty in the past, with enormous political consequences.

Yet Germany's economy clearly does dominate Europe. Germany makes the rules and is the overwhelming beneficiary of all forms of economic engagement. In the west this has been most evident in the capacity of the Germans to define the future of EMU, in the east in the policies of *Osthandel* and *Ostpolitik* that have laid the foundation for dynamic growth in trade and investment.

The costs and benefits are palpable. Germany makes the most, and Germany pays the most—and, on balance, Germany wins. Some others also benefit, but the beneficiaries are consistently the same group of small states in western Europe, who are not (and never will be) in a position to challenge Germany's economic domination. Few others win. Many small states vie for German investments in vain and suffer from the discipline imposed by German monetary policy. As for the states of eastern Europe, collectively they benefit: in terms of hard currency; from German investment and aid; from Germany as a destination for exports; and from expenditures by German tourists. But they pay a twofold price.

First, imports from Germany grow faster than exports to Germany in both relative and absolute terms. Second, they risk what Czechs refer to as the Germanization of the economy: scarce foreign investment will focus on them as a source of cheap labor, concentrated in low value-added jobs, generating uneven sectoral development, and designed to serve local rather than export markets. These fears may be unjustified, and early entry into the European Union would go a long way to relieving such concerns. At present, however, the issue of mutual benefits is unresolved, but the Germans are the dominant economic force to the countries of Eastern Europe.

The big losers are the major economies of western Europe. The French are driven by domestic agricultural concerns, a desire to reign in German power through multilateral fora, and the belief that France can regain lost international prestige by exerting leadership in an EU transformed from a bureaucratic project into a political one. For this they pay the price in terms of trade balances. They are caught between a rock and a hard place; their only alternative, if any real alternative exists, is to shift away from a regional focus and expose themselves to direct competition from American, Japanese, and Southeast Asian producers. Within the EU they can often hide behind sectoral agreements such as those in steel and autos, and have to deal only with the Germans. The French could not do so, however, on a regular basis with the Americans and the Japanese.

The French dilemma is explicable, driven by domestic and foreign policy considerations, but the British and Italian positions are so bad as to defy explanation. The British lost dramatically in terms of trade and yet remained the second largest net contributors to the EU budget across the 1980s. Italian losses through trade were dramatic. EU exports account for less than 15 percent of exports in both countries. It is conceivable that their imports are primarily intermediate goods, which they then re-export in the form of finished products and so generate a net surplus. But aggregate trade statistics for the two countries provide no basis for such a claim.

We therefore conclude that the German position is not only strong but getting stronger. The propensity of eastern countries to discourage imports from beyond the EU (through tariffs and content requirements) will only enhance Germany's position. Unification may have been costly for Germany, but all the indicators suggest a wealthier and more dominant future for the German economy in Europe, both east and west.

CHAPTER TWELVE

Foreign Cultural Policy

with Carolyn Höfig

God protect us from storm and wind and Germans abroad.
—Old European adage

For one heady moment in the early 1960s, an expert deemed the Federal Republic ripe for a new political age marked by the primacy of cultural policy—*Primat der Kulturpolitik*.[1] The German border had just become a permanent installation of concrete, barbed wire, and land mines, and power-political foreign relations (*Außenpolitik*) seemed out of date in the new age of transatlantic alliances and intercontinental missiles. At the height of the Cold War, mutual understanding offered the clearest hope for a peaceable future. Contemporary thinking held that foreign cultural policy would help effect this understanding. In the course of the next thirty years West Germany developed a cultural-political apparatus to address the legacy of National Socialism, soothe relations with Western allies, open an exchange with the developing nations of the southern hemisphere, and advance coexistence in the Soviet bloc.

When Hilmar Hoffmann, the city of Frankfurt's long-time cultural commissioner (*Kulturdezernent*), assumed the presidency of the Goethe Institute on July 2, 1993, he identified cultural policy as the "third pillar" of German foreign policy, alongside security and economic policy.[2] Willy Brandt had minted the image of the third pillar in 1967, and since then, other practitioners and promoters of international cultural relations have used it. In 1995, for instance, Hagen Graf Lambsdorff, a senior member of the German Foreign Ministry, reiterated the point in Washington D.C., emphasizing the centrality of culture in Germany's "bridging function," which he deemed necessary for successful consolidation of a democratic political system and a prosperous economic order in the new Europe.[3] Indeed, the official description of German foreign cultural policy begins: "Foreign cultural policy is, next to the cultivation of political and economic relations, an integral component of foreign policy."[4]

Post-unification Germany, however, seems to have revised its opinion about international cultural relations. *Kulturpolitik*, some critics believe, no longer forms the third pillar of foreign policy but serves rather as an instrument of short-sighted initiatives for enhancing German national standing.[5] Cultural policy finds itself cast as the handmaiden of power politics. Cultural policy makers have contested the issue almost since the beginning of the Federal Republic, and many

183

current concerns—the government's desire to control dissemination of German culture beyond its border, pressure to present a more politicized and less controversial message, struggles over funding and unfunding programs—echo earlier debates. Still, united Germany faces different challenges now, and old cultural-political conflicts assume a new significance.

The official description of German foreign cultural policy establishes the task as not "unilateral export of culture . . . , but dialogue, exchange and cooperative partnership," not one-way cultural propaganda.[6] Foreign cultural policy stands out as something of a hybrid. It may be a central part of state strategy to enhance interest in foreign relations. Yet culture in a liberal democracy claims independence. For the purposes of foreign policy, legitimate and effective culture must emanate from civil society. Unlike external economic policy, and most decidedly unlike security policy, cultural policy occurs on behalf of and not at the behest of the nation state.

Culture distinguishes itself by its "stickiness," its reflexive orientation to its own past, and its strong particularism. Whereas economics is the most universal, international, and modern of the three pillars, and politics operates in the arena of the state (a thoroughly modern structure), culture works in such amorphous areas as identity, art, creativity, music, and literature. Moreover, culture is inextricably tied to language, which overlaps to a great extent with the collectivity of the nation. It reflects something at once more specific and more elusive about its purveyors. A balance between the unique and the universal aspects of German culture to the general advantage of both for thirty years formed the basis of the Bundesrepublik's foreign cultural policy.

As yet, we cannot know how the new Berlin Republic may alter this approach. Foreign cultural policy after unification must build on the recent record of crafting, at the most basic human level, reconciliation, cooperation, and understanding between Germany and its neighbors. We believe that it is in the sphere of culture that German power faces its greatest and most lasting obstacle. It is in this sphere that Germany lacks the requisite acceptance by other Europeans to develop into a hegemon.

In international politics, hegemonic power constitutes a form of rule exercised not so much by armies as by markets, not so much by the threat of physical force as by the attractiveness of ideas and values. It was in this realm that the Soviet Union proved inadequate to match America's power. What better way to demonstrate the compelling presence of American hegemony than by the irresistible appeals of American popular culture?

One need not love the hegemon to accept its rule. We know how complex are feelings and attitudes vis-à-vis the United States in Europe and the rest of the world.[7] Yet one of the major differences in postwar Europe is that, in the West, American hegemony, no matter how resented, was accepted by the vast majority precisely because it was seen as based on a voluntary agreement entered into by the people and their democratically elected governments. In the East, in sharp contrast, Soviet domination was never accepted. The Soviets had to rely on coercion, which in turn made their rule brittle.

Hegemonies are further defined by the longevity of their ideological and cultural power, which may extend well beyond the de facto powers of the hegemon's institutions. Thus, one of the qualities of a hegemony is that it can survive without its original agents. It develops into structures that assume independence of original intent. One can well imagine the survival—indeed, the flourishing—of Americanism without the United States, well beyond original geography and politics.

Without cultural power, a dominant country either resorts to force or fails to establish hegemony. There is no doubt in our mind that the Berlin Republic, like its predecessor, will not take up arms to further its interest. We are equally confident that Germany will remain a hegesy and not become a hegemon, largely because German culture cannot become the common European discourse in key areas of public and private life.[8]

Germany offers many attractive values—constitutional patriotism, moderation, conflict mediation, economic wealth and material comfort—but it is mainly through its institutions that the Bundesrepublik justly attained its status as a model. "Modell Deutschland" was more than a self-congratulatory election slogan by Social Democrats for their 1976 parliamentary campaign. The concept conveys the success of institutional arrangements that have helped Germany become economically prosperous and political stable. Institutions are transferable on a limited basis and then only with great difficulty, however, as witnessed by the serious problems confronting the transfer of West German institutions into the former GDR.[9] Of course, culture transfer is far from easy, too. Yet, we believe, it is only through the transfer of both institutions *and* culture that a hegemonic relationship can flourish. Europeans may have a high regard for the institutions of codetermination and the social market economy, but German culture does not attract and engage them as American culture does.

Cultural policy may be part of the tripod of German foreign policy, but the objective of that policy differs fundamentally from the projection of German power in Europe. Its objective is not power but acceptance, from the peoples of Europe and the world. It is part of German identity's response to historical events and their presence in the collective memories of contemporary Europeans; it is part of the burning desire to be normal in the context of Germans' and others' perceptions that fifty years after Auschwitz, Germany remains abnormal.

German Cultural Policy

Before the advent of the nation-state, cultural and linguistic influences diffused easily across borders. With the sovereign state arose the practice of country-to-country relations, and so cultural policy entered the repertoire of statecraft. Culture bespoke national (or nationalistic) glory, and not surprisingly, international cultural undertakings remained the preserve of the largest European states. Germany participated in these developments with the other major Continental powers.

German thinking on foreign cultural affairs has gone through four phases, reflected in the changing denomination of the cultural department of the Foreign Ministry.[10] Almost since 1871, the foreign-policy makers of the German Reich clung to a course of "preserving Germandom" abroad (*Erhaltung des Deutschtums*). Of primary concern was the maintenance of schools in other countries to "keep the children of German descent from becoming denationalized, . . . [and] to give these children the benefits of the German language, a German education, and the German point of view."[11] The Foreign Ministry's budget for 1875 included aid for the German school in Constantinople, and by 1879, Reich subsidies aided German schools in Athens, Cairo, Genoa, New York, Rio de Janeiro, and Rome, as well as Belgrade and Bucharest. The schools gradually acquired libraries and other facilities not only to support the local German community but also to proselytize for the German perspective on matters of political concern. The Foreign Ministry received its first cultural division in 1906; it was a schooling office (*Schulreferat*).

By the eve of World War I, Wilhelmstraße had begun to focus on culture in terms of a world-economic policy, even as the Reich government was preparing for war.[12] Only in 1912 did the more inclusive term "foreign cultural policy"—*auswärtige Kulturpolitik*—enter official discourse.

The Department for German Culture Abroad and Cultural Affairs—*Kulturabteilung*, for short—began operations within the Foreign Ministry in 1920, starting the second phase of cultural policy abroad.[13] Trade-related aspects of international cultural relations still figured in ministerial deliberations, and the German language abroad was a rather distant concern, although the sentiment "whoever speaks German buys German" ("*Wer deutsch spricht, kauft auch deutsch*") was gaining currency. Foreign schools and the preservation of Germandom remained explicit duties for German international policy, and special rights for German minorities were sought from the Versailles settlement, with an eye toward eventual political unity.[14] Some practitioners persisted in regarding Germany's international cultural presence as an "intellectual weapon."[15]

By the mid-1920s, the Weimar government had initiated an integrated foreign cultural policy, characterized most succinctly in a much-quoted observation by Theodor Heuss, then a member of parliament: "One cannot make culture with politics; perhaps one can make politics with culture." A new consensus began to coalesce around the necessity of mutual communication and understanding, "a policy of cultural promotion and presentation in the best sense."[16] The Germans began various exchange programs involving scholars, scientists, church groups, and youth, particularly with France, as first steps toward improving international relations.[17]

The National Socialists curtailed this development. More precisely, the Nazis returned to a conception of foreign cultural relations as *Machtpolitik*, with updated means and ends, turning progressive Weimar programs to the advantage of their foreign policy in the process. Under Hitler—and despite Goebbels's efforts to claim foreign cultural policy for his Propaganda Ministry—international culture remained officially the task of the Foreign Ministry, which pointedly renamed its cultural division the *Kulturpolitische Abteilung* (Committee for Culture). The 1936 Berlin Olympic Games were the readiest example of National Socialist cultural self-promotion. The foreign organization of the NSDAP—the *Auslands-Organisation*—identified itself as a "community of destiny for all Germans,"[18] an extreme version of the preservation of Germandom. Although the AO did not succeed in supplanting the Foreign Ministry, it became an increasingly active force in international cultural relations. The AO spent the initial years of the Third Reich on such projects as reverse exchanges, bringing German nationals, notably children and young mothers, from outside the Reich to Germany for vacations. Once war started, the AO supported the invading German army in some countries, although it may overstate the AO's influence to identify it as an actual fifth column.[19]

The postwar settlement presented the new Federal Republic with distinct challenges for cultural policy. For the normalization of its international relations, and more important for the thorough democratization of the country, Germany had to reconstruct its official position on culture and its promotion. Thus, the makers of the Bundesrepublik's foreign cultural policy returned to Weimar projects, charged them with the urgency of postwar political reform, and gradually renewed the country's earlier approach to cultural relations. The fourth phase of German cultural affairs abroad began, then, in 1952, with the return of a Kulturabteilung to the Foreign Ministry.[20]

The Foreign Ministry's contemporary goals include the encouragement of "world openness and understanding" and "information, exchange and cooperation."[21] Cultural programs abroad necessitate planning that is much longer-range and more incremental than in other areas of foreign policy. As a result, the foreign-cultural apparatus is more independent from daily parliamentary and partisan concerns (though to be sure practitioners have often lamented the absence of interest in the German parliament.)[22] Nonetheless, final authority rests with the federal Finance Ministry, which apportions the annual budget. Makers of cultural policy have viewed the direct interventions of federal budgeting as a threat.[23] Still, for its first three decades the *Kulturabteilung* enjoyed a steady increase in governmental funding from the Bonn Republic. It started with an operating budget of DM2.8 million, rising to DM171 million in 1965, and by the mid-1970s Bonn attained the so-called "Foreign Cultural Billion"—DM, that is.[24]

Nominally, the budget rose slightly from 1980 to 1982 as well, but inflation and exchange rates conspired to effect a real reduction. In 1980/81, the Goethe

Institute faced a round of painful program cuts, and for the first time, the Finance Ministry raided cultural policy coffers to pay for other programs. The total foreign cultural budget continues to hold at the ten-digit level, but since the early 1980s it has risen and fallen sharply with Germany's economic fortunes. In 1995, for example, foreign-cultural funding dropped 10 percent from the 1994 budget.[25]

The money supports a complex but resilient structure of foreign-cultural organizations that has grown—and changed—with financing. As far as internal cultural policy is concerned, Article 5 of the Basic Law states simply that culture is free. The individual states bear the highest official authority for culture within the country; no German Ministry of Culture exists to coordinate cultural funding at the national level. Instead, a variety of ministries address cultural policy where it intersects with their other functions, most notably the Foreign Ministry, the Interior Ministry, and increasingly the Education Ministry. In all cases, policy arises only in cooperation among the ministry or ministries, the states, regional bodies, and assorted independent organizations. Even then, ministries act mostly in an advisory capacity: subsidiary groups retain ultimate autonomy, and all carry out their programs accordingly.

This scrupulously decentralized approach to German cultural policy applies just as much in the international realm, where a tangle of organizations—some private, some state-funded—promote various aspects of German culture. To many observers of the early years of the Federal Republic, this cultural-political apparatus was an ad hoc attempt to address grave concerns about free expression and democratic administration. The "improvised" system came to offend some politicians, who in the late 1950s sought to professionalize the premise and practice of foreign cultural policy.[26] As models, the reformers took the quasi-independent, extra-governmental British Council and the Swiss organization Pro Helvetia. The Foreign Ministry objected that cultural policy is an *integral* part of foreign policy, and the "improvised" system prevailed. Indeed, by the mid-1960s, when the demand for German cultural programs plainly exceeded the capacities of the *Kulturabteilung*, the Foreign Ministry was trumpeting the virtues of its system of independent contractors.[27]

By the early 1970s, the ministry directly programmed only German schools abroad, and then in consultation with the educational offices of the individual federal states. The actual implementation of most foreign cultural initiatives falls to so-called intermediary organizations (*Mittlerorganisationen*)[28] with more specific charters: the German Academic Exchange Service (*Deutscher Akademischer Austauschdienst*), the Alexander von Humboldt Foundation, the Carl Duisberg Society, Inter Nationes, the foundations of the political parties, the German Music Council, the National Olympic Committee.

The largest and perhaps best known is the "Goethe Institute for the Encouragement of the German Language Abroad and for the Promotion of International Cultural Cooperation, Inc." Headquartered in Munich, the Goethe Institute runs more than 150 cultural institutes in 78 countries, as well as sixteen language schools and nine branches within Germany.[29] The federal budget of 1992 set aside DM 331 million for the Goethe Institute, which dropped to about DM 300 million for the fiscal year 1994–95.[30] (The 160 or so other foreign-cultural organizations shared about DM 7 million in subsidies in 1992.) A series of agreements bind the Goethe Institute and the Foreign Ministry, including a cooperation treaty in 1969 and a more detailed working agreement, seven years later.[31]

Immediately after World War II, of course, Germany's primary concern was restoring bombed-out cities and discredited institutions. As the Federal Republic took shape, the government looked to cultural policy to resurrect Germany's esteem in the eyes of its neighbors, and above all at the elite level, for straightforward political or trade-related reasons.[32] Bruno E. Werner, who held the cultural desk in the West German embassy in Washington, D.C., from 1950 to 1952, noted with equal parts pique and envy that although Charles de Gaulle irritated American lawmakers, a century of carefully tended cultural enterprises paid off in a deeply held affinity for things French among Americans on Main Street. He quoted an unnamed congressman on the subject: "Every disagreement that we have with France, any political strife immediately turns around as compassion and sympathy among us Americans through a few tears from charming Marianne."[33]

In the drive toward a new kind of foreign cultural policy, the FRG turned to the classic means of cultural influence, primarily German foreign schools and academic exchanges. Not until after 1955 did programs with a broader focus and, more important, a reciprocal component take their place in FRG policy. Internationalism began to replace the goal of national advantage and sublimated *Machtpolitik*, especially as the Federal Republic devised vaguely paternal schemes of "educational aid"—*Bildungshilfe*—to help newly decolonized countries foster their own cultural identities.[34] The *Kulturabteilung* was no longer professional exile to Foreign Ministry staff but instead attracted the most gifted people. The reformers of the early 1960s were no longer willing to sit back and wait for German classical music to reach listeners around the world (which would foster trade and improve Germany's image within the community of nations). Ludwig Erhard's chancellorship witnessed the first significant steps toward a fully elaborated foreign cultural policy.

The golden age of *Kulturpolitik* abroad arrived with the social-liberal coalition government. In 1970, a parliamentary commission of inquiry, led by Ralf Dahrendorf, began to investigate FRG foreign cultural policy. The federal government responded with thorough-going operational reforms in the Foreign Ministry in 1977.[35] In 1980, a 42-nation symposium with the ambitious title "Bridges across Frontiers" took place in Bonn, exploring the farthest reaches of cultural policy's potential.[36] To latter-day cultural politicians this conference—and the "Foreign Culture Billion" that helped make it possible—crowned the achievements of German international cultural affairs.

Even then, all that glistered was not 24 karat. By 1982, the foreign-cultural subcommittee's exuberant endorsement of the Dahrendorf commission report no longer attracted the necessary consensus, and the Foreign Ministry tabled the initiatives. In the end, measures did clarify authority among the branches of government and inaugurated a more active international presence for the Federal Republic. But the "bold plan for the next millennium" began to fray mere moments into its authors' thousand-year expectations.[37]

The Enquête-Kommission had noted that its primary task entailed "the legitimation of the Federal Republic as a cultural state in a changing world." In its response, the government of Helmut Schmidt and Hans-Dietrich Genscher insisted that only a "well-balanced self-representation" of Germany abroad would serve such ends.[38] The timing of this declaration is crucial, for the 1968 student revolts, increasingly violent acts of terrorism, the international debate over *Berufsverbote* (the screening of public servants for constitutional conformism and political loyalty) had all caused an identity crisis in the FRG of the early and middle 1970s.[39] Self-representation abroad became sensitive for Bonn. The struggle to control the international German image played out in the government's dealings with the Goethe Institute.

Even critics concede that the government used great discretion, and the Foreign Ministry canceled only a handful of programs: in 1977 the presentation of Peter Lilienthal's Chile film in Ottawa; in 1978/79 a planned seminar in Genoa on the movement for autonomy in southern Tyrol; and in 1979 a showing of the film *The Tin Drum* in Singapore, because local officials would allow uncensored movies to run only on extraterritorial property and without invitations.[40] Some authors, such as Günter Grass and Heinrich Böll, canceled foreign appearances to protest official statements that in their view impinged on artistic freedom, but in fact Bonn never vetoed programs that featured critical intellectuals.

Nevertheless, the Goethe Institute's independence depended heavily on the favorable disposition of the federal government.

Cultural Policy after Unification

Before 1989, cultural policy makers in the FRG insisted on the unified and, by implication, unifying nature of German culture.[41] In fact, because of its stickiness and particularism, culture remained relatively immune to the effects of communism in the German Democratic Republic (rather as German culture had weathered Nazism intact). Without question, both regimes used culture for propagandistic purposes, censored extensively, and used the state apparatus to produce and consume culture made to specification. Yet neither system could quite rid cultural production of its particularly German elements. Crudely put, Goethe and Schiller remain Goethe and Schiller regardless of the political spin that regimes might seek to put on them.

Of course, Bonn's refrain of "unified German culture" plainly served political ends. The GDR posed problems for international cultural relations. For one thing, German–German relations remained tentative, and cultural policy reflected this atmosphere: the Germanies did not sign any kind of cultural agreement until May 6, 1986, though the GDR had done so earlier with several other communist countries. Right up to the signing, Bonn's purveyors of cultural policy regarded most of their activities—from carefully guided youth exchanges to the obligatory school outings to East Berlin and the maintenance of television towers that broadcast into the GDR—as part of the West's obligatory cultural offensive against the East.[42]

Moreover, conflicting images arose of Germany abroad. Section 1.6 of the Foreign Ministry's 1987 guidelines on cultural policy stated, "Our cultural mission abroad does not seek competition with the GDR; but it also need not shy away from [competition]."[43] The guidelines note that most countries received FRG cultural measures more enthusiastically than they did the GDR's. Nonetheless, wherever the GDR directed its foreign cultural policy, including "the attempt to assert the development of a 'socialist' or 'East German national' culture," the West German Foreign Ministry promised counterinitiatives. After 1986 the GDR generally abandoned open polemics against the FRG beyond its own borders. Still, a proposed rationalization of German orthography and disputes concerning cultural property evoked high-level reactions from both German states.

To some extent, the Federal Republic developed its foreign cultural policy expressly to challenge the political division of the country, and even the heyday of *Bildungshilfe* for the developing southern hemisphere did not eclipse Bonn's self-appointed mission in Eastern Europe.[44] Hoffmann observes that the foreign-policy significance of cultural relations derived from bloc competition in Europe: "I was supposed to present to the world the 'better,' culturally richer [and] democratic Germany."[45] Needless to say, unification called into question much of what cultural politicians in the FRG had long taken for granted.

Unification presented Bonn with a chance to explore new cultural possibilities in the east. One might expect cultural cooperation to have come hard to West German officialdom after unification. In fact, German cultural unification attests to the strength and resilience of the Federal Republic's institutions. Curiously, unification also confirms East German cultural stickiness.

Cultural cohesiveness carried East German culture more or less intact through unification. Whole edifices—politics, economic, law, education—toppled between November 9, 1989, and October 3, 1990, but culture persisted. The question German cultural politicians, as Manfred Ackermann notes, was "not so much: how do I change the cultural 'system' of the former GDR? but rather: how in times of radical institutional and material change do I preserve the cultural 'substance' and how do I improve the cultural infrastructure?"[46] Indeed, culture was one of the few areas in which East Germany had something to offer united

Germany, arguably something specifically German.[47] After all, the GDR claimed to be the direct descendant of the "good Germans," meaning of course the Left, whereas the West Germans were direct descendants of the "bad Germans," mainly Nazis and their capitalist allies. In the 1980s, the GDR began to rediscover national icons such as Martin Luther and Frederick the Great in the (ultimately futile) effort to anchor the East German state in German national history, and there developed the widely held view that the GDR was the more German of the two states: the place where German culture remained pure and pristine, untainted by western commercialism and American influences. Even West Germans, particularly in the country's cultural elite, extolled East Germany as the only protector of true German culture.

Never mind that East Berlin centralized its cultural undertakings, controlled them through a ponderous Ministry of Culture, and organized culture from above. The apparatus regulated the ideological content of culture and lavished resources on acceptable venues: festivals and exhibitions abounded, theaters and concerts were subsidized, books were cheap, and artists became state-financed heroes. But the GDR decommodified culture, and that alone won the admiration of many a West German intellectual on the Left as well as the Right.

The West's shock treatment for the East threatened to dismantle the GDR's bureaucratic accoutrements for culture, at least at first. What if culture were simply cut loose, to thrive or shrivel on its own in the free market, "American style"? In united Germany, paper and printing materials no longer enjoy high subsidies; cinemas and theaters have to accommodate the tastes of the public; and artists, like most other professionals, face the demands of the economy more directly. As one observer noted, "before [unification], the artists and the cultural performers were the 'court jesters of the regime'—and nowadays most of them would not at all mind being the 'court jesters of the market economy.' "[48]

Article 35 of the Unity Treaty of August 31, 1990, expressly assured the cultural practitioners of the east of the same rights, privileges and assistance that their western counterparts enjoyed.[49] Unification brought the FRG's decentralized system of cultural administration, but the new Länder did not have the financial resources to meet their new cultural responsibilities. In fact, some experts worried that economic hardship would claim culture as its first victim. Apparently, the federal executive shared this concern, and shortly after unification the government approved a one-time grant of DM 900 million. DM 300 million provided for a "cultural infrastructure program," and the five states of the East and eastern Berlin divided the remaining DM 600 million. The state of Saxony, home to Dresden, Leipzig, and a host of major cultural sites, came away with just over DM 191 million; Berlin received DM 100 million for renovations and restorations.[50] These steps might not guarantee the survival of all of East Germany's culture and cultural figures, but they do provide the means to effect the cultural unification.

The extent of that unification remains unclear. Some evidence suggests that the particularisms of each cultural tradition have gained acceptance.[51] East German artists such as Willi Sitte and Werner Tübke have found welcoming audiences in the west.[52] On the other hand, the internal debate about Christa Wolf's association with the East German secret police betokens the lingering sentiment that everything from "over there" belongs on the trash heap of history. (A TV comedy series about East Germans, complete with exaggerated Saxon dialect, and the persistence of GDR nostalgia[53] represent more ambivalent positions.) Officially, however, integration prevails, and culture from the GDR has found its way into the unified German identity.[54] Despite four decades of contentions, Germans from east and west have come together to rival, perhaps to supersede, what was touted before 1989/1990 as a major success of cultural policy: the European Community.

In the European Union, the stickiness of culture was first an insurmountable hurdle but then the fundamental strength of interstate cultural relations. Certainly the goal of a common cultural policy would be a collective European identity; and just as certainly, no such identity exists. But then, Bonn viewed as its foremost cultural task "to connect the culture of civilization of Germany with the culture and civilization of other peoples, to instruct and to learn, to bring about the give and take among nations in cooperative partnership."[55] The countries of the EU have realized many of the traditional objectives of foreign cultural policy in practical progress toward unity. Mutual understanding and cooperation may still be imperfect, but the European Union rests on the foundation of Franco-German friendship, a relationship secure thanks to years of conscientious effort.[56]

This is an immense achievement. But is Western Europe a discrete cultural unit? Is the European Union even close to being more than the sum of its parts? Can we really speak of a coherent European culture, experienced by Europeans on a daily level?

Culture does not even appear in the Treaty of Rome, except in Article 7 (on nondiscrimination) and Article 36, which exempts "national treasures" from the prohibition on import and export restrictions.[57] A European Cultural Convention was established in 1954, and the Council for Cultural Cooperation of the Council of Europe has existed in abject obscurity since the mid-1960s. Indeed, few examples so clearly attest to the predominance of economic relations among the triad of economics, politics, and culture than the current reality of the European Union. To be sure, the founding fathers envisioned an integrated political entity, but the community of fifteen has barely advanced beyond the European Economic Community of the original six. Despite the Single European Act of 1992 and the much more ambitious Maastricht Treaty, the political integration of the European Union is still in its infancy. "Europe" in a political sense means little more than

Brussels, the Eurocracy, and the European Commission—that is, agents of administration, regulation, and coordination—and does not involve elected officials and true political agents, such as parliaments, parties, and all-European leaders.

This particularism resonates in contemporary culture. The French conceive of Continental culture only to the extent that they perceive an (exaggerated) American threat to their own cultural industry. Jack Lang, the Socialist party's long-term minister of culture, characterized policy as *culture et économie—même combat*.[58] The Germans seem equally inclined to defend their national culture, though they conceal their anti-Americanism better than the French do. As for Maastricht, its vague European cultural policy reveals three objectives: the protection of European culture from foreign, particularly American, influences; the complete freedom of movement for culture and the guarantee of its autonomy and independence from political interference; and respect, tolerance, and encouragement of national customs and regional particularisms. Not only do these resolutions conflict one with another, they all but rule out Europe-wide cultural policy, thereby, in effect, leaving culture to each of the EU's member countries.

It is appropriate to recall that the European Union works on a federal model, which does not promote collective identification. Ultimately the individual states treat culture quite differently. How to reconcile the half-governmental German system of cultural administration with the French Ministry of Culture and the nominally independent British Council? Culture remains nationally or regionally oriented, not only in its expression but also in its institutional support.

Particularism in the EU manifests itself in the matter of language, in many ways the primary conduit for culture. No one seriously proposes a single European language, and such a move would clearly contravene the prerogatives of member states. As it happens, English is a functional equivalent: it remains the most common language in the EU, spoken by 42 percent of the population either as native-speakers, or with conversational competence.[59] French retains its official-language status, with 29 percent of EU inhabitants able to converse in it. Since unification, the proportion of German speakers has increased, and with Austria's accession to the EU in 1995, some 33 percent of the EU speaks German. Only 7 percent of those speak it as a second language, however, compared with the 25 percent of the EU that speak English as non-natives, and the 13 percent that learned French to proficiency. German policy makers realize the disadvantages involved, and in June 1996 Helmut Kohl urged further public spending to promote the learning of German worldwide.[60]

Appropriate cultural policy for the EU would not seek to level differences, we believe, but to make differences more acceptable. After years of legal and administrative maneuvering, the European Union has finally arrived at a cultural policy to accommodate diversity. Since 1987, there has emerged a comprehensive multilateral exchange program covering students, professors, teachers, apprentices, and workers in the EU as well as the former EFTA countries, with parallel programs involving eastern Europe. On January 1, 1995, three overarching programs—Socrates, Leonardo, and Youth for Europe—combined a dozen or so programs. The exchange emerged primarily to encourage foreign-language skills among younger Europeans, by supporting language educators and by tempting students at all levels to try study abroad. (Early programs also offered students the opportunity to experience other approaches in their field, which had particular appeal in the hard sciences.[61]) With the Treaty on European Unity, however, the various programs acquired a single legal framework in Articles 126 and 127 and the expressed mission of fostering "the interrelationship between education, training, employment, social stability and economic performance."[62]

The new EU programs provide grants to cover study fees and additional living expenses. For the period from 1995 to 1999, the Commission of the European Communities proposes to spend more than ECU 1 billion ($1.26 billion) on the Socrates program for academic exchanges at all levels; more than ECU 800 million ($1 billion) on the Leonardo scheme for international vocational training; and some ECU 157 million (nearly $200 million) for Youth for Europe III.[63] Funding has increased as the programs have grown. The ERASMUS university exchange, part of the Socrates program, provides an example of the EU's undertaking.

Proponents of ERASMUS aimed to have about 10 percent of the European university population studying outside their home institutions. Its first year, the academic year 1987–88, saw some 3,000 students take advantage of mobility grants; about 13,000 signed up for the following year. For 1994–95, 145,800 students applied for grants.[64] Funding has grown to accommodate this increase, but problems of timely grant disbursement and securing local accommodation required prolonged Commission attention. Another issue concerned the disparities in student "flows" into and out of EU countries. As recently as 1991–92, far more German students studied abroad with ERASMUS than foreign students came into the Federal Republic, whereas British universities hosted far more students than they sent onto the Continent. The numbers of incoming and outgoing students have since leveled out.[65]

Only about 3 percent of applications come from fine arts students. Engineering students submitted 13 percent of the applications for 1994–95; law students accounted for 10 percent, and business management students for 9 percent. Foreign teaching methods and other cultural particularities do not deter some budding European professionals and may, in fact, attract them to the exchange programs. Artists, however, remain more closely tied to their own cultural framework.

Some 18 percent of employed ERASMUS alumni were working abroad thirty months after their exchange period.[66] Three years after their stay abroad, as many as 92 percent of ERASMUS graduates maintained contact with their host country; they visited, on average, more than three times a year, and they overwhelmingly mean to maintain their foreign-language fluency. Program veterans have an updated view of "national characteristics," at least where the national approach to education is concerned: German universities pay special regard to students' freedom, place little emphasis on regular class attendance, and focus on imparting theories, concepts, and paradigms. By contrast, French postsecondary institutions value the acquisition of facts and make the instructor the center of the informational exchange. In general, such differences earn positive reactions from students, and at this level, Europeans seem a step closer to realizing the vaunted goal of "diversity in unity."

A recent German-French partnership may serve as another EU model. The Germans and the French have gone into genuinely bicultural television programming with the "arte" TV channel. The channel, which Helmut Kohl and François Mitterrand christened with great ceremony in late April 1991, bills itself as the European Culture Channel and serves, as one early backer put it, "to break down mental tariff barriers."[67]

With a yearly budget of DM 250 million, "arte" has editorial offices in Strasbourg, which tend to the station's informational programming. Officially independent, "arte" began life as a cooperative undertaking of the French and German state-supported television stations, and it remains within their purview. Just the same, "arte" scrupulously serves as more than a conduit for translated fare from the French La Sept and the two German national channels. Programming tends to mix dark British comedy series, solidly entertaining films, and culture fora with either a bilingual soundtrack or subtitles. "Arte" airs no game shows or sports broadcasts. An unscientific survey of its first several months reveals an entire evening dedicated to Polish director Krzysztof Kieslowski; so-called theme evenings dedicated to "voyeurs" or "chaos" or German resistance to Hitler; the American film *Bird*—directed by Clint Eastwood—about the great jazz musician Charlie Parker; a French-Italian Middle Ages epic; a live broadcast from journalists in Sarajevo "to the European Council"; Wim Wenders' *Himmel über Berlin* (released as *Wings of Desire* in the United States); Billy Wilder comedies from the 1960s; and *Mr. Bean*.

Even before "arte" hit the airwaves on March 30, 1992, the scheme attracted doubters. Critics took the view that the French exercised the dominant role in the "arte" partnership and that they would drag the European culture channel down into the commercial morass of the burgeoning cable television industry. These doubting reports occasionally invoke persistent cultural differences, whether organizational or intellectual between France and Germany. (Our unscientific content-analysis revealed, it must be noted, neither endless Wagner nights nor a single Jerry Lewis film festival.) Still, "arte" has survived detractors and the pitfalls of niche cable-programming. In Germany, watching "arte" has been called a "virtual intellectual necessity," though the channel can claim a respectable entertainment value as well.[68]

"Arte" bodes well for the cultural cohesion of the European Union, even though, or rather *because*, it embodies the principle of cultural distinctiveness. Here, as in ERASMUS and other promising policies, Germany and its EU neighbors have finally realized success in the "failure" of Euro-culture. So far, programs in western Europe have continued, despite budget cuts. The debate on German foreign cultural policy now concerns whether the EU experience will provide the model for the next round of initiatives in eastern Europe.

Cultural Policy in Eastern Europe

The Federal Republic of Germany maintained a phantom presence in Eastern Europe, but official relations remained limited. In 1969 Yugoslavia concluded a cultural agreement with West Germany, as a partial reaffirmation of its independent status in Eastern Europe, and Romania followed suit in 1973.[69] A Soviet-German cultural accord preceded Bucharest's agreement with Bonn by six weeks, but it was only a formality until Kohl and Gorbachev worked out a more substantive arrangement in late 1988. The Yugoslavian treaty brought the Goethe Institute to Belgrade in 1970 and Zagreb in 1971; the Romanians helped implement joint two-year cultural programs. Otherwise, all was quiet on the Eastern cultural front from 1949 until quite recently.

The final agreement of the Conference for Security and Cooperation in Europe held out some promise when it was concluded in Helsinki on August 1, 1975. In the accord the Western states of Europe acknowledged the sovereignty and borders of their Eastern European counterparts, promising to open East-West relations to greater reciprocity. In the wake of the agreement, Bonn concluded its first series of cultural treaties with all East bloc countries except East Germany. Despite the promise of a cultural thaw, however, little else developed, and one expert deemed the ten years after Helsinki "a decade of stagnation."[70]

The CSCE Culture Forum of 1985 in Budapest marked an end to the rigid East-West cultural divide. Artists, writers, filmmakers, and other promoters of culture met for the first time to discuss their fields. (Many of the same personalities rode the crest of the reform wave in their respective countries a few years later.) The habit of East-West cultural cooperation began to form, then, even before the blocs came apart. Once the Cold War ended, cultural relations with Germany enjoyed a boom in eastern and east central Europe. New Goethe Institutes operate in Sofia, Prague, Bratislava, Warsaw, Cracow, Budapest, Riga, Moscow, Kiev, St. Petersburg, and Minsk; Tallinn and Vilnius are slated to receive institutes as well.[71] The sprawling complex of the former GDR embassy in the Russian capital houses the new German presence, including the Goethe Institute. In Warsaw, the institute occupies the eleventh story of the "wedding cake" Palace of Culture, still the most prominent feature in the city. In Prague and in Cracow, Hilmar Hoffmann's deputies have restored prominent historical buildings in the heart of the cities.

There remain sizable German minority populations in many of the countries of eastern Europe, toward whom the FRG recognizes a "moral obligation."[72] However, policy focuses on their successful integration into the society in which

they find themselves. The issue of German schools abroad reveals this fundamental realignment of foreign cultural policy. As late as 1964, *Kulturpolitiker*
could posit foreign schools as "the core of German foreign cultural policy" and
"the prerequisite for farther-reaching intellectual relations."[73] In 1992, the federal
parliament approved some DM 340 million to assist 123 foreign-based German
schools. The stated mission of these schools, however, now involves qualifying
Germans for higher education or vocational training in Germany. Furthermore,
such schools now enroll native students alongside German ones. The implicit
message is clear: keep your German-ness but learn to get along with the surrounding community—after all, you do live in its country.[74]

Language instruction is the primary task for purveyors of German culture in
eastern Europe: approximately 20 million people worldwide are learning German,
and more than 13 million of them are from eastern Europe. (About 330,000
Americans currently struggle with gender, cases, and separable verbs *auf deutsch*.)
Ukraine has more than 1 million students of German. The German language is
the most-taught tongue in the primary and secondary schools of the Czech Republic (with nearly 51 percent of pupils learning the language in 1990–91) and
Slovakia (40.5 percent).[75]

Since German unification, German has been surpassing Russian as the second
foreign language for eastern and central Europe. Indeed, it is rapidly closing in
on English, still the leader, and has surpassed it in certain circles in Budapest,
Prague, Zagreb, Ljubljana, and Warsaw. It may be regaining the prominence it
enjoyed as a lingua franca of the region, from the end of the Napoleonic Wars
until 1945. German would spread faster still if Germans stopped speaking English
to East Europeans (to the great chagrin of the *Frankfurter Allgemeine Zeitung* and
the German conservatism it represents) and conversed with them in German
only.[76]

A brief survey illustrates the proliferation of German. In Bulgaria, the German
language is the most widely known second language in the country, even though
there never existed a German-speaking minority in Bulgaria. As of the 1992–93
academic year, Russian no longer counts as a mandatory school subject. Currently, German trails French and English in terms of interested pupils, although
this statistic obscures the fact that some 100,000 of nearly 135,000 Bulgarian
students of German attend classes at one of the sixteen German-speaking gym-
nasiums in the country.[77]

The Czech connection to German culture can be traced back to Habsburg
rule, and some 2 million Czechs speak German today. Only a small remnant of
the German-speaking minority, about 60,000 people, still calls the Czech Republic home and the language is on the decline among them. In Slovakia, the
Carpathian-German minority today is fewer than 6,000. Nonetheless, interest in
German has increased in both countries, particularly after secondary schools
ceased to require Russian instruction after 1989.

In Hungary, the German linguistic and cultural presence is particularly well-developed. Socialist Hungary provided early opportunities for international cultural cooperation, and, the German language retains some currency from the days of the Austro-Hungarian Empire. About 220,000 Germans still live within the Hungarian borders, and Hungarian policy on national minorities has encouraged the development of a whole German-speaking infrastructure in the country, including schools, cultural projects, and media offerings. In 1990–91, more than 200,000 primary and secondary students signed up for German instruction, compared to the 151,000 who opted for English.[78]

Poland also abolished mandatory Russian classes in the 1980s, but German continues to lag behind Russian and now English. Only about 9 percent of Polish primary-school students learn German, whereas nearly 34 percent study Russian and more than 15 percent take English. In the secondary schools, not quite 50 percent study German, again less than Russian (71.1 percent) and English (59 percent), according to 1990–91 figures. Still, a healthy interest exists at the universities and professional schools. Only since 1989 has the Polish government officially acknowledged the presence of a German-speaking minority in the country, almost all in Upper Silesia, numbering perhaps 500,000 people by Polish counts and up to 800,000 in German estimates.[79]

In Romania, German ranks fourth among foreign languages taught at school, behind (in order) French, English, and Russian. However, interest in German has increased steadily since schools dropped the Russian requirement. Even though Ceausescu pursued an often violent policy of forced Romanization, some 200,000 native German speakers survived the regime, concentrated in the Banat (Timisoara/Temesvar and Arad) and the Carpathian Mountains (Sibiu/Hermannstadt and Cluj/Klausenburg). There even existed a full-time German theater in Timisoara/Temesvar and a German repertory company in Sibiu/Hermannstadt. Following the opening to the West, the FRG undertook, with the blessing of the new government in Bucharest, a massive support campaign for such cultural establishments as schools and university departments that teach German. Bonn lays particular emphasis on stabilizing conditions in traditionally German regions, because since 1990 an overwhelming proportion of Romania's German minority has migrated to the Federal Republic—111,150 in 1990 alone.[80]

Even in the countries of the former Yugoslavia, German maintains a strong presence behind English and Russian. The dwindling German minority, perhaps 8,000 people in all, lives predominantly in Croatia. Although the Croatian Germans themselves are rapidly losing their interest in the German language, certain German politicians have attained saint-like stature in Croatia as a consequence of their engagement on behalf of Croatia's independence, promising to increase the preeminence of German there.

With nine million students of German, the lands of the former Soviet Union offer by far the largest audience for Bonn's cultural endeavors. Russia alone accounts for more than 4.2 million German learners, and in the new republics with a significant German minority, such as Kazakhstan, German edges out even

English as the most sought-after foreign language. Indeed, 2 million or so Germans were the fourteenth largest ethnic group in the USSR, which helps explain the broad appeal of the language.[81]

Potential troubles threaten German foreign cultural policy in eastern and east central Europe, and in particular wrangles over the ownership of cultural products lost as booty in previous wars, from the (now) Russian collections of artworks and books and the famed Amber Room to the (now) Polish display of historical German aircraft.[82] At stake here is more a legal precedent than a cultural principle, though all sides make much of their desire to keep what they view as rightfully theirs. In general, however, the FRG seems committed to maintaining the level and intensity of German cultural promotion in the erstwhile Soviet bloc. As one long-time cultural policy maker in the Foreign Ministry wrote recently, "As pressing as it is to arrest the economic collapse in Central and Eastern Europe and to minimize the social disparities as much as possible, one cannot expect politics and economics alone to solve the enduring European questions."[83]

German Culture as Power

"We are once again somebody—without knowing rightly who," Hildegard Hamm-Brücher said of Germany in 1976.[84] The diagnosis applies just as poignantly today to united Germany. In the new political order on the Continent Germany is a dominating structural presence that is not manifestly to the detriment of the dominated parties. A large number of German scholars resist this characterization of Germany's position, out of intellectual habit and an understandable longing for the power-political certainties of the Cold War. Still, German cultural relations with eastern Europe belie the treasured image of the Federal Republic as the well-behaved pupil of greater Western powers. The East certainly expects a degree of leadership.[85]

Perhaps 80 percent of foreign students of German really do care more about vocabulary exercises in business German than about the intricacies of Kleist. (To be sure, the remaining 20 percent conceive of their language training as an entrée into German culture, classical or contemporary. For instance, German poetry readings and dance recitals consistently sell out in Moscow, all the more impressive when one considers that a large portion of the audiences commanded no more German than they needed as children to play Russians and Germans—a local variant of Cowboys and Indians—that is, *"Halt!"*, *"Achtung!"*, and *"Hände hoch!"*[86]) Young Russians pay several rubles for plastic bags emblazoned with trade names like Schwarzkopf and Boss, and Moscow prostitutes greet prospective clients with the opening line of "Loreley": *"Ich weiß nicht, was soll es bedeuten, daß ich so traurig bin* [I don't quite know why I am so sad]." German is effectively the language of trade and business throughout much of the former

East bloc, but to many citizens of the new democracies it also represents initiation to German-style prosperity. Increased contacts have only reinforced the phenomenon; for better or worse, Germany provides the model of development—democratic, internationally integrated, capitalist—to which eastern and east central Europeans aspire.

Naturally enough, German economic predominance has prompted a kind of linguistic backlash. One cynical interpretation from east of the Oder holds that "Poles should learn German so that they can later translate for their colleagues what the boss wants."[87] But English clearly remains, as in western Europe, the "gateway to the world." Eastern European school children clamor for Snickers, Coca-Cola, and Chicago Bulls T-shirts; they do not wear *Lederhosen*, sing advertising jingles for Haribo candies, or stand in line overnight for tickets to Nina Hagen concerts. As in Germany, American popular culture overshadows all other contenders. As one American entrepreneur located in Hungary said of the owner of the first Pizza Hut in Budapest, "He's not selling pizza, he's selling the speed and glitz of US culture."[88]

The overwhelming international presence of American culture limits German cultural hegemony in eastern Europe as elsewhere. Unified Germany is a partial or undeveloped hegemon vis-à-vis its eastern neighbors, at least where culture is concerned. Poles may react with alarm to the imperialist potential of Germany's economic might, but the structure of post–Cold War Europe has focused the potential of German influence abroad. If anything, the logic of this new order calls for greater cultural efforts in the widest sense, an expanded program for emerging Europe, east and west. An adage from the country's past prayed, "God protect us from storm and wind and Germans abroad." Today, Germans abroad are more likely to serve as messengers of openness, cooperation, and democracy. The good school-child of the West has graduated.

It is, however, just at this crucial moment that the Kohl administration seems intent on restoring a degree of *Machtpolitik* to Germany's international profile.[89] The Federal German government is now seeking to cut more esoteric cultural events—to decouple, after more than three decades, the cultural and linguistic components of the Goethe Institute's mission—and to politicize the remaining programs: to pluck the wings of Pegasus by turning foreign cultural policy "into the dray-horse of diplomacy and trade," as one worried policymaker prognosticated. One critic claimed, "Money is wasted on unreal and illusory things, for example [a] poetry reading before four old spinsters [at a] cost [of] some thousands of marks."[90] One can imagine the Kohl government's annoyance about a 1991 poetry reading in the Moscow Goethe Institute with contributions from the East German artist Sacha Anderson. Anderson was later revealed as a long-term informant who had provided the GDR's notorious Stasi with frequent reports on his artist colleagues. His appearance at the Moscow reading, which no doubt began as an effort to provide an all-German cultural program in the newly inaugurated institute, left the Goethe Institute and, by implication, the Foreign Ministry looking as though they supported one of the perpetrators of the old regime.

It bears mentioning that confronting the worst aspects of the German past has always topped the list of the *Kulturabteilung*'s appointed tasks. Gustaf Gründgens was perhaps Germany's finest stage actor before, during, and after World War II, but he refused to leave Germany after the Nazi seizure of power despite ample opportunity and sought out Göring's patronage.[91] Gründgens appeared in officially sponsored guest performances abroad before he committed suicide in 1963. In the early period, the Bunderepublik presented its cultural legacy in all its ambiguities. Indeed, this understanding of international cultural relations as open exchange serves Germany well.

Culture and cultural policy will necessarily change as the new Germany supplants the old Federal Republic. Still, cultural policy is more than mere economics or security. Indeed, the history of the Federal Republic's cultural policy suggests that in times of great change, intensified *Kulturpolitik* helps smooth the passage. It may still be premature to call for the primacy of cultural policy, but the German record since 1945 argues forcefully for the preservation of foreign cultural achievements.

It is striking that culture, for all its particularism, has not withered to parochial curiosities but rather opens itself to export and exchange in an era of interdependence. We find it no surprise that German culture has flourished along with German trade in this new environment. Culture is an instrument of power: the stickiness of culture simply means that its strategies differ from those of economics and politics.[92] But still, Germany's neighbors observe strict limits on their cultural acceptance of things German. Ultimately, the limits of German political ambition, the commodified nature of the newly desired German culture, and the still uncontested hegemony of American culture in Europe combine to protect Germany's European neighbors from a renewed German hegemony.

Conclusion:

The Predicament of the Berlin Republic

The Germans will never forgive us for Auschwitz
—Zvi Rex, Israeli psychoanalyst

Politics in the Berlin Republic will barely vary from politics in its Bonn predecessor. The new Germany is geographically larger, by the magnitude of the state of Indiana, and more populous by 17 million people. However, in its qualitative features and characteristics this new entity will not differ much from the immensely successful republic headquartered in a sleepy university town on the Rhine. This is in essence how optimists, in Germany and abroad, see the future of German politics and society. As we have argued, there is plenty of strong evidence for such a view, and indeed we share much of this optimism. Focusing on the durability of the Bonn Republic's democratic institutions and political culture, we count ourselves among the most optimistic interpreters of the Berlin Republic's future.

The democratic structures of Modell Deutschland are so well entrenched, domestically and multilaterally, that the benefits of loyalty far exceed any that a possible exit or new voice might yield. In its latest incarnation (how many more will there be in decades and centuries to come?), Germany will remain democratically exemplary.

Still, the Berlin Republic will be significantly different from its Bonn predecessor. Changes in quantity and geography, accompanied by epochal rearrangements of global affairs in the wake of the eruptions of 1989 and 1990, entail a major shift in the very character and identity of Germany. This shift, the pessimists fear, may not bode well either for the future of Germany's democracy or for the political stability and autonomy of Germany's European neighbors.

Although we found virtually no evidence to support concerns about the continued flourishing of German democracy, we do wonder whether optimism may be misplaced in the context of German power. It is here, we argue, that Germany's self-understanding remains murky. Germany vacillates between an overbearing projection of power (mainly, though not exclusively, in the realm of the economy) and a reticence about admitting that power; the country's identity remains uncertain and ill-defined in the area of power as it is crystal clear in the domain of democracy. The analogy to the United States in the interwar period, able to lead but unwilling to do so, still holds.

203

The new Germany will remain loyal to the tenets of democracy, but there are legitimate competitors to current policies regarding power. This loyalty appears to be weakening, pitting a neopacifist, neo-isolationist exit on the Left against a renewed desire for voice on the Right and the center. Indeed, this debate is vital for the future identity of the Berlin Republic. If the essence of the Bonn Republic was the institutional anchoring of democracy on German soil, then the essence of the Berlin Republic will be how the Germans resolve the proper deployment of German power in Europe and the world. There exists only one certainty: because of the Bonn Republic's success in establishing a flourishing democracy, the debate about German power will be lively and unfettered. The outcome remains contested.

The contest will be decided in the post-Kohl era, and several developments seem quite likely to us. It is very doubtful, for instance, whether Kohl's successor as the leader of Germany's largest political party and most powerful conservative institution will share Helmut Kohl's deep commitment to, and identity-shaping affection for, the West in general and the United States in particular. We believe that Kohl's Atlanticism is a collective memory for a specific generation, a memory that existed by necessity within the Bonn Republic's political class but will do so only by choice within the Berlin Republic's. It will undoubtedly be more ephemeral and more contested as a result.

Furthermore, we are skeptical whether Kohl's successor will exhibit the Europeanism that has been such a hallmark of this particular chancellor and of the Bonn Republic. We are *not* saying that Kohl's successors will develop an anti-Europeanism akin to the sentiment regularly encountered among important segments of the British political class. But the texture of this new German Europeanism will be different. It will be a means rather than an end (the true change in identity sought by Kohl's political and generational cohort). Germans will become good Europeans to further their own economic and political interests, not because they perceive such an identity as morally desirable and perhaps even superior to their own national identity. Germany has always pursued self-interested policies in the context of Europe, but that impulse, we believe, will strengthen.

The Social Democrats have threatened not to support the third stage of European economic and monetary union (better known as Maastricht II) if revisions of the treaty do not include explicit improvements in EU labor market and social policies. Without the Social Democrats' support, the government will not have the requisite two-thirds majority to pass the necessary legislation. The Social Democrats' criticism of the EU regarding social policy and protection of the weak is not new. What is new is their willingness to erect roadblocks on the path to European unity. Europe, even to the Social Democrats, has become negotiable.[1]

Much of this is crude electioneering and campaign posturing. But its new acceptability among German Social Democrats, traditionally among the most pro-European constituents in Germany, exemplifies the qualitative shift that is occuring in the German public debate over Europe. This was once a sacrosanct topic. All Germans upheld the desirability of a European political identity, which was to coexist with and perhaps someday even supersede the German one. The primacy of Europeanism is, however, now gradually eroding in Germany's political circles. "Europe" is devolving into a means instead of constituting a desirable end. Nobody will yet admit publicly to holding such views; but in many private discussions it is evident that the Germans' love affair with Europe as a substitute for their national identity is coming to an end in the 1990s.

Polls show consistently that German exuberance for Europe has been waning. Indeed, one eminent survey research center, the Forschungsgruppe Wahlen, is now finding that a significant number of Germans want to see their national government maintain its sovereignty in virtually all matters of policy. In fact, a majority of Germans does not want Brussels to exercise governmental authority in Germany. The verdict is clear: Germans, formerly the Continent's most enthusiastic Europeans, are acquiring a much more measured view of European unification.[2] They are trading a European identity for a German one.

All of this is part of what some conservative intellectuals have recently labeled "fluid contours" (*fliessende Grenzen*): everything is up for grabs, is subject to redefinition. No taboos are exempt, not even Auschwitz. An increasing number of highly influential, young intellectuals, sporting superb credentials and occupying major positions of cultural and social power, have gradually begun to dismantle the Bundesrepublik's most solid consensus: that National Socialism, and the Holocaust in particular, were among the most heinous expressions of human evil in history.

These are not fringe historians of the radical Right; nor are they neo-Nazis or Holocaust-deniers. They are merely revisionists, relativizers, "historicists." They do not want to deny Germany's culpability for the past. Instead, they give voice to new interpretations, uncover hitherto neglected nuances, to create an atmosphere in which competing interpretations of Auschwitz are as legitimately debated as those of any other period in German history. Their intent is to "normalize" Auschwitz, to render it part of Germany's lively pluralist political culture like any other topic.

These proliferating reinterpretations of the Nazi past attempt nothing short of committing Auschwitz to the realm of history—thereby relieving, if not exculpating, the Germans' collective memory from this immense burden. Adherents do not necessarily object to such recent activities as building monuments to the victims of the Holocaust (most prominently, one in Berlin), constructing a Jewish museum in Berlin, and declaring January 27, when Auschwitz was liberated in 1945, as a day to honor the victims of National Socialism. Indeed, they even welcome these activities as long as they finally liberate the new Berlin Republic from the burdens that shackled its Bonn predecessor.

In order for Germany to normalize its political activities and identity, above all its relations to power, the country will have to normalize relations with its recent past. This does not entail denial of the Holocaust. Instead it demands that the Holocaust be treated as dispassionately as National Socialism's many other features.[3] The Holocaust is not to be denied, but it is not to be given special attention. This normalization of the Holocaust is essential for a normalization of German history, which in turn is a fundamental prerequisite for the normalization of German power.

When these new, legitimate revisionists talk about the need to transform Germany into a normal country, they invariably have in mind the issue of power and not that of democracy. Indeed, few regimes could have done a more admirable job than the old Bonn Republic's in creating a stable democracy. It is now up to Berlin to complete a second and complementary task: to make Germany a normal country by normalizing its power as well. This, however, can happen only if the Germans' psyche about Auschwitz becomes normal. Until this happens, Germany's power will remain limited and impaired. If conservative intellectuals and their increasingly numerous admirers have their way, the transformation will occur in the Berlin Republic. Exorcised of Auschwitz, the new Germany will no longer face institutional and cultural constraints on the proper deployment and projection of power.

In a way we have returned again to the issue of the German *Sonderweg*. But which epoch in German history was exceptional, what constitutes one's basis of comparison? Nazi Germany differed from western countries on the dimension of democracy but not on that of power. What rendered Germany "exceptional"— as compared to Britain, France, the United States, the Low and the Scandinavian countries—was its deficit in democracy. (This deficit was explained, by adherents of the *Sonderweg* interpretation, as a result of Germany's excessive preoccupation with power.)

Exactly the opposite was the case with the Bonn Republic. Here "German exceptionalism" pertained to a deficit not in democracy but rather in power. What rendered the Bonn Republic special was that it did not project political and military power commensurate with its economic might.

For the Berlin Republic to become genuinely normal on the two key dimensions of power and democracy, it would have to normalize its relations with the past. The debate pits two memories, two histories, against each other, the Nazi preoccupation with power against Bonn's reluctance to admit power. This debate and its outcome will, we believe, define the political identity of the Berlin Republic.

That history and collective memory matter in the exercise of contemporary power is the core of our understanding of Germany. In few instances is this claim clearer than with the National Socialist episode, Auschwitz in particular. We venture to predict that what has cynically (but realistically) come to be known as the "Auschwitz bonus," a phenomenon that distinguished the political culture of the Bonn Republic, will gradually diminish in the Berlin Republic. Auschwitz will fade from memory because the mechanisms of political legitimation and collective identity will be quite different in the new Germany from those that defined the Bundesrepublik. Increasingly historicized, Auschwitz will attain a different meaning for Germans of the Berlin Republic. Guilt, shame, and responsibility will gradually transform themselves into knowledge, acknowledgment, and analysis. By necessity, this will lead to debate. Indeed, one leading conservative thinker told us confidentially that he expected to see a bevy of revisionist books on all aspects of Germany's Nazi interlude, particularly the Holocaust, in the coming years.

If our observation that victimization and victimhood are particularly potent in the political expression of collective memory is true, then the revision of Auschwitz makes good sense. The customary view of Auschwitz made the Germans such vicious ogres that it rendered the self-perception of Germans-as-victims all but impossible. German victimhood was crowded out by the magnitude of the Holocaust, skewing the Germans' collective memory.[4] With the historicization of Auschwitz this, too, will change. Germans will soon be able to express freely Germany's victimization as a legitimate ingredient of their collective memory. This then will comprise yet another stage in the lengthy and complex predicament that we have come to know as the German Question. We leave it to the reader to judge whether this major change bodes well for the future of the Berlin Republic and its neighbors.

NOTES

Introduction: The Latest Stage of the German Question

1. These events are chronicled in Gordon A. Craig, *Germany 1866–1945* (Oxford: Oxford University Press, 1978).

2. See, for example, Heinrich Gotthard von Treitschke, *History of Germany in the Nineteenth Century*, ed. Gordon A. Craig (Chicago: University of Chicago Press, 1975); *Politics* (New York: Harcourt, Brace & World, 1963); Adolf Hausrath, *Treitschke, His Doctrine of German Destiny and of International Relations* (New York: G. P. Putnam's, 1914).

3. See Albert O. Hirschman, *National Power and the Structure of Foreign Trade* (Berkeley: University of California Press, 1945).

4. Steven Lukes, *Power: A Radical View* (New York: Macmillan, 1974), p. 23. See also Peter Bachrach and Morton Baratz, *Power and Poverty: Theory and Practice* (New York: Oxford University Press, 1970). According to Elke Thiel, such agenda-setting influence is exemplified by the negotiations of the Economic Monetary Union treaty. See "German Politics with Respect to the European Economic and Monetary Union," American Institute for Contemporary German Studies, 18 May 1995.

5. For accounts of such attitudes, see "Today's Germans: Peacable, Fearful—and Green," *Financial Times*, 4 January 1991; and "Germans Favor a Low Profile in World Affairs," *Financial Times*, 4 January 1991.

6. See, for example, "Bündnis '90/Die Grünen: Von Krise zu Krise," *Focus*, 11 December 1995, pp. 28–30.

7. See Charles Kindleberger, *The World in Depression, 1929–1939* (Berkeley: University of California Press, 1973), chaps. 1 and 14.

8. See, in particular, Robert Gilpin, *The Political Economy of International Relations* (Princeton: Princeton University Press, 1987).

9. For this historical comparison see Robert Gilpin, *U.S. Power and the Multinational Corporation: The Political Economy of Foreign Direct Investment* (New York: Basic Books, 1975).

10. See Nicos Kotzias, "Die Rolle der Bundesrepublik Deutschland in der neuen Architektur Europas," in Caroline Thomas and Klaus-Peter Weiner, eds., *Auf dem Weg zur Hegemonialmacht? Die deutsche Aussenpolitik nach der Vereinigung* (Cologne: Papyrossa Verlag, 1993), pp. 111–129. See also Joseph Nye, *Bound to Lead: The Changing Nature of American Power* (New York: Basic Books, 1990). For a contrasting analysis on "soft" power in Germany as well as Japan, see Hanns W. Maull, "Germany and Japan: The New Civilian Powers," *Foreign Affairs* 69 (Winter 1990/91), pp. 91–106.

11. See, for the most notable example, Robert Gilpin, *War and Change in World Politics* (New York: Cambridge University Press, 1981).

12. For the multilaterally beneficial effects of European integration into the EU, however, see Richard Baldwin, "The Growth Effects of 1992," *Economic Policy* 9 (1989), pp. 247–283.

13. For representatives of this Right position see Arnulf Baring, *Deutschland, was nun?* (Munich: Goldmann Verlag, 1992); Wolfgang Schäuble, "Überlegungen zur europäischen Politik: Positionspapier der CDU/CSU Bundestagsfraktion vom 1. September 1994," *Blätter für deutsche und internationale Politik*, October 1994, pp. 1271–1280; Hans-Peter Schwarz, *Die Zentralmacht Europas: Deutschlands Rückkehr auf die Weltbühne* (Berlin: Siedler Verlag, 1994).

14. See, for example, Lewis E. Lehrman and John Mueller, "The Curse of Being a Reserve Currency," *Wall Street Journal*, 4 January 1993.

15. See Alexander Gerschenkron, *Bread and Democracy in Germany* (New York: Howard Fertig, 1966); Hans-Ulrich Wehler, *The German Empire, 1871–1918* (Dover, N.H.: Berg, 1985); Wolfgang J. Mommsen, *Der autoritäre Nationalstaat: Verfassung, Gesellschaft und Kultur des deutschen Kaiserreiches* (Frankfurt: Fischer Taschenbuch, 1990).

16. As a clear statement of this position see Carsten Hefeker, "German Monetary Union, the Bundesbank and the EMS Collapse," *Banca Nazionale del Lavoro Quarterly Review*, December 1994, pp. 379–398.

17. See Timothy Garton Ash, *In the Name of Europe* (London: Random House, 1993), especially p. 396; Gus Fagan, "German Foreign Policy: The Conflict over the Recognition of Croatia and Slovenia 1991," *Labour Focus on Eastern Europe*, no. 48 (Summer 1994), p. 17.

18. See Beverly Crawford, "Domestic Pressures and Multilateral Mistrust: Why Germany Unilaterally Recognized Croatia in 1991," *German Politics and Society* 13 (Summer 1995), pp. 1–34. Different views stress German economic self-interest in recognizing Croatia and Slovenia: see Fagan, "German Foreign Policy." We agree with Crawford's interpretation, which focuses on how a noble, neo-Wilsonian impulse led to disaster.

19. This argument is laid out in Peter Katzenstein, *Policy and Politics in West Germany: The Growth of a Semi-Sovereign State* (Philadelphia: Temple University Press, 1987). Katzenstein is currently working on a collaborative project on Germany's relationships with small European trading partners which emphasizes the positive-sum aspect of this relationship.

20. Robert A. Dahl, "The Concept of Power," *Behavioral Science* 2 (1957). Subsequent formulations of power, reflected in the capacity to set agendas and to define the ways in

which decision makers think about problems, are, we believe, more reflective of German power.

21. There is an extensive literature on German external power in the Bonn Republic prior to unification. See for example Simon Bulmer, *The Domestic Structure of European Community Policy Making in Germany* (New York: Garland, 1986); Bulmer and William Paterson, *The Federal Republic of Germany and the European Community* (London: Allen and Unwin, 1987); Renata Fritsch-Bournazel, *Confronting the German Question: Germans on the East-West Divide* (Oxford: Berg, 1988); Karl Kaiser and John Roper, eds., *British-German Defence Co-operation: Partners within the Alliance* (London: Royal Institute of International Affairs, 1988).

22. For a discussion of the inner core of Realist assumptions see Joseph Grieco, *Co-operation among Nations: Europe, America, and Non-Tariff Barriers to Trade* (Ithaca: Cornell University Press, 1990), pp. 3–4.

23. See Stanley Hoffmann, "An American Social Science: International Relations," in his *Janus and Minerva: Essays in the Theory and Practice of International Relations* (Boulder, Colo.: Westview, 1987). Exceptions, of course, exist to his generalization, but the general thrust of Realist theory (in all its contemporary forms) has been away from domestic factors and towards systemic ones.

24. For responses to common problems in NATO, see Christoph Bertram, "Power and the Past: Germany's New International Loneliness," in Arnulf Baring, ed., *Germany's New Position in Europe: Problems and Perspective* (Oxford: Berg, 1994), pp. 96–97. Some recent commentators have suggested that NATO has taken on renewed importance—and with it, a centripetal force.

25. See Wolfram Hanrieder, *Germany, America, Europe: Forty Years of German Foreign Policy* (New Haven: Yale University Press, 1989).

26. For Germany's role as a bridge between East and West in the Bonn Republic, see Christoph Bertram, "Power and the Past: Germany's New International Loneliness," in Arnulf Baring, ed., *Germany's New Position in Europe: Problems and Perspectives* (Oxford: Berg, 1994), pp. 91–105.

27. John J. Mearsheimer, "Back to the Future: Instability in Europe after the Cold War," reprinted in Sean Lynn-Jones, ed., *The Cold War and After: Prospects for Peace* (Cambridge: MIT Press, 1991), p. 174.

28. "Responsibility, Realism: Providing for the Future German Foreign Policy in a World Undergoing a Process of Restructuring," *Statements and Speeches* 16, 5 (New York: German Information Center, 1993).

29. Germany and Japan deal differently with their World War II pasts. Whereas Auschwitz has not permitted the Germans to claim the role of victim (though the bombing of Dresden in February 1945 has certainly been invoked for that purpose, especially by the German Right), Japan has had Hiroshima. The "Hiroshima Effect" has allowed the Japanese to belittle, even deny, their own war crimes in Asia (particularly in China). To this day, Japanese politicians seem unable to apologize for Japan's war crimes without couching such an apology in relativistic obfuscation. An institutional difference is also important: Japan was permitted greater continuity with its prewar existence by the U.S. decision to leave the emperor as head of state. In sum: for contemporary Germany, Auschwitz is a German crime against humanity; for Japan, Hiroshima is humanity's crime against the Japanese. Auschwitz bears a burden of guilt and responsibility, whereas Hiroshima confers

a halo of righteousness. See Ian Buruma, *Wages of Guilt: Memories of War in Germany and Japan* (New York: FSG, 1994), and Steven D. Wrage, "Germany and Japan Handle History Very Differently," *International Herald Tribune*, 17 August 1995.

30. Some exemplars of notable work in this tradition include Irving Janis and Leon Mann, *Decision Making: A Psychological Analysis of Conflict, Choice, and Commitment* (New York: Free Press, 1977); Robert Jervis, *Perception and Misperception in International Politics* (Princeton: Princeton University Press, 1976); Richard Ned Lebow, *Between Peace and War: The Nature of International Crisis* (Baltimore: Johns Hopkins University Press, 1981); Lebow and Janice Gross Stein, *We All Lost the Cold War* (Princeton: Princeton University Press, 1995); John D. Steinbruner, *The Cybernetic Theory of Decision* (Princeton: Princeton University Press, 1974). The attempt to aggregate is best represented in Janis, *Groupthink: Psychological Studies of Policy Decisions and Fiascoes* (Boston: Houghton Mifflin, 1982).

31. See Richard Ned Lebow, "General Learning and Conflict Management," *International Journal* 40 (Autumn 1985), p. 555.

32. For a domestic perspective on the relationship between the domestic politics of the *Handelsstaat* and foreign policy, see Christian Hacke, "Deutschland und die neue Weltordnung: Zwischen innenpolitischer Überforderung und außenpolitischen Krisen," *Aus Politik und Zeitgeschichte* 46 (November 1992), pp. 3–16.

33. We did not coin *hegesy*; the earliest formulation we have found is Nicos Kotzias, "Die Rolle der Bundesrepublik," pp. 111–129.

34. This quotation is from an alternative critique of the Realist position that focuses on Germany's external relations in arguing against German expansionism. See Stanley Hoffmann, "Reflections on the German Question," in *The European Sisyphus: Essays on Europe, 1964–1994* (Boulder, Colo.: Westview, 1995), p. 264.

35. The assumptions of liberalism and neoliberalism are described in detail in Andrew Moravcsik, "Preferences and Power in the European Community: A Liberal Intergovernmentalist Approach to the EC," in Simon Bulmer and Andrew Scott, eds., *Economic and Political Integration in Europe: Internal Dynamics and Global Context* (Oxford: Blackwell, 1994), pp. 29–80.

36. See Richard Samuels, *"Rich Nation, Strong Army": National Security and the Technological Transformation of Japan* (Ithaca: Cornell University Press, 1994), pp. 33–78.

37. Kohl warned the Congress of the Christian Democrats of the prospect of a twenty-first-century European war in the absence of sustained European integration. See Alan Cowell, "Kohl Presses Case for European Integration," *New York Times*, 17 October 1995.

38. Maurice Halbwachs, *The Collective Memory*, trans. Francis J. Ditter, Jr., and Vida Yazdi Ditter (New York: Harper and Row, 1980).

39. We have used three papers from the 1995 meeting of the American Historical Association, Chicago: Alon Confino, "Collective Memory: A Useful Analytical Tool or a New Historical Catch-Word?"; Susan Crane, "Loss vs. Preservation: The Difference between Historical Memory and Collective Memory"; and Elliot Neaman, "Gravediggers of Memory: Young Conservatives and the Nazi Past in Post-Unified Germany."

40. On collective memory in the destruction of former Yugoslavia see Laura Silber and Allan Little, *Yugoslavia: Death of a Nation* (New York: TV Books/Penguin, 1995). On collective memory as a crucial arena of contestation, see Chris Hedges, "After the Peace, the War against Memory," *New York Times*, 14 January 1996.

41. Emile Durkheim, *The Division of Labor in Society* (New York: Free Press, 1952).

42. On the distinction between shame cultures and guilt cultures, see Ruth Benedict,

The Chrysanthemum and the Sword: Patterns of Japanese Culture (Cambridge, Mass.: The Riverside Press, 1946), pp. 222–224.

43. For a comparative account of victimhood see Mark J. Osiel, "Ever Again: Legal Remembrance of Administrative Massacre," *University of Pennsylvania Law Review* 144 (December 1995), pp. 463–704. For the importance of victimhood in Germany, see Jane Kramer, *The Politics of Memory: Looking for Germany in the New Germany* (New York: Random House, 1996).

44. Tony Judt, "The Past Is Another Country: Myth and Memory in Postwar Europe," *Daedalus* 121 (Fall 1992), pp. 83–118.

45. For the Austrian case, see Robert E. Clute, *The International Status of Austria, 1938–1955* (The Hague: Martinus Nijhoff, 1962). Not until the Waldheim affair of the middle 1980s was Austria's official status as National Socialism's first foreign victim publicly debated in postwar Austria. On the Waldheim affair and its ramifications, see Richard Mitten, *The Waldheim Phenomenon in Austria: The Politics of Anti-Semitic Prejudice* (Boulder, Colo.: Westview, 1992). For the French case, see Henri Rousso, *The Vichy Syndrome: History and Memory in France since 1944*, trans. Arthur Goldhammer (Cambridge: Harvard University Press, 1991). The issue continues to preoccupy France: President Jacques Chirac was the first French president who publicly apologized to the victims of Nazi terror in France for complicity by many French people, without whose active participation the Nazi occupiers would not have been as successful. Chirac chose this very topic to differentiate himself from his predecessor François Mitterrand.

46. A useful bibliography is Iwona Irwin-Zarecka, *Frames of Remembrance: The Dynamics of Collective Memory* (New Brunswick, N.J.: Transaction, 1994). But see Benedict Anderson's superb *Imagined Communities: Reflections on the Origin and Spread of Nationalism* (London: Verso, 1983).

47. For a fine critique of the social sciences, particularly political science, and their failure to study collective memory, see Herbert Hirsch, *Genocide and the Politics of Memory: Studying Death to Preserve Life* (Chapel Hill: University of North Carolina Press, 1995), especially chap. 7.

48. Two notable recent exceptions are Thomas Banchoff, "Historical Memory and German Choices: The Cases of Adenauer and Brandt," American Institute for Contemporary German Studies, Washington, D.C., February 1996; and Gideon Rose, "Victory and Substitutes: Foreign Policy Decision-Making at the Ends of Wars" (Ph.D. diss., Harvard University, October 1994).

49. We owe point 7 of this section to Thomas Banchoff's insights in correspondence with Andrei Markovits, January 1996.

50. For a fine discussion of this point, see Yael Zerubavel, *Recovered Roots: Collective Memory and the Making of Israeli National Tradition* (Chicago: University of Chicago Press, 1995).

1: Europe and the German Question

1. See, for example, Renata Fritsch-Bournazel, *Das Land in der Mitte: Die Deutschen im europäischen Kräftefeld* (München: Iudicium Verlag, 1986).

2. These events play crucial roles in the relativization of history and the historicization of the past. The 1995 exhibit in Hamburg on the 200 days between the liberation of

Auschwitz and the dropping of the atomic bomb on Hiroshima was organized by the well-known left-wing intellectual Jan Philip Reemtsma, director of the Institute of Social Research, Hamburg. The exhibit universalizes cruelty, thus relativizing Auschwitz and Hiroshima.

3. See Geoff Eley, *From Unification to Nazism: Reinterpreting the German Past* (Boston: Allen and Unwin, 1986); Richard J. Evans, "Introduction: Wilhelm II's Germany and the Historians," in Richard J. Evans, ed., *Society and Politics in Wilhelmine Germany* (New York: Barnes and Noble, 1978); Fritz Fischer, *The War of Illusions* (New York: Norton, 1975); John. A. Moses, *The Politics of Illusion: The Fischer Controversy in German Historiography* (New York: Barnes and Noble, 1975); Hans-Ulrich Wehler, *The German Empire, 1871–1918* (Dover, N.H.: Berg, 1985).

4. See Ralf Dahrendorf, *Society and Democracy in Germany* (New York: Norton, 1979), pp. 3–16.

5. Alan Riding, "Union in Europe Strongly Backed by Danish Voters," *New York Times*, 19 May 1993, p. A1.

6. When influence is the product of unintended behavior but nevertheless pervasive, we characterize it as structural capacity rather than a material, coercive form of power. See Stephen Gill, *American Hegemony and the Trilateral Commission* (Cambridge: Cambridge University Press, 1990), p. 64.

7. See the discussion in the *Independent*, 19 December 1991.

8. The poll on Maastricht, the retention of the DM, and the German influence on Maastricht are all discussed by Peter Gumbel, "German Parliament Moves Closer to Approving Maastricht Treaty," *Wall Street Journal*, 9 October 1992, p. A8.

9. Leopold von Ranke was a major proponent both of an early, primitive form of a xenophobic *Realpolitik* and of the warlike nature of Prussian society. See his *Memoirs of the House of Brandenburg and History of Prussia during the Seventeenth and Eighteenth Centuries* (New York: Greenwood Press, 1968); *The Secret of World History: Selected Writings on the Art and Science of History* (New York: Fordham University Press, 1981); *The Theory and Practice of History* (Indianapolis: Bobbs-Merrill, 1973); *Völker und Staaten in der neueren Geschichte* (Zürich: E. Rentsch, 1945); *Weltgeschichte* (Leipzig: Duncker & Humblot, 1883). For his influence on subsequent conservative German historians, see Fischer, *The War of Illusions*, p. 30, and Moses, *The Politics of Illusion*.

10. Volker Berghahn, *Germany and the Approach of War in 1914* (New York: St. Martins, 1973), p. 9.

11. Evans, "Introduction: Wilhelm II's Germany," p. 19.

12. Discussed in Moses, *The Politics of Illusion*, pp. 31–41 and 48.

13. For the claim that domination was the primary objective, see Fischer, *The War of Illusions*, p. 30. For the alternative claim that Germany merely sought to become an equal partner among world powers, see Moses, *The Politics of Illusion*, p. 24.

14. See Alexander Gerschenkron, *Economic Backwardness in Historical Perspective* (Cambridge: Belknap Press of Harvard University, 1962), p. 23.

15. See Moses, *The Politics of Illusion*, p. xiii and Fritz Fischer, *Germany's Aims in the First World War* (New York: Norton, 1967), p. 8.

16. For the assumptions of Ranke and his successors see Moses, *The Politics of Illusion*, foreword, preface, and pp. 1–29.

17. Cf. Moses, *The Politics of Illusion*, pp. 31–41 and 48.

18. Eckart Kehr, *Der Primat der Innenpolitik* (Berlin: de Gruyter, 1965).

19. See Berghahn, *Germany and the Approach of War in 1914*; Geoff Eley, *Reshaping the German Right: Radical Nationalism and Political Change after Bismarck* (New Haven: Yale University Press, 1980); Fischer, *Germany's Aims in the First World War*; Wolfgang Mommsen, "Domestic Factors in German Foreign Policy before 1914," *Central European History* 6 (1973), pp. 3–43; and Wehler, *The German Empire, 1871–1918*.

20. See Alexander Gerschenkron, *Bread and Democracy in Germany* (New York: Howard Fertig, 1966), p. 25.

21. In comparative politics, see Carl Friedrich and Zbigniew Brzezinski, *Totalitarian Dictatorship and Autocracy* (Cambridge: Harvard University Press, 1956); Gerschenkron, *Bread and Democracy*; Juan Linz, "Totalitarian and Authoritarian Regimes," in Fred Greenstein and Nelson Polsby, eds., *The Handbook of Political Science* Vol. 3 (Reading, Mass.: Addison-Wesley, 1975); Seymour Martin Lipset, *Political Man: The Social Basis of Politics* (New York: Doubleday, 1963); and Barrington Moore, Jr., *The Social Origins of Dictatorship and Democracy: Lord and Peasant in the Making of the Modern World* (Boston: Beacon, 1966).

22. Gerschenkron, *Bread and Democracy*, pp. 16–17, 53, 153; David Abraham, *Collapse of the Weimar Republic* (Princeton: Princeton University Press, 1981). For a differing view see Henry A. Turner, *German Big Business and the Rise of Hitler* (New York: Oxford University Press, 1985). See also the debate between Abraham and Gerald Feldman in *Central European History*, 17 (June/September 1984), pp. 159–290.

23. Wehler defines social imperialism as a diversionary tactic meant to weaken efforts at domestic reform by liberals and the workers' movement. See Wehler, *The German Empire, 1871–1918*, p. 173.

24. For one interesting analysis of the consequences of Auschwitz see Alexander and Margarethe Mitscherlich, *The Inability to Mourn: Principles of Collective Behavior* (New York: Grove Press, 1975).

25. However, the so-called Stalin Notes of March and April 1952 seemed to suggest that reunification might be possible in return for neutrality on the part of a reunified Germany, but they were rejected by Adenauer. For an excellent discussion of reunification during the Adenauer period, see Timothy Garton Ash, *In Europe's Name* (New York: Random House, 1993), pp. 48–53. On U.S. support for German unification, see Philip Zelikow and Condoleezza Rice, *Germany Unified and Europe Transformed: A Study in Statecraft* (Cambridge: Harvard University Press, 1995).

26. For details see Bruce Jentleson, *Pipeline Politics: The Complex Political Economy of East-West Energy Trade* (Ithaca: Cornell University Press, 1986).

27. For a recent comprehensive discussion see U.S. Congress, Office of Technology Assessment, *Multinationals and the U.S. Technology Base* (Washington, D.C.: GPO, September 1994).

28. For our earlier discussion see Andrei S. Markovits and Simon Reich, "Should Europe Fear the German?" *German Politics and Society* 23 (Summer 1991), pp. 1–20.

29. The classic statement is in Mancur Olson, *The Rise and Decline of Nations: Economic Growth, Stagflation, and Social Rigidities* (New Haven: Yale University Press, 1982), especially pp. 75–77.

30. Neither the East Germans nor the West German Left used the term National Socialism often, preferring the generic "fascism" instead. "Fascism" delineates an internationally recognizable form of repressive rule, but it decidedly fails to give the particular case its home-grown flavor. By using the term fascism instead of "national socialism," the GDR and the

West German Left tried to universalize a political rule whose German particularism was in many ways much more telling than its universal characteristics of its true nature.

31. The conservative position, among others, is presented in *Historikerstreit: Die Dokumentation der Kontroverse um die Einzigartigkeit der nationalsozialistischen Judenvernichtung* (Munich: Piper, 1987). For a summary of the debate, see Norbert Kampe, "Normalizing the Holocaust? The Recent Historians' Debate in the Federal Republic of Germany," *Holocaust and Genocide Studies* 2 (1987), pp. 61–90. A comprehensive critique is offered by Charles Maier in *The Unmasterable Past: History, Holocaust, and the German National Identity* (Cambridge: Harvard University Press, 1988).

32. See Lipset, *Political Man.*

33. On Modell Deutschland, see Andrei S. Markovits, ed., *The Political Economy of West Germany: Modell Deutschland* (New York: Praeger, 1982).

34. See Norman M. Naimark, *The Russians in Germany: A History of the Soviet Zone of Occupation, 1945–49* (Cambridge: Belknap Press of Harvard University Press, 1995).

35. For a comprehensive discussion and criticism of the reaction to Goldhagen's book in Germany, see Andrei S. Markovits, "Störfall im Endlager der Geschichte: Daniel Goldhagen und seine deutschen Kritiker," *Blätter für deutsche und internationale Politik*, June 1996, pp. 667–674.

2: Optimists and Pessimists

1. See, for example, Flora Lewis, "Bringing In the East," *Foreign Affairs* 69 (Fall 1990), p. 25.

2. Stephen Kinzer, "Germany Now Leading Campaign to Strengthen the European Community," *The New York Times*, December 2, 1991, p. A3.

3. See Robert Gilpin, *U.S. Power and the Multinational Corporation* (New York: Basic Books, 1975), p. 107.

4. Cf. Wolfram Hanrieder, *Germany, America, Europe: Forty Years of German Foreign Policy* (New Haven: Yale University Press, 1989), pp. 5–7.

5. For the assumption that states are interested in absolute rather than relative gains, see Joseph Grieco, *Cooperation among Nations* (Ithaca: Cornell University Press, 1990), especially p. 10.

6. Ronald Tiersky, "France in the New Europe," *Foreign Affairs* 71 (Spring 1992), p. 145.

7. See John Cole, "Federalism or Barbarism?" *New Statesman and Society*, 12 June 1992, p. 9.

8. Tiersky, "France in the New Europe," p. 133.

9. For an influential analysis of the broad effects of the enlargement of the European Union, see Richard E. Baldwin, *Towards an Integrated Europe* (London: Center for Economic Policy Research, 1994).

10. Quoted in "Kohl Pledges Global Role for Germany," *Manchester Guardian Weekly*, 7 October 1990.

11. See, for an example of this argument, Martin Wolf, "Some Myths about Economic Power," *Financial Times*, 1 November 1990.

12. See Alexander Gerschenkron, *Bread and Democracy in Germany* (rpt. Ithaca: Cornell University Press, 1989).

13. For two exceptions to this view of a total break with the past, see Ralf Dahrendorf, *Society and Democracy in Germany* (New York: Norton, 1979), and Simon Reich, *The Fruits of Fascism: Postwar Prosperity in Historical Perspective* (Ithaca: Cornell University Press, 1990).

14. Philip H. Gordon, "The Normalization of German Foreign Policy," *Orbis* 38 (Spring 1994), p. 242. Gordon's optimistic assessment contains institutional as well as "elite learning" elements.

15. Tiersky, "France in the New Europe," p. 138.

16. Some German exponents of the *Handelsstaat* interpretation of the new Germany—Reinhard Rhode and Volker Rittberger, for example—extol the fact that the Germans have become "a nation of shopkeepers" (*Krämerseelen*). Formerly an epithet, this word is now used as empirical verification of the Federal Republic's success in creating a completely new political culture operating on a logic different from previous German states.

17. For a comprehensive rejection of the notion that Germany is either able or willing to lead in Europe, see Michael Kreile, "Übernimmt Deutschland eine Führungsrolle in der Europäischen Gemeinschaft?" in Werner Weidenfeld, ed., *Was ändert die Einheit?* (Gütersloh: Verlag Bertelsmann Stiftung, 1993).

18. Johann Gottlieb Fichte, *Der geschlossene Handelsstaat* (Tübingen: J. G. Cottaschen Buchhandlung, 1800). For the numerous interpretations of Fichte's work over the years, see Andreas Verzar, *Das autonome Subjekt und der Vernunftsstaat: Eine systematisch-historische Untersuchung zu Fichtes "geschlossenen Handelsstaat" von 1800* (Bonn: Bouvier Verlag, Herbert Grundmann, 1979).

19. A more extreme but logical extension of this argument was offered by the CDU/CSU in the "Schäuble paper," officially "Überlegungen zur europäischen Politik. Position der CDU/CSU Bundestagsfraktion vom 1. September 1994," and discussed in greater detail in the following chapter. See *Blätter für deutsche und internationale Politik*, October 1994, pp. 1271–1280.

20. Hanns W. Maull, "Germany and Japan: The New Civilian Powers," *Foreign Affairs* 69, (Winter 1990/1991), pp. 97, 98, 105.

21. See Marc Fisher, *Germany, Germans and the Burdens of History* (New York: Simon and Schuster, 1995).

22. See *Blätter für deutsche und internationale Politik*, October 1994, pp. 1271 and 1276.

23. Mary Hampton, "Die deutsche Vision von einer sich wandelnden Welt," in Bruno Schoch, ed., *Deutschlands Einheit und Europas Zukunft* (Frankfurt a.M.: Suhrkamp, 1992), pp. 290–314.

24. Albert Statz, "Zwischen neuer Machtpolitik und Selbstbeschränkung. Deutsche Aussenpolitik am Scheideweg," in Schoch, *Deutschlands Einheit und Europas Zukunft*, p. 252.

25. See Friedbert Pflüger, *Deutschland driftet: Die Konservative Revolution entdeckt ihre Kinder* (Düsseldorf: Econ, 1994).

26. See John Ely, "The 'Black-Brown Hazelnut' in a Bigger Germany: The Rise of a Radical Right as a Structural Feature," in Michael G. Huelshoff, Andrei S. Markovits, and Simon Reich, eds., *From Bundesrepublik to Deutschland* (Ann Arbor: University of Michigan Press, 1993), pp. 235–68.

27. See Andrei Markovits, Seyla Benhabib, and Moishe Postone, "Rainer Werner Fassbinder's 'Garbage, the City and Death': Renewed Antagonisms in the Complex Relationship between Jews and Germans in the Federal Republic of Germany," *New German*

Critique 38 (Fall 1986), pp. 3–27. See David B. Morris, "Bitburg Revisited: Germany's Search for Normalcy," *German Politics and Society* 13 (Winter 1995), pp. 92–109. The standard works on Bitburg include Geoffrey Hartman, ed., *Bitburg in Moral and Political Perspective* (Bloomington: Indiana University Press, 1986), and Ilya Levkov, ed., *Bitburg and Beyond* (New York: Shapolsky, 1987). On the historians' debate, for the participants' own articles and letters, see *Historikerstreit* (Munich: Piper, 1987), published in English as *Forever in the Shadow of Hitler?* (Atlantic Highlands, N.J.: Humanities, 1993).

28. See "Die Entdeckung der D-Mark als Wahlkampfthema," *Süddeutsche Zeitung*, 31 October 1995.

29. See Ely, "The 'Black-Brown Hazelnut' in a Bigger Germany," pp. 235–268.

30. See Jeffrey Herf, *War by Other Means: Soviet Power, West German Resistance, and the Battle of the Euromissiles* (New York: Free Press, 1991).

31. See "Epilogue" to the German-language edition of Andrei S. Markovits and Philip S. Gorski, *The German Left: Red, Green and Beyond* (New York: Oxford University Press, 1993) *Grün schlägt Rot: Die deutsche Linke seit 1945* (Hamburg: Rotbuch Verlag, 1997).

32. Arthur Heinrich, "Danke, Amerika! Dayton und die Deutschen," *Blätter für deutsche und internationale Politik* 1 (1996), pp. 35–44.

33. See Alan Cowell, "Memories of Wartime Brutalities Revive Czech-German Animosity," *New York Times*, 9 February 1996, pp. A1, A12.

34. See "Today's Germans: Peaceable, Fearful—and Green," and "Germans Favor Low Profile in World Affairs," both *Financial Times*, 4 January 1991.

3: Germans and Germany

Parts of this chapter were published as Andrei Markovits, "Germany and the Germans: A View from the United States," *German Politics and Society* 13 (19XX), pp. 142–165.

1. See Robert Gilpin, *War and Change in World Politics* (Cambridge: Cambridge University Press, 1981).

2. Virtually everybody writing on this topic divides Germany into two groups corresponding to what we here call mass or public opinion and elite opinion. See, for example, Charles Doran, "The Superpowers: The United States I," in Robert Spencer, ed., *Perceptions of the Federal Republic of Germany* (Toronto: Centre for International Studies, University of Toronto, 1986), pp. 65–69.

3. See Chicago Council on Foreign Relations, "American Public Opinion and US Foreign Policy 1995," ed. John E. Rielly (Chicago, 1995), p. 6.

4. This poll by the Gallup Organization was taken in February, July, and September 1990 and found virtually no changes in percentages in favor or opposed to the statement.

5. See Chicago Council on Foreign Relations, "American Public Opinion and US Foreign Policy 1991," ed. John E. Rielly (Chicago, 1991), p. 21.

6. See Chicago Council on Foreign Relations, "American Public Opinion and US Foreign Policy 1995," ed. John E. Rielly (Chicago, 1995), p. 22.

7. See the superb paper by Karin Böhme-Dürr, "Amerikanische Perspektiven: Öffentliche, offizielle und veröffentlichte Deutschlandbilder," in Ewald König, ed., *Typisch Deutsch: Wie uns die ausländische Presse sieht* (Munich: Olzog Verlag, 1996).

8. As quoted in William Safire, "Cap over the Wall," *New York Times*, 15 February 1996.

9. See Chicago Council on Foreign Relations, "American Public Opinion and US Foreign Policy 1995," ed. John E. Rielly (Chicago, 1995), p. 7.

10. All these figures come from Chicago Council on Foreign Relations, "American Public Opinion and US Foreign Policy 1991," ed. John E. Rielly (Chicago, 1991), p. 19.

11. These numbers are from the Chicago Council on Foreign Relations, "American Public Opinion and US Foreign Policy 1995," ed. John E. Rielly (Chicago, 1995), p. 20. Good-sized countries such as Italy and Spain were not even part of the survey.

12. See Chicago Council on Foreign Relations, "American Public Opinion and US Foreign Policy 1991," ed. John E. Rielly (Chicago, 1991), p. 22.

13. See Chicago Council on Foreign Relations, "American Public Opinion and US Foreign Policy 1995," ed. John E. Rielly (Chicago, 1995), p. 25.

14. See ibid., p. 24.

15. Ronald D. Asmus, "Germany in the Eyes of the American Security Elite" (Santa Monica: RAND, 1993), p. 20.

16. Asmus, "Germany in the Eyes," p. 6. See also Marc Fisher, *Germany, Germans and the Burdens of History* (New York: Simon and Schuster, 1995).

17. Böhme-Dürr, "Amerikanische Perspektiven," and her "In Search of Orientation: How the Past Contributes to Foreign News Construction," *Communication Review*, forthcoming, special issue on "Collective Memory."

18. As quoted in Böhme-Dürr, "In Search of Orientation," p. 11.

4: Reactions among the Europeans

1. Ludwig Fleck, as quoted in Ingo Kolboom, "Deutschlandbilder der Franzosen: Der Tod des 'Dauerdeutschen,' " in Günter Trautmann, *Die hässlichen Deutschen? Deutschland im Spiegel der westlichen und östlichen Nachbarn* (Darmstadt: Wissenschaftliche Buchgesellschaft, 1991), p. 213,

2. Karl Mannheim, "The Problem of Generations," in Mannheim, *Essays in the Sociology of Knowledge*, ed. Paul Kecskemeti (London: Routledge and Kegan Paul, 1952).

3. In addition to gathering local surveys from as many countries as we could, we also relied on cross-European surveys that gauged the perception of Germans by Europeans. Most notable among these pan-European surveys were the ones conducted by the *Economist*, the Belgian newspaper *Le Soir*, the French paper *Libération* and the Allensbach Institute published in the Allensbacher Berichte of 1990. Here is a comprehensive list of the newspapers we consulted:

Austria: *Der Standard, Die Presse, Kurier, Kronen-Zeitung, Salzburger Nachrichten, Profil, News.*

Belgium: *Het Laatste Nieuws, La Libre Belgique, Le Soir.*

Denmark: *Politiken.*

France: *Le Canard Enchainé, L'Express, L'Humanité, Le Figaro, Le Monde, Le Nouvel Observateur, Le Point, Libération.*

Great Britain: *New Statesman, Economist, Financial Times, Guardian, Independent, Spectator, Times.*

Greece: *Anti, Avghi, Eleftheros Tipos, Kathimerini, Ta Nea, To Vima.*

Hungary: *Magyar Hírlap, Népszabadság.*

Ireland: *Irish Independent, Irish Times.*

Italy: *Corriere della Serra, Il Messagero, La Repubblica, La Stampa, L'Expresso, L'Unità.* The Netherlands: *Algemeen Dagblad De Telegraaf, Het Parool, NRC/Handelsblad.* Portugal: *Correio da Manha, Expresso, Journal de O Dia, O Diàrio.* Spain: *ABC, Diàrio 16, El Pais, Ya.*

Three anthologies proved immensely useful for our research: Ulrike Liebert and Wolfgang Merkel, eds., *Die Politik zur deutschen Einheit: Probleme—Strategien—Kontroversen* (Opladen: Leske & Budrich, 1991); Günter Trautmann, ed., *Die hässlichen Deutschen? Deutschland im Spiegel der westlichen und östlichen Nachbarn* (Darmstadt: Wissenschaftliche Buchgesellschaft, 1991); and Harold James and Marla Stone, eds., *When the Wall Came Down: Reactions to German Unification* (New York: Routledge, 1992).

4. This periodization was first used by Andrei S. Markovits in his "Die deutsche Frage—Perzeptionen und Politik in der Europäischen Gemeinschaft," in Liebert and Merkel, *Politik zur deutschen Einheit*, pp. 321–341.

5. For a prototypical example, see Lothar Kettenacker, "Englische Spekulationen über die Deutschen" in Trautmann, *Die hässlichen Deutschen?* p. 207.

6. German sport teams and sport stars are invariably associated with warlike images; see Manfred Schneider, "Die Erotik des Fernsehsports. Beobachtungen zur heroischen Mystik des Alltags" (lecture on the panel "Forum 2: Sport im internationalen Fernsehgeschäft" at the Cologne Conference—Medienforum, Cologne, Germany, 1 June 1992). On the positive connotation of "Aatu" in Finnish, see Antti S. Vihinen, "Das Deutschenbild aus finnischer Sicht—viel Positives, selten Negatives," in Trautmann, *Die hässlichen Deutschen?* op. cit. p. 268.

7. Ludwick Fleck, as quoted in Kolboom, "Deutschlandbilder."

8. Gian Enrico Rusconi as quoted in Luigi Vittorio Ferraris, "Die hässlichen Deutschen," in Trautmann, *Die hässlichen Deutschen?*, p. 245.

9. Moshe Zimmermann, " 'Deutschland' als Ersatz für die zerfallenden Feindbilder: Zur Entstehung einer israelischen Schizophrenie," *Frankfurter Rundschau*, 29 July 1995. This is the source for Israeli data reported hereafter.

10. On the German Left's traditions of vehement hostility toward Israel and the peace movement's openly anti-American and anti-Israeli attitudes during the Gulf War, see Andrei S. Markovits and Philip S. Gorski, *The German Left: Red, Green and Beyond* (New York: Oxford University Press, 1993), esp. pp. 136–138.

5: The European Rim

1. European Commission, *Eurobarometer*, no. 33, June 1990, p. 38.

2. European Commission, *Eurobarometer*, no. 35, June 1991, p. A24.

3. The Serbs have resorted to calling all Bosnian Muslims "Turks."

4. "Portuguese Revolution Settles into Stability," *New York Times*, 29 April 1990.

5. European Commission, *Eurobarometer*, no. 33, June 1990, p. 38.

6. European Commission, *Eurobarometer*, no. 35, June 1991, p. A24.

7. *Expresso*, "Portugal e a Europa de hoje," 25 November 1989.

8. *Expresso*, " 'A Grande Alemanha' e o realinhamento europeu," 17 February 1990.

9. European Commission, *Eurobarometer*, no. 33, June 1990, p. 38.

10. European Commission, *Eurobarometer*, no. 35, June 1991, p. A24.

11. *El Pais*, 22 March 1990.

12. European Commission, *Eurobarometer*, no. 33, June 1990, p. 38.

13. European Commission, *Eurobarometer*, no. 35, June 1991, p. A24.

14. *Irish Times*, 15 February 1990.

6: Four Small Northern States

1. European Commission, *Eurobarometer*, no. 33, June 1990, p. 38.

2. *Le Soir*, 6–7 January 1990.

3. European Commission, *Eurobarometer*, no. 35, June 1991, p. A24.

4. For the comparison between the antipathy exhibited toward Count Alba and the Germans, see Horst Lademacher, "Der ungleiche Nachbar: Das Bild der Deutschen in den Niederlanden" in Günter Trautmann, ed., *Die hässlichen Deutschen? Deutschland im Spiegel der westlichen und östlichen Nachbarn* (Darmstadt: Wissenschaftliche Buchgesellschaft, 1991), p. 181.

5. Moreover, *mof* also characterizes how members of small or weaker states view people from larger and more powerful nations. Some aspects of the Dutch perception of the Germans are generic.

6. Thomas Rose, " 'Schrecklich, überall so unbeliebt zu sein,' " *Berliner Zeitung*, 19 October 1995.

7. On anti-Americanism in Germany, see Andrei S. Markovits, "Anti-Americanism and the Struggle for a West German Identity," in Peter H. Merkl, ed., *The Federal Republic of Germany at Forty* (New York: New York University Press, 1989), pp. 35–54; and Markovits and Andreas Hess, "Terra incognita: Oder: Mit dem Westen über den Westen hinausdenken," in *Blätter für deutsche und internationale Politik*, January 1992, pp. 99–105.

8. Lutsen B. Jansen, *Bekend en onbemind: Het beeld van Duitsland en Duitsers onder jongeren van vijftien tot negentien jaar* (Clingedael, 1993), as quoted in Hans Süssmuth, "Deutschlandbilder im Ausland: Wahrnehmungsmuster und Imagebildung," in Hans Süssmuth, ed., *Deutschlandbilder in Polen und Rußland, in der Tschechoslowakei und in Ungarn* (Baden-Baden: Nomos Verlagsgesellschaft, 1993), pp. 13–14. See also Martin van Traa, "Wohlbekannt aber ungeliebt? Der deutsche Nachbar aus niederländischer Sicht," *Europa-Archiv* 49 (1994), pp. 491–498.

9. "Sudden death is Duitse specialiteit" in *Algemeen Dagblad*, Rotterdam, August 15, 1996. Bayer, which was once part of I.G. Farben, one of the most complicitous German companies in the Nazis' many atrocities and notoriously the manufacturer of Zyklon B gas used in the extermination of millions of Jews, withdrew this slogan in its Guatemalan advertising rather promptly.

10. European Commission, *Eurobarometer*, no. 33, June 1990, p. 38.

11. European Commission, *Eurobarometer*, no. 35, June 1991, p. A24.

12. *NRC/Handelsblad*, 8 December 1989.

13. *NRC/Handelsblad*, 2 December 1989.

14. Alan Cowell, "After 50 Years, a German-Dutch Military Partnership," *New York Times*, 12 September 1995.

15. As quoted in ibid.

16. This episode is discussed in Dorothee Heisenberg, "Loud and Clear: Germany's EMU Agenda-Setting after Maastricht," presented at the Tenth International Conference

of Europeanists, Chicago, 14–17 March 1996, p. 2. The secret memo was reported in the *Financial Times*, 26 October 1994.

17. For an excellent discussion, see Bernd Henningsen, " 'Der Deutsche wird nie ein guter Däne': Zum Bild der Deutschen in Dänemark," in Trautmann, *Die hässlichen Deutschen?* pp. 167–180.

18. European Commission, *Eurobarometer*, no. 33, June 1990, p. 38.

19. Henningsen, " 'Der Deutsche wird nie ein guter Däne,' " p. 176.

20. As quoted in Trautmann, *Die hässlichen Deutschen?* p. 179.

21. European Commission, *Eurobarometer*, no. 35, June 1991, p. A24.

22. Trautmann, *Die hässlichen Deutschen?* p. 177.

23. Ibid., p. 169.

24. For this characterization see Günter Trautmann, "Die hässlichen Deutschen? Die Deutschen im Spiegel der westlichen und östlichen Nachbarn," in Trautmann, ed., *Die hässlichen Deutschen?*, p. 17.

25. See Antti S. Vihinen, "Das Deutschenbild aus finnischer Sicht—viel Positives, selten Negatives," in Trautmann, *Die hässlichen Deutschen?*, pp. 265–270.

7: Austria

Parts of this chapter were published as Andrei Markovits, "Austrian-German relations in the New Europe: Predicaments of Political and National Identity Formation," *German Studies Review* XIX (1996), pp. 91–111.

1. We find particularly useful Harald von Riekhoff and Hanspeter Neuhold, eds., *Unequal Partners: A Comparative Analysis of Relations between Austria and the Federal Republic of Germany and between Canada and the United States* (Boulder: Westview Press, 1993).

2. Hans Heinz Fabris, "Medienkolonie—na und?" in Margit Scherb and Inge Morawetz, eds., *In deutscher Hand? Österreich und sein grosser Nachbar* (Vienna: Verlag für Gesellschaftskritik, 1990), p. 55.

3. Hans Heinz Fabris, "Media Relations between Austria and the Federal Republic of Germany," in von Riekhoff and Neuhold, pp. 243–246.

4. Ibid., p. 250.

5. Ibid., p. 253.

6. Austrians and Germans often speak of the common language that divides them. Austrians do in fact have different names for certain foods, for example, but the overwhelming power of quotidian affinity and the deep understanding between these two peoples is only possible because of a common language.

7. For a brilliant critique of this Austrian self-congratulation, see the remarks by Sigrid Löffler at the symposium "Österreich und Deutschland in Europa," Frankfurt am Main, 4 May 1995.

8. For an insightful analysis as to how Austria has used its smallness not in genuine self-reflection but in a calculated exculpatory politics vis-à-vis the Nazi past, see the comments made by Rudolf Burger at the symposium "Österreich und Deutschland in Europa," Frankfurt am Main, 4 May 1995. Invoking smallness means relinquishing responsibility.

9. See Ernst Bruckmüller, *Österreichbewußtsein im Wandel: Identität und Selbstverständnis in den 90er Jahren* (Vienna: Signum Verlag, 1994), pp. 134–136.

10. Ibid., p. 26.

11. Ibid., p. 150. Though a distant second to the Germans, the Hungarians are way

ahead in the Austrians' affection compared to other neighbors. The legacy of the Habsburg monarchy lives on vividly in a continuing mutual admiration between the Hungarians and the Austrians.

12. It is telling about how large numbers of Austrians still feel about the Third Reich, that when Austrians mention *Besatzungszeit* (occupation period), everybody takes it to mean the period between 1945 and 1955, i.e., the period of Allied occupation. Only to a few left-wing intellectuals might the term connote the period between 1938 and 1945. Despite the obvious political distancing by Austrians from Germans over the past fifty years, the Nazi period still enjoys immense legitimacy, admiration, and goodwill among Austrians—far higher than among Germans. See ibid., particularly pp. 58 and 59.

8: The World of Post-Communism

1. See Jerzy Holzer, "Der widerliche Schwabe, der brutale Preusse . . . ," in Günter Trautmann, ed., *Die hässlichen Deutschen? Deutschland im Spiegel der westlichen und östlichen Nachbarn* (Darmstadt: Wissenschaftliche Buchgesellschaft, 1991).

2. On the 1913 law see Rogers Brubaker, *Citizenship and Nationhood in France and Germany* (Cambridge: Harvard University Press, 1992). On *polnische Wirtschaft* see Hans-Adolf Jacobsen, "Polen und Deutsche: Kontinuität und Wandel gegenseitiger Bilder im 20. Jahrhundert," in Hans Süssmuth, ed., *Deutschlandbilder in Polen und Rußland, in der Tschechoslowakei und Ungarn* (Baden-Baden: Nomos Verlagsgesellschaft, 1993), p. 157.

3. Grzegorz Ekiert, "The Return of the German Minority to Poland," *German Politics and Society*, no. 26 (Summer 1992), p. 92.

4. For the expulsion of the Germans from Poland and Czechoslovakia, see A. M. de Zayas, *Nemesis at Potsdam* (Lincoln: University of Nebraska Press, 1988).

5. See Klaus Ziemer, "Können Polen und Deutsche Freunde sein? Polnische Befürchtungen bei der Vereinigung Deutschlands," in Trautmann, *Die hässlichen Deutschen?* p. 90.

6. Quoted in Dieter Bingen, "Oder-Neiße-Grenze," in Ewa Kobylinska, Andreas Lawaty, and Rüdiger Stephan, eds., *Deutsche und Polen: 100 Schlüsselbegriffe* (Munich: Piper, 1992), p. 410.

7. See Ludwig Mehlhorn, "Die Sprachlosigkeit zwischen Polen und der DDR: Eine Hypothek," in Kobylinska, Lawaty, and Stephan, *Deutsche und Polen*, pp. 522–528.

8. See Ziemer, "Können Polen und Deutsche Freunde sein?" p. 96.

9. See "Furcht, Neid und Respekt," *Der Spiegel*, 2 September 1991, p. 49.

10. See European Commission, *Eurobarometer*, no. 34, December 1990, p. A47.

11. See Michael Ludwig, *Polen und die deutsche Frage* (Bonn: Forschungsinstitut der deutschen Gesellschaft für Auswärtige Politik, Europa Union Verlag, 1991), pp. 22–25.

12. Ibid., pp. 27, 39.

13. Ibid., p. 140.

14. "Furcht, Neid, und Respekt," *Der Spiegel*, 2 September 1991, p. 48.

15. Ibid., pp. 49, 57.

16. Ibid., p. 55.

17. See Jacobsen, "Polen und Deutsche," p. 153.

18. See "Deutsche bei den Polen am Ende der Beliebtheitsskala," *Frankfurter Allgemeine Zeitung*, 31 July 1995, p. 8.

19. For Polish-German economic (and cultural) relations before and after 1989, see

Patricia Davis, "Polish-German Relations in the New Europe: From Sensitivity to Vulnerability," paper presented at the 19th Annual Conference of the German Studies Association, Chicago, 1995.

20. European Commission, *Central and Eastern Eurobarometer*, March 1994, Annex Figure 10.

21. European Commission, *Central and Eastern Eurobarometer*, March 1995, Annex Figure 9.

22. All public opinion data refer to Czechoslovakia until the formation of separate Czech and Slovak states on 1 January 1993. Data thereafter refer only to the Czech Republic.

23. See Jan Kren, "Deutschlandbilder bei den Tschechen," in Süssmuth, *Deutschlandbilder in Polen und Rußland*, pp. 224–225.

24. See Ferdinand Seibt, *Deutschland und die Tschechen: Geschichte einer Nachbarschaft in der Mitte Europas* (Munich: Piper, 1993), pp. 322–323, 348.

25. Ibid., p. 350. See Alan Cowell, "Memories of Wartime Brutalities Revive Czech-German Animosity," *New York Times*, 9 February 1996.

26. Kren, "Deutchlandbilder," p. 228.

27. Ibid., p. 229.

28. Seibt, *Deutschland und die Tschechen*, p. 403.

29. Quoted in "One Germany Is No Threat, Says Czechs' Leader," *Daily Telegraph*, 3 January 1990, p. 10.

30. European Commission, *Eurobarometer*, no. 33, June 1990, p. 38.

31. European Commission, *Eurobarometer*, no. 34, December 1990, p. A47.

32. Seibt, *Deutschland und die Tschechen*, p. 404.

33. Kren, "Deutschlandbilder," pp. 230–231.

34. Berthold Kohler, "Gefürchtet und bewundert: Was die Tschechen über die Deutschen denken," *Frankfurter Allgemeine Zeitung*, 17 July 1995.

35. E.g., Vaclav Havel in an interview with *Süddeutsche Zeitung*, 13 April 1993.

36. "Neuer Spuk um altes Gespenst," *Süddeutsche Zeitung*, 8 February 1996.

37. "Tschechien—wieder ein strategisches Bollwerk?" *Süddeutsche Zeitung*, 27 February 1996.

38. *Magyar Hírlap*, 16 May 1990.

39. European Commission, *Eurobarometer*, no. 34, December 1990, p. A47.

40. In April 1990, after all, Hungary's third largest political party, the Party of Citizens and Independent Smallholders, then a member of the governing coalition, seriously thought about asking Otto von Habsburg to return to Hungary and assume the office of the president. Otto, in notable contrast to Franz Josef, his grandfather, speaks fluent Hungarian. The plan was never realized because Otto preferred to remain a member of the CSU's delegation to the European Parliament in Strassburg.

41. See József László, "Das Deutschlandbild in Ungarn," in Süssmuth, *Deutschlandbilder in Polen und Rußland*, p. 267.

42. Ibid., pp. 267–269.

43. *Népszabadság*, 5 May 1990.

44. Quoted in Kathrin Sitzler, "Das aktuelle Deutschlandbild der Ungarn," in Süssmuth, *Deutschlandbilder in Polen und Rußland*, p. 279.

45. Ibid., pp. 282, 277.

46. European Commission, *Central and Eastern Eurobarometer*, March 1995, Annex Figure 9.

9: The Big States

1. European Commission, *Eurobarometer*, no. 33, June 1990, p. 38.

2. European Commission, *Eurobarometer*, no. 35, June 1991, p. A24.

3. See "Mayhem," *Economist*, 19 September 1992, pp. 15–16; and "A Ghastly Game of Dominoes," *Economist*, 19 September 1992, pp. 89–90.

4. See Robert Graham, "Italians Upset at Waigel's Remarks," and Lionel Barber, "EMU Turmoil Hits EU's Majorca Summit," *Financial Times*, 22 September 1995, p. 2; and "Europe's Dream of Common Currency: A German Warning Shot," *New York Times*, 22 September 1995, p. A13.

5. As cited in Elisabeth Geffers and Michael Struebel, "Die 'häßlichen' Deutschen aus italienischer Sicht," in Guenter Trautmann, ed., *Die häßlichen Deutschen? Deutschland im Spiegel der westlichen und östlichen Nachbarn* (Darmstadt: Wissenschaftliche Buchgesellschaft, 1991), p. 259.

6. Cited in ibid., p. 254.

7. *Corriere*, 28 December 1989.

8. *Corriere*, 1 January 1990.

9. *Corriere*, 20 March 1990.

10. *Corriere*, 12 November 1989.

11. *Corriere*, 14 February 1990.

12. This was the height of the Left's scholarly preoccupation with "fascism." Fascism was explained as an extension, even a deformity, of capitalism. These were the days when Louis Althusser and Nicos Poulantzas, the latter a prolific writer on fascism, were all but required reading on the Parisian scene.

13. *New York Times*, 20 February 1990.

14. *Canard Enchaîné*, 14 February 1990.

15. European Commission, *Eurobarometer*, no. 33, June 1990, p. 38.

16. European Commission, *Eurobarometer*, no. 35, June 1991, p. A24.

17. *Le Monde*, 10 February 1990.

18. *Le Monde*, 16 February 1990.

19. Quoted in *Le Monde*, 23 February 1990.

20. *Le Monde*, 21 February 1990.

21. *Le Monde*, 21 March 1990.

22. Ibid.

23. *Le Monde*, 24 March 1990.

24. *Le Monde*, 27 March 1990.

25. *Figaro*, 8 December 1989.

26. *Figaro*, 24 March 1990.

27. *Figaro*, 30 March 1990.

28. *Figaro*, 9 and 19 February, 1990.

29. *Figaro*, 27 February 1990.

30. *Figaro*, 15 March 1990.

31. Nathaniel C. Nash, "Leader Calls Cutbacks Vital for French Role in Europe," *New York Times*, 8 December 1995.

32. See Nicholas Pyke, "Ginger v. the Red Baron," *Times Educational Supplement*, 6 December 1991, p. 10. The Goethe Institute and the British Council later collaborated in publishing *How Do We See Each Other? Stereotypes of England and Germany in the Chil-*

dren's and Youth Literature of Both Countries (Munich: Internationale Jugendbibliothek, 1993).

33. "Michel und John Bull auf neuen Wegen," *Süddeutsche Zeitung*, 10 August 1995.

34. As quoted in Timothy Garton Ash, "The Chequers Affair," *New York Review of Books*, 27 September 1990.

35. Quoted in "Michel und John Bull auf neuen Wegen," *Süddeutsche Zeitung*, 10 August 1995.

36. European Commission, *Eurobarometer*, no. 33, June 1990, p. 38.

37. Public opinion polls are extremely volatile and vary according to the phrasing of questions asked. In a similar survey designed to measure the European reaction to German unification conducted by the *Economist*, the British appear much more negatively disposed. Moreover, they also appear to be decidedly more opposed than the French. Results: 45 percent of the British respondents favor unification, 30 percent oppose it; 61 percent of the French favor unification, 15 percent oppose it. See the *Economist*, 27 January 1990.

38. *Spectator*, 14 July 1990.

39. Ibid.

40. Much of the public saw German unification as a *positive* development. When questioned in the spring of 1991, 10 percent of U.K. respondents answered that a unified Germany made them personally feel very hopeful about the future of the U.K., 43 percent rather hopeful, 26 percent rather fearful, 7 percent very fearful, and 14 percent did not know. See European Commission, *Eurobarometer*, no. 35, June 1991, p. A24.

10: The Deployment of German Soldiers Abroad

1. See Andrei S. Markovits and Philip S. Gorski, *The German Left: Red, Green and Beyond* (New York: Oxford University Press, 1993), pp. 136–138.

2. Dieter Deiseroth, "Die Bundesrepublik—Transitstelle für US-Militäreinsätze außerhalb des NATO-Gebietes? Anmerkungen zum 'Wartime-Host-Nation-Support-Abkommen' zwischen den USA und der Bundesrepublik Deutschland vom 15. April 1982," in *Kritische Justiz*, no. 4 (1985), pp. 412–434.

3. See Jeffrey Herf, *War by Any Other Means: Soviet Power, West German Resistance and the Battle of the Euromissiles* (New York: Free Press, 1991); and Markovits and Gorski, *The German Left*.

4. Thomas Giegerich, "The German Contribution to the Protection of Shipping in the Persian Gulf: Staying out for Political or Constitutional Reasons?" *Zeitschrift für ausländisches öffentliches Recht und Völkerrecht*, no. 1 (1989), pp. 1–40.

5. Oskar Hoffmann, *Deutsche Blauhelme bei UN-Missionen: Politische Hintergründe und rechtliche Aspekte* (Munich: Verlag Bonn Aktuell, 1993), pp. 82, 83.

6. Other examples included a three-month support mission following floods in Algeria and Tunisia in 1970; the transport of 9,000 tons of first aid material to the Sahel region of Africa in 1973/74; first-aid missions to Turkey and Italy in the wake of earthquakes in 1985; and help to the victims of the earthquake in Armenia in 1988. See ibid.

7. For a compilation of the Bundeswehr's participation in UN missions and humanitarian activities since 1991, see Karen Donfried, "German Foreign Policy: Regional Priorities and Global Debuts" (Washington: Congressional Research Service, Library of Congress, 1995), p. 16.

8. Ibid., p. 86; see also Caroline Thomas and Klaus-Peter Weiner, "Neuer Interventionismus—die deutsche Aussenpolitik nach der Vereinigung," in Caroline Thomas and Klaus-Peter Weiner, ed., *Auf dem Weg zur Hegemonialmacht? Die deutsche Aussenpolitik nach der Vereinigung* (Cologne: Papyrossa Verlag, 1993), pp. 150, 151.

9. See Hoffmann, *Deutsche Blauhelme*, p. 89.

10. All quotations are from the official English translation: *The Basic Law of the Federal Republic of Germany* (Bonn: Press and Information Office of the Federal Government, 1986).

11. For a superb discussion of Constitutional Court decisions, see Manfred H. Wiegandt, "Germany's International Integration: The Rulings of the German Federal Constitutional Court on the Maastricht Treaty and the Out-of-Area Deployment of German Troops," *American University Journal of International Law and Policy* 10 (Winter 1995), pp. 889–916.

12. Hoffmann, *Deutsche Blauhelme*, p. 76.

13. Volker Rühe, "Zunkunftsaufgaben deutscher Sicherheitspolitik," *Europäische Sicherheit* (Winter 1992), pp. 421–426.

14. Michael Jach and Klaus Schrotthofer, "Bundeswehr: Start ins Ungewisse," *Focus*, 3 July 1995, pp. 20–23.

15. See "Bundestag stimmt Einsatz von 'Tornados' zu. Kinkel: Es geht um die Glaubwürdigkeit Deutschlands," *Süddeutsche Zeitung*, 1–2 July, 1995.

16. For a step-by-step account of the German recognition of Croatia and Slovenia and the Greens' key role, see Beverly Crawford, "German Foreign Policy and European Political Cooperation: The Diplomatic Recognition of Croatia in 1991," *German Politics and Society* 1 (Summer 1995), pp. 1–34.

17. Permission was contingent on the following provisions: that these activities occurred under the aegis of the United Nations (not NATO), that all German personnel were fully integrated into this UN command (that is, that they were wearing "blue helmets"), and that their tasks were purely auxiliary and under no circumstances combative.

18. Joschka Fischer, "Die Katastrophe in Bosnien und die Konsequenzen für unsere Partei Bündnis '90/Die Grünen: Ein Brief an die Bundestagsfraktion und an die Partei," published in abridged version as "Wir müssen für den militärischen Schutz der UN-Zonen sein," in the Dokumentation section of *Frankfurter Rundschau*, 2 August 1995.

19. Joschka Fischer, "Auf der Flucht vor der Wirklichkeit," letter, Monday, 27 November 1995.

20. On Germany's identity as a "normal" rather than a "civilian" power, see Mary M. McKenzie, "Competing Conceptions of Normalcy in the Post-Cold War Era: Germany, Europe and Foreign Policy Change," *German Politics and Society* 14 (Summer 1996).

21. See Ronald D. Asmus, *Germany's Geopolitical Maturation: Public Opinion and Security Policy in 1994* (Santa Monica: RAND, 1995), p. 42. Quotation from "Today's Germans: Peaceable, Fearful—and Green," *Financial Times*, 4 January 1991.

11: Germany's Economic Power in Europe

Parts of this chapter were published as Andrei S. Markovits, Simon Reich, and Frank Westermann, "Does Germany's Economic Dominance in Europe Yield Hegemonic Power?" *Review of International Political Economy* 3 (1996).

1. Hans-Peter Schwarz, *Die gezähmten Deutschen: Von der Machtbessessenheit zur Machtvergessenheit* (Stuttgart: Deutsche Verlags-Anstalt, 1985), pp. 116–117.

2. Susan Strange, *States and Markets* (London: Pinter, 1994), pp. 24–25.

3. Rick Atkinson, "Germans Invest in East Europe but Curb Image of Empire," *Washington Post*, 17 April 1994, pp. A25, A30.

4. See Robert Gilpin, *War and Change in World Politics* (Cambridge: Cambridge University Press, 1981) pp. 42–43, and Stephen D. Krasner, "State Power and the Structure of International Trade," *World Politics*, April 1976, pp. 317–347.

5. Sachverständigenrat zur Begutachtung der gesamtwirtschaftlichen Entwicklung, "Den Aufschwung sichern—Arbeitsplätze schaffen," *Jahresgutachten 1994/95* (Stuttgart: Metzler-Poeschel, 1994), pp. 317, 324.

6. *European Economy*, no. 3, 1994, p. 155.

7. W. R. Smyser, *The Economy of a United Germany* (New York: St. Martins, 1992), p. 4.

8. Georg Winckler, "The Impact of the Economy of the FRG on the Economy of Austria," in Harald von Riekhoff and Hanspeter Neuhold, eds., *Unequal Partners: A Comparative Analysis of Relations between Austria and the Federal Republic of Germany and between Canada and the United States* (Boulder: Westview Press, 1993), p. 158. All contributions were written before German unification and so refer to West Germany instead of Germany.

9. Margit Scherb, "Wir und die westeuropäische Hegemonialmacht: Die Beziehungen zwischen Österreich und der Bundesrepublik Deutschland in den Bereichen Währung, Aussenhandel und Direktinvestitionen," in Scherb and Inge Morawetz, eds., *In deutscher Hand? Österreich und sein grosser Nachbar* (Vienna: Verlag für Gesellschaftskritik, 1990), p. 55.

10. Harald von Riekhoff, "Introduction: Toward a Comparison of Relations Between Austria/FRG and Canada/United States," in von Riekhoff and Neuhold, eds., *Unequal Partners*, pp. 14, 15.

11. Relying on Granger-style causality measures Winckler cites a study that found "that about 60 percent (of a possible 100 percent) of Austria's GNP and consumption is 'caused' (in the sense of Granger) by the FRG's GNP and consumption." Winckler concludes this part of his analysis by stating "that at the level of real aggregates the Austrian economy is highly influenced by the West German economy." Winckler, "Impact of the Economy," p. 157.

12. As quoted in Scherb, "Wir und die westeuropäische Hegemonialmacht," p. 56.

13. Poehl and Kohl are quoted in ibid., pp. 35 and 56 respectively.

14. See Robert Holzmann and Georg Winckler, "Austrian Economic Policy: Some Theoretical and Critical Remarks on Austro-Keynesianism," *Empirica* 10 (1983), pp. 183–203. Also Hans Seidel, "Social Partnership and Austro-Keynesianism," in Günter Bischof and Anton Pelinka, eds., *Contemporary Austrian Studies* vol. 4 (1995), pp. 94–118.

15. D. Mark Schultz, "Austrian-EC Trade Relations: Evolution toward Integration," in von Riekhoff and Neuhold, *Unequal Partners*, p. 171; for data after 1985, we use personal information from economists of the Creditanstalt, one of Austria's leading banks.

16. Scherb, "Wir und die westeuropäische Hegemonialmacht," p. 47.

17. To be sure, the amazing jump in German foreign direct investment in Austria in the 1960s had much to do with the complicated compensatory processes involving German-held property during the Nazi period. For this interesting aspect of Austrian-

German relations, see Rosmarie Atzenhofer, "Wie das deutsche Eigentum wieder 'deutsch' wurde," in Scherb and Morawetz, *In deutscher Hand?* pp. 61–85. For early 1990s data see Winckler, "Impact of the Economy," p. 161.

18. On Germany's growth as a foreign investor as a consequence of Austria's privatization efforts of the 1980s, see Inge Morawetz, "Schwellenland Österreich? Aktuelle Veränderungen der österreichischen Eigentumsstruktur im Sog der Internationalisierungsstrategien der Bundesrepublik Deutschland," in Scherb and Morawetz, *In deutscher Hand?* pp. 87–112.

19. Here causality is inferred when lagged values of a variable, say ge(t), have explanatory power in a regression of another variable (in our case bln [t]).This means that a regression of the variable bln (t) would have a lower standard error if lagged values of ge (t) were included than in a pure autoregression. See C. W. J. Granger, "Investigating Causal Relations by Econometric Models and Cross-Spectral Methods," *Econometrica*, 37 (1969), pp. 222–312. This kind of analysis can be carried out by employing a multivariate vector autoregression (VAR). See William H. Greene, *Econometric Analysis*, 2d ed. (New York: Maximilian Publishing, 1993), pp. 549–559.

To reach a significance level of 95 percent for our results and to keep sufficient degrees of freedom for the regressions, we limit our data in the following way: we use the Benelux countries, which have the highest potential spillover effect from Germany, as one aggregate variable; and the U.K. as the clearest loser in EU trade relations as a counterexample. Germany is the third country included in the VAR. Using the backshift operator notation and noting that first differences of natural logs are approximate percentage changes—see Andrew C. Harvey, *Time Series Models*, 2d ed. (Cambridge: MIT Press, 1993), we define the variables as:

$bln(t) = (1-B)\ln bln(t)$: Percentage change in total exports of the BENELUX countries from period t-1 to period t

$ge(t) = (1-B)\ln ge(t)$: Percentage change in total exports of Germany from period t-1 to period t

$uk(t) = (1-B)\ln uk(t)$: Percentage change in total exports of U.K. from period t-1 to period t

We use annual export data of each country from 1960 to 1992, retrieved from the International Financial Statistics CD-Rom, May 1995, of the International Monetary Fund.

20. Looking at the correlation between the variables at various lags, we find that Germany has a spillover effect on the Benelux countries at lag 3 to lag 6. Germany's F-statistic for the U.K. as the dependent variable indicates that the effect of Germany's export growth on British export growth is jointly zero at all six lags. We also ran vector autoregressions using other EU countries as variables. The results supported our argument but did not reach a significance level of 95 percent.

21. For a more geographical interpretation of output correlations between Germany and the Benelux countries, see Tamim Bayoumi and Barry Eichengreen, "Shocking Aspects of European Monetary Integration," in Francesco Torres and Francesco Giavazzi, eds., *Adjustment and Growth in the European Monetary Union* (Cambridge: Cambridge University Press, 1993), pp. 193–229.

22. "Will Germany Tow Europe into Trouble?," *Economist*, 31 August 1991, p. 53.

23. Albert O. Hirschman, *National Power and the Structure of Foreign Trade* (Berkeley: University of California Press, 1945).

24. For figures see *Sachverstündigenrat zur Begutachtung der gesamtwirtschaftlichen Entwicklung, Jahresgutachten 1994/95* (Stuttgart: Metzler-Pöschel, 1995), pp. 347, 445.

25. Some have argued that "Germany inhabits within Europe today roughly the same position the U.S. did in the world of the 1950s," in terms of the role of the D-Mark. Lewis E. Lehrman and John Mueller, "The Curse of Being a Reserve Currency," *Wall Street Journal*, 4 January 1993. For growing signs of German monetary independence from the United States, see Ferdinand Protzman, "Inflation in Germany Averaged 3.1% in 1991," *New York Times*, 10 January 1992; Peter Passell, "Bonn Punches, the Dollar Rolls," *New York Times*, 27 August 1992; and, most pointedly, in Tom Buerkle, "Germany Scolds U.S. for Failing to Defend Dollar," *International Herald Tribune*, 6 April 1995, p. 1.

26. Reinhard Rhode, "Deutschland: Weltwirtschaftsmacht oder überforderter Euro-Hegemon?" in Bruno Schoch, ed., *Deutschlands Einheit und Europas Zukunft* (Frankfurt am Main: Suhrkamp, 1992), p. 214.

27. See, for example, recent evidence about the need for the Bundesbank to purchase U.S. Dollars as a means of supporting its value against the Deutsche Mark. Craig R. Whitney, "Germans Reduce 2 Interest Rates," *New York Times*, 12 May 1994, p. A1.

28. Lewis E. Lehrman and John Mueller, "The Curse of Being a Reserve Currency," *Wall Street Journal*, 4 January 1993.

29. For the former see John Marcom, Jr., "Bundesbank über alles," *Forbes*, 24 December 1990, pp. 36–38; for the latter, somewhat less pessimistic view, see Roland Leuschel, "Why the Bundesbank Raised Rates," *Wall Street Journal*, 15 January 1992, p. A12. For a more neutral position, in terms of optimism and pessimism see Milton J. Ezrati, "Germany's Hands Are Tied on Rates," *New York Times*, 7 February 1993.

30. See Helmut Schlesinger, then Bundesbank president, on why German interest rates, then choking the economies of Europe, were not excessively high, in Richard W. Stevenson, "Bundesbank's Chief Holds the Line on Rate Policy," *New York Times*, 2 February 1993.

31. For a discussion see Craig R. Whitney, "Kohl Denies Secret Plan to Force European Union," *New York Times*, 25 September 1992.

32. The first quotation comes from Ferdinand Protzman, "Bundesbank Increases Rates to Highest Level since 1948," *New York Times*, 20 December 1991, p. C1. The second comment, by Peter Peitsch, an economist at the Commerzbank A.G. in Frankfurt, comes from the same article.

33. This point is made, for example, by Hans-Peter Stihl, president of the German Association of Chambers of Commerce and Industry, in David Marsh, "German Warns on German Influence," *Financial Times*, 30 August 1992.

34. Craig R. Whitney, "Bundesbank: Sound Money Bastion," *New York Times*, 22 October 1992, p. C1. Whitney makes a comparable argument in his piece entitled "Germany's Well-Defended Mark," *New York Times*, 23 September 1992, p. A16.

35. For an insightful journalistic account of German deliberations on the ERM crisis and the future of the European Monetary System, see Craig R. Whitney, "Blaming the Bundesbank," *New York Times Magazine*, 17 October 1993, pp. 19, 44, 48, 59.

36. Jon Stein, "D-Mark Bullying but Protecting Pound," *Futures*, December 1990, p. 24.

37. C. Randall Henning, *Currencies and Policies in the United States, Germany and Japan* (Washington, D.C.: International Institute for Economics, 1994), pp. 98–99.

38. Ibid., p. 230.

39. Peter Gumbel, "German Parliament Moves Closer to Approving Maastricht Treaty," *Wall Street Journal*, 9 October 1993, p. A8.

40. Henning, *Currencies and Policies*, p. 232.

41. See, for example, Ferdinand Protzman, "Germany's Top Banker Gives Europe a Warning," *New York Times*, 20 March 1991, p. D2; "As Independent as Judges," *Economist*, 20 April 1991, p. 17; David Marsh, "Bundesbank to Criticize Kohl's Maastricht Deal," *Financial Times*, 29 January 1992, p. 1.

42. Karl Otto Pöhl, quoted in Dieter Balkhausen, *Gutes Geld und schlechte Politik* (Düsseldorf: Econverlag, 1992), p. 177.

43. Henning, *Currencies and Policies*, p. 235. For the claim that the terms of the Maastricht Agreement reflected German governmental influence as the principal architect for EMU, see also "Made in Germany," *Economist*, 2 November 1991, p. 77.

44. For a summary see "Nightmare on ERM Street, II," *Economist*, 28 November 1992, pp. 87–88. See also Craig R. Whitney, "Europeans Agree to Let Currencies Fluctuate Widely," *New York Times*, 2 August 1992, p. A1, and Richard W. Stevenson, "Europeans' Currency System Shaken as Britain Cuts Free," *New York Times*, 17 September 1992.

45. See Peter Marsh, "Tietmeyer Firm on Re-entry to ERM," *Financial Times*, 6 February 1993; "Bundesbank Says European Bank Must Be in Frankfurt," *Financial Times*, 30 March 1992, p. 1.

46. For examples of this point drawn from the 1990s, see "Bundesbank Strikes Back," *Financial Times*, 5 November 1990, p. 16; Jonathan Fuerbringer, "The Bundesbank's One-Two Punch," *New York Times*, 22 December 1991, and Martin Wolf, "Germany Faces More Pressure to Ease Interest Rates," *Financial Times*, 6 July 1993. The same argument, about the centrality of the Bundesbank's Lombard rate, is made by Leslie Gelb, "Love Lombard Rates," *New York Times*, 20 September 1992, p. E17.

47. For versions of this argument see Craig R. Whitney, "Germany Focuses on German Unity; European Unity Will Wait," *New York Times*, 13 May 1992, p. A1; Keith Rockwell, "EC Monetary Union Set Back by Germany's Policy Fears," *Journal of Commerce*, 28 February 1991, p. 3A; Charles Bean, "Why EMU's Critics Are Wrong," *Financial Times*, 3 July 1992, p. 15.

48. See "Die Entdeckung der D-Mark als Wahlkampfthema," *Süddeutsche Zeitung*, 31 October 1995.

49. Not only could the Bundesbank precipitate a rise in interest rates and a concomitant recession, it could also generate a fall in rates to trigger a European recovery—albeit for domestic reasons. For examples in the early 1990s see Terence Roth, "Bundesbank May Be Forced to Lower Rates," *Wall Street Journal*, 29 September 1992, p. A2; "Cutting It Fine," *Economist*, 20 March 1993, p. 85; "German Move Triggers Further Rate Cuts," *Financial Times*, 20 February 1994, p. 2; Ferdinand Protzman, "German Central Bank Lowers Discount Rate," *New York Times*, 18 February 1994, p. C2; Craig R. Whitney, "In Surprise Move, Germans Cut Both Key Interest Rates," *New York Times*, 15 April 1994, p. C1. For a more "internationalist," optimistic interpretation of the Bundesbank's behavior see Craig R. Whitney, "A Benign Bundesbank?" *New York Times*, 17 May 1994, p. C1; Stephen Kinzer, "Bundesbank Takes Europe View," *New York Times*, 20 September 1992, p. C5.

50. For examples of optimists, see Samuel Brittan, "Better Frankfurt Than Liverpool," *Financial Times*, 9 January 1992, p. 11; "The Bank They Love to Hate," *Economist*, 18

January 1992, pp. 17–18; "The Bundesbank Gets a Bashing," *Economist*, 5 December 1992, p. 81. For a journalistic account that suggests a more "enlightened" Bundesbank response to external requirements, see Steven Greenhouse, "Bundesbank Gives In," *New York Times*, 14 September 1992, p. C2.

51. As an example see David Marsh, "Germany Cedes the Lead on European Rates," *Financial Times*, 8 January 1993, p. 2.

52. This observation is consistent with stylized facts from the business cycle literature. After a (technology) shock (such as German unification), the increased marginal productivity of capital causes further investment (domestic and foreign). Consequently, investment plus consumption exceed output (C+I is greater than Y). The difference (Y-C-I) is accounted for by net imports, which explains the negative trend in the trade balance.

53. Sachverständigenrat, *Jahresgutachten 1994/95*, pp. 317, 65, 67.

54. Jane Perlez, "Polish-German Border an Economic Frontier," *New York Times*, 14 May 1994, p. A5.

55. *Business Europe*, 14–20 November 1994, p. 8.

56. Robert Keohane, *After Hegemony: Cooperation and Discord in the World Political Economy* (Princeton: Princeton University Press, 1984), and Andrei S. Markovits and Simon Reich, "Deutschlands Neues Gesicht," *Leviathan: Zeitschrift für Sozialwissenschaften*, 1/1992.

57. See, for example, David Gardner, "Germany Calls for Check on Britain's EC Rebate," *Financial Times*, 11 February 1992, p. 18, or "The Fight for EC Finances," *Financial Times*, 12 May 1992, p. 18.

58. See David Buchan, "Southern EC States Fight Plan to End Tied Aid," *Financial Times*, 6 May 1992, p. 6.

59. For a general outline see "Deutschland ist größter Geber und zweitgrößter Investor in Osteuropa," *Deutschland Nachrichten* 7 October 1994.

60. See, for example, the comments by Foreign Minister Klaus Kinkel, in "Kohl, Visiting Russia, Agrees to Debt Relief," *New York Times*, 17 December 1992.

61. Craig R. Whitney, "Germany's East Wing of the Common European Home," *New York Times*, 28 July 1991, p. E5.

62. David E. Sanger, "In New Diplomatic Struggles, Money Is an Unreliable Ally," *New York Times*, 9 April 1995, Section 4, p. 1.

63. For examples see Rick Atkinson, "Germans Invest in East Europe but Curb Image of Empire," *Washington Post*, 17 April 1994, p. A25, A30.

64. See Helmut Kohl as quoted in "The Stabilization of Central and Eastern Europe," German Information Center, April 1994, p. 2.

65. "Germany's Eastern Question," *Economist*, 29 February 1992, pp. 51–52.

66. All data are from "The Stabilization of Central and Eastern Europe," German Information Center, April 1994, p. 2.

67. Michael Koop, "Joining the Club: Options for the Integration of Central and Eastern European Countries into the EU," a paper prepared for "Europe's Economy Looks East," American Institute for Contemporary German Studies, 15–16 May 1995, p. 20. Dieter Schumacher, in "Impact of Increased Division of Labor with Eastern Europe on German Trade," argued that German trade with the Visegrad countries was expanding dynamically. This change had the effect of enlarging trade relations and increasing the division of labor between Germany and these countries, with Germany supplying high

value added products such as investment goods, in particular products from mechanical engineering, electrical machinery, and transport equipment industries (p. 5). German imports from these countries were clearly more labor-intensive (p. 22). Schumacher further noted that while trade with Germany approached 25 percent of overall trade for each Visegrad country, it was only 7 percent of all German trade. This maldistribution appears to replicate the dependency relationship described by Hirschman in *National Power and the Structure of Foreign Trade.*

68. Nancy Dunne, David Buchan, and Louise Kehoe, "Polish Tariffs Biased to the EC, Says US," *Financial Times*, 15 May 1992, p. 4. Under 1992 provisions, for example, Poland imposed import tariffs averaging 20 percent on a range of products that were previously duty-free, and 60 percent local content rules on non-EU products. The Czech Republic invoked selective tariffs against western products, such as used cars, in 1992. See Richard W. Stevenson, "In a Czech Plant, VW Shows How to Succeed in the East," *New York Times*, 22 June 1993.

69. Sachverständigenrat, *Jahresgutachten 1994/95*, p. 42.

70. "The Stabilization of Central and Eastern Europe," German Information Center, April 1994, p. 3.

71. "The Trouble with Kohl and Yeltsin," *Economist*, 12 December 1992, p. 56.

72. "Experts Advise Caution on Czech Investments," *FBIS* WEU-95–007, 11 January 1995, pp. 20–21.

73. See comments about the VW purchase of Skoda in Richard W. Stevenson, "In a Czech Plant, VW Shows How to Succeed in the East," *New York Times*, 22 June 1993. In confidential interviews with one of the authors of this book, in autumn 1993, senior banking officials presented figures indicating very limited amounts of German direct investment in eastern Europe. Subsequent interviews with German industrialists who had invested in the region contradicted this claim, suggesting that in many cases their firms had been offered assets at nominal prices or for free in eastern countries—just to get the economy stimulated. The figures that banking officials provided did not represent the real value of assets.

74. *Business Eastern Europe*, 4 June 1990, p. 188.

75. *Privatization Newsletter of Czechoslovakia*, no. 1, October 1991, p. 2.

76. James Juracka, "Getting Information on Companies within the Jurisdiction of the Ministry of Industry for the Czech Republic," *Privatization Newsletter of Czechoslovakia*, no. 1, October 1991, p. 7.

77. Burton Bollag, "Welcome to Prague, Boom Town," *New York Times*, 21 October 1992.

78. Ariane Genillard and Anthony Robinson, "Czechs Go Globe-Trotting to End Euro-dependency," *Financial Times*, 15 May 1992, p. 4.

79. "Experts Advise Caution on Czech Investments," *FBIS* WEU-95–007, 11 January 1995, p. 20; and "Germany's Eastern Question," *Economist*, 29 February 1992, pp. 51–52.

80. Leszek Miller, deputy leader of the Democratic Left Alliance, which had just had tremendous electoral success, quoted in Jane Perlez, "Ex-Communists in Poland Try to Reassure Foreign Investors," *New York Times*, 22 September 1993.

81. Nicholas Denton and Anthony Robbins, "Hungary: Robust Little Exporter in Heart of Europe," *Financial Times*, 20 May 1992, p. 6, and Denton, "Poised on the Verge of Recovery," *Financial Times*, 17 November 1993, p. 30.

82. Nicholas Denton and Anthony Robbins, "Hungary: Robust Little Exporter in Heart of Europe," *Financial Times*, 20 May 1992, p. 6.

83. "In Search of Full Integration," *Financial Times*, 17 November 1993, p. 4.

84. See Nicholas Denton, "Hungary Makes Striking Switch to Privatization," *Financial Times*, 9 October 1992, p. 3; *Business Eastern Europe*, 23 July 1990, p. 242.

85. Commercial Law and Practice Course Handbook Series, *A New Look at Doing Business with the Soviet Union* (New York: Practicing Law Institute, 1989), p. 27.

86. Figures from Peter Marsh, "Marriage Contracts," *Financial Times*, 20 September 1991, p. 12.

87. See Craig R. Whitney, "Investment Needs for a New Russia Are Mostly Unmet," *New York Times*, 14 December 1992, p. A1; "The Wild East," *Economist*, January 4, 1992, pp. 40–41; Ferdinand Protzman, "Germany Curbs Trade Aid for Former Soviet States," *New York Times*, 23 January 1992, p. C1.

88. See "German Support for the Reform Process in the Former Soviet Union," German Information Center (New York, March 1995).

89. See, for example, "The Stabilization of Central and Eastern Europe," German Information Center, April 1994, pp. 1–2.

90. On this issue see, for example, Quentin Peel and George Graham, "Kohl to Ask US to Step Up Assistance for Moscow," *Financial Times*, 26 March 1993; and Serge Schmemann, "Who Hails Russia? Nixon, No Less," *New York Times*, 19 February 1993; Anthony Lewis, "For Want of a Nail," *New York Times*, 16 February 1992; Steven Greenhouse, "Bush and Kohl Unveil Plan for 7 Nations to Contribute $24 billion in Aid for Russia," *New York Times*, 2 April 1992, p. A1.

91. "The Stabilization of Central and Eastern Europe," German Information Center, April 1994, p. 4.

92. "German Support for the Reform Process in the Former Soviet Union and the Countries of Central, Southeastern and Eastern Europe," German Information Center, March 1995, p. 1.

93. "EC to Participate in Washington Coordinating and Conference," *European Community News*, no. 2/92, 21 January 1992, p. 2.

94. "German Support for the Reform Process in the Former Soviet Union and the Countries of Central, Southeastern and Eastern Europe," German Information Center, March 1995, p. 3.

95. David E. Sanger, "In New Diplomatic Struggles, Money Is an Unreliable Ally," *New York Times*, 9 April 1995, Section 4, p. 1.

12: Foreign Cultural Policy

1. Hellmut Becker, "Außenpolitik und Kulturpolitik," in *Merkur*, no. 155–166 (1961), reprinted in Dieter Braun, ed., *Deutsche Kulturpolitik im Ausland*, Schriftenreihe des Goethe-Instituts, vol. 2 (Munich: Süddeutscher Verlag, 1966), pp. 88–103. Compare Becker, "Kultur—ein Mittel unserer Außenpolitik," *Süddeutsche Zeitung*, 23 August 1962, reprinted in Braun, ed., pp. 103–110.

2. "Hilmar Hoffmann: Kulturpolitik is die dritte Säule deutscher Außenpolitik," in *Deutschland Nachrichten*, 9 July 1993, p. 6.

3. Hagen Graf Lambsdorff, "Foreign Affairs and Cultural Policies: Current Trends

and Initiatives," speech at the workshop "Foreign Affairs and Cultural Policies: American and German Strategies after the Cold War," American Institute for Contemporary German Studies, Washington, D.C., 28 April 1995.

4. "Auswärtige Kulturpolitik," *Almanach der Bundesregierung 1993/94* (Bonn: Presse- und Informationsamt der Bundesregierung, 1994), pp. 149–151.

5. Hilmar Hoffmann, "Vorwort," in Hoffmann and Kurt-Jürgen Maaß, eds., *Freund oder Fratze?* (Frankfurt a.M.: Campus, 1994), p. 7.

6. "Auswärtige Kulturpolitik," p. 149.

7. See Klaus von Beyme, *Vorbild Amerika? Der Einfluß der amerikanischen Demokratie in der Welt* (Munich: Piper, 1986); Emil-Peter Müller, *Antiamerikanismus in Deutschland: Zwischen Care-Paket und Cruise Missile* (Cologne: Deutscher Instituts-Verlag, 1986); Sebastian Knauer, *Lieben wir die USA? Was die Deutschen über die Amerikaner denken* (Hamburg: Stern-Verlag, 1987); Andrei S. Markovits, "On Anti-Americanism in West Germany," *New German Critique*, no. 34 (Winter 1985); and Josef Joffe, "Europe and America: The Politics of Resentment," *Foreign Affairs* 61 (1983). Americanism in a political and economic sense combines the Lockean attributes of liberal rule and market capitalism.

8. For the relationship between culture and hegemony, see Antonio Gramsci, *Selections from the Prison Notebooks*. Edited and translated by Q. Hoare and G. Nowell Smith (New York: International Publishers, 1971); *Selections from Political Writings, 1910–1920*. Edited and translated by Q. Hoare (New York: International Publishers, 1977); and idem, *Selections from Political Writings, 1921–1926*. Edited and translated by Q. Hoare (New York: International Publishers, 1978).

9. See Wade Jacoby's superb doctoral thesis, "The Politics of Institutional Transfer: Two Postwar Reconstructions in Germany, 1945–1995" (Cambridge, MIT, 1996).

10. This handy linkage of institutions and ideas also appears in Dieter Sattler, "Einleitung" to *Jahresbericht der Kulturabteilung des Auswärtigen Amtes 1964*, reprinted in Braun, *Deutsche Kulturpolitik*, p. 147.

11. "Reichshaushalts-Etat für das Jahr 1878–79. Etat für das Auswärtige Amt," quoted in Ruth Emily McMurry and Muna Lee, *The Cultural Approach: Another Way in International Relations* (Chapel Hill: University of North Carolina Press, 1947), pp. 40–41.

12. See Jürgen Kloosterhuis, "Deutsche auswärtige Kulturpolitik und ihre Trägergruppen vor dem Ersten Weltkrieg," in Kurt Düwell and Werner Link, eds., *Deutsche auswärtige Kulturpolitik seit 1871, Beiträge zur Geschichte der Kulturpolitik*, vol. 1 (Cologne and Vienna: Böhlau, 1981), pp. 7–36.

13. For the new department's inception and objectives, see Kurt Düwell, "Gründung der kulturpolitischen Abteilung, Auswärtiges Amt 1919/20 als Neuansatz," in Düwell and Link, *Deutsche auswärtige Kulturpolitik*, pp. 44–61.

14. McMurry and Lee, *Cultural Approach*, make rather too much of this continuity—see pp. 47–63—informed by their vantage point of 1945.

15. See on Karl Haushofer, geopolitics, and the German Academy: Hans-Adolf Jacobsen, "Auswärtige Kulturpolitik als 'geistige Waffe,' " in Düwell and Link, *Deutsche auswärtige Kulturpolitik*, pp. 218–256. Not surprisingly, Haushofer and his notions on foreign cultural policy survived well into the National Socialist regime.

16. Hans Arnold, *Foreign Cultural Policy: A Survey from the German Point of View*, trans. Keith Hamnett (London: Wolff, 1979), p. 16.

17. See Edwina S. Campbell, *Germany's Past and Europe's Future* (Washington, D.C.: Pergamon-Brassey's, 1989), particularly pp. 49–72. The lessons of the Franco-German interwar experience, according to this book, figured significantly in the foreign policy of the young Federal Republic.

18. Emil Ehrich, "Die Auslands-Organisation der NSDAP," *Schriften der deutschen Hochschulen für Politik*, Heft 13 (Berlin, 1927), quoted in McMurry and Lee, *Cultural Approach*, p. 63.

19. Hans-Adolf Jacobsen, *Nationalsozialistische Außenpolitik, 1933–1938* (Frankfurt am Main and Berlin: Alfred Metzner, 1968), pp. 156, 143.

20. In January 1950 the Federal Chancellery's Liaison Office to the Allied High Commission gained a cultural desk. In the fall of 1950, this liaison office became the office for foreign affairs, which, in turn, became the Foreign Ministry of the Federal Republic of Germany on 1 April 1951. The new *Kulturabteilung* began its work "in a few rooms of a villa on the Rhine" the following year. See Sattler, "Einleitung," p. 149.

21. See the December 1970 guiding principles that the Foreign Ministry established on its foreign cultural mission, in "Zur auswärtigen Kulturpolitik" (Document no. 128: Leitsätze des Auswärtigen Amtes für die auswärtige Kulturpolitik, Dezember 1970 [Auszüge]) in *40 Jahre Außenpolitik der Bundesrepublik Deutschland* (Stuttgart: Bonn Aktuell, 1989), pp. 230–233.

22. See Becker, "Außenpolitik und Kulturpolitik," p. 89, for example. Hildegard Hamm-Brücher issues a similar lament in "Die gefährdete Dimension unserer Außenpolitik," in Hoffmann and Maaß, *Freund oder Fratze?*, pp. 22–29.

23. See for the 1958 perspective the comments of Werner Richter, then president of the DAAD, in Theodor Steltzer, "Vorschlag zur Bildung einer Körperschaft zur Förderung der deutschen Kulturarbeit im Ausland," in Braun, *Deutsche Kulturpolitik*, pp. 59–68.

24. Sattler, "Einleitung," p. 149. For the intervening years, see Becker, "Außenpolitik und Kulturpolitik," p. 100. Arnold, *Foreign Cultural Policy*, p. 17.

25. "Genscher stellt sich vor Hoffmann," *Süddeutsche Zeitung*, 12/13 August 1995, p. 13.

26. See Bruno E. Werner, "Geist, Kunst und Diplomatie," in Braun, *Deutsche Kulturpolitik*, pp. 50–59.

27. See the excerpts from *Jahresbericht der Kulturabteilung des Auswärtigen Amtes 1964* in Braun, *Deutsche Kulturpolitik*, pp. 158–166

28. The Germans settled on "intermediary organizations" as the appropriate translation for the term *Mittlerorganisationen*. A more accurate translation—not only linguistically but also in terms of the role these bodies play—might be "mediating organizations."

29. *Almanach der Bundesregierung*, p. 149. The almanac gives the number of foreign-based Goethe operations as 152 in 1993.

30. *Almanach der Bundesregierung*, p. 149. In comparison, this same source shows the DAAD receiving about DM 228 million in the 1992 budget. "Deutsch für die Welt," *Der Spiegel*, no. 36, 5 September 1994, p. 199.

31. For excerpts from the 1969 agreement, see "Die Aufgaben des 'Goethe Instituts' " (Document no. 119), in *40 Jahre Außenpolitik*, pp. 213–214. The 1976 accord is excerpted in "Rahmenvertrag zwischen der Bundesrepublik Deutschland und dem Goethe-Institut" (Document no. 174) in *40 Jahre Außenpolitik*, pp. 337–340.

32. This early periodization appears in the comments of Foreign Minister Gerhard

Schröder in the "Bundestagsprotokoll" (11 December 1963), pp. 130–132. Chancellor Ludwig Erhard also included it in his remarks on cultural policy abroad in his "Regierungserklärung" (10 November 1965), excerpted in Braun, *Deutsche Kulturpolitik*, p. 12.

33. Werner, "Geist, Kunst," p. 54.

34. See Winfried Böll, "Die kulturelle Stellung der Bundesrepublik in der Völkergemeinschaft," speech to a conference of the Friedrich-Ebert-Stiftung (24–26 November, 1958), reprinted in Braun, *Deutsche Kulturpolitik*, pp. 70–78. *Bildungshilfe* lost many of its imperialist overtones as time went by. For the initial phases of its development, however, see Becker, "Außenpolitik und Kulturpolitik," pp. 91–94, and the entire section "Fachlicher Austausch—Bildungshilfe," in Braun, *Deutsche Kulturpolitik*, pp. 169–225.

35. For a full discussion of the inquiry and its ramifications, see Witte, "Die Enquête-Kommision des Bundestages," in Düwell and Link, *Deutsche auswärtige Kulturpolitik*, pp. 295–343.

36. An edited, English-language version of the proceedings is *International Cultural Relations—Bridge across Frontiers*, vol. 13 of Materialien zum Internationalen Kulturaustausch / Studies in International Cultural Relations, trans. H. K. Bonning et al. (Stuttgart: Institut für Auslandsbeziehungen, 1980).

37. Wolfgang Jäger and Jürgen Link, *Republik im Wandel, 1974–1982*, vol. 5/II of Karl Dietrich Bracher et al., eds., *Geschichte der Bundesrepublik Deutschland* (Stuttgart: Deutsche Verlags-Anstalt, 1994), pp. 412–413.

38. Hansgert Peisert, *Die auswärtige Kulturpolitik der Bundesrepublik Deutschland* (Stuttgart: Klett, 1978), pp. 356–358.

39. For the *Berufsverbote* in German politics, see Gerard Braunthal, *Political Loyalty and Public Service in West Germany: The 1972 Decree against Radicals and Its Consequences* (Amherst: University of Massachusetts Press, 1990).

40. See Jäger and Link, *Republik im Wandel*, p. 416.

41. See, for example, Paragraph 1.6 of the 1970 guidelines: "The emphasis of these commonalties are the goal of our policy." *40 Jahre Außenpolitik*, p. 231. See also Barthold C. Witte, *Dialog über Grenzen* (Pfullingen: Neske, 1988), pp. 23–24.

42. For instance, the remarks of Federal Minister Heinrich Windelen, "Intra-German Cultural Policy—Part of an Offensive in Our Policy on Germany?" Lecture delivered to the Educational Institute of the Konrad Adenauer Foundation, 10 April 1984.

43. This sentence and the following references to the 1987 guidelines come from *40 Jahre Außenpolitik*, p. 499.

44. Becker, "Außenpolitik und Kulturpolitik," pp. 91–92.

45. Hoffmann, "Foreword," p. 7.

46. Manfred Ackermann, *Der kulturelle Einigungsprozess, Forum Deutsche Einheit: Perspektiven und Argumente* no. 7 (Bonn and Bad-Godesberg: Friedrich-Ebert-Stiftung, 1991), p. 5.

47. Ibid., p. 8. With this same issue of focus, audience, and context—international versus German—Ackermann also seeks to explain why "the majority of West German artists" had reservations about unification, whereas East German artists supported it.

48. Wolf Oschlies, *Agonie oder Aufschwung der Kultur? Osteuropäische Kulturpolitik unter den Bedingungen einsetzender Marktwirtschaft* (Bonn: Berichte des Bundesinstituts für ostwissenschaftliche Studien, 1991), p. 44.

49. The article also provides for the restoration of collections that had been split between the two German states and the preservation of East German cultural elements. Article 35 is reprinted, with subsequent remarks, in the first appendix of Ackermann, *Kulturelle Einigungsprozess*, pp. 54–57.

50. Ibid., pp. 24, 57–59.

51. Compare Friedrich Bischoff, "Kulturfreundlichkeit als Ziel," *Weltkunst* no. 11, 1 June 1992, pp. 1449–1451.

52. "Aufsässig grün," *Der Spiegel*, 11 July 1994, pp. 166–167.

53. Thomas Koch describes this phenomenon succinctly when he compares the "myth" of East German social security and egalitarianism to popular refrains about the Third Reich as a time when one could walk the streets in safety. Both notions completely miss the abiding experience of either system. Koch, "Deutsch-deutsche Einigung als Kulturproblem," *Deutschland Archiv*, January 1991, pp. 16–25. Recent survey data reveal an increasingly differentiated "Ostalgie" that may reverberate in German politics. See "Stolz aufs eigene Leben," in *Der Spiegel*, 3 July 1995, pp. 40–64.

54. One might not see many East German paintings in museums in the West or exhibits abroad—yet. But the Foreign Ministry has happily taken over some GDR foreign-cultural programs and personnel, in part because East Germany had strong contacts with countries that remained out of Bonn's reach but also because they had proved effective.

55. Becker, "Kultur—ein Mittel unserer Außenpolitik?" p. 106.

56. The Franco-German *Annäherung* has inspired an enormous literature. For specifically cultural aspects, see Arnold, *Foreign Cultural Policy*, pp. 72–76; Witte, *Dialog über Grenzen*, pp. 93–121; and Bernard Trouillet, *Das deutsch-französische Verhältnis im Spiegel von Kultur und Sprache, Studien und Dokumentation zur vergleichenden Bildungsforschung*, vol. 20 (Weinheim and Basel: Betz, 1981). A helpful chronology appears in *20 Jahre Deutsch-Französiche Zusammenarbeit, Reihe Berichte und Dokumentation* (Bonn: Presse- und Informationsamt der Bundesregierung, 1983), pp. 97–109.

57. See Brigitte Mohr, "Education and Culture," in Carl-Christoph Schweitzer and Detlev Karsten, eds., *The Federal Republic of Germany and EC Membership Evaluated* (London: Pinter, 1990), pp. 232–245. Actually, the phrasing of Article 36 demonstrates the even deeper problem of different working conceptions of culture in the EU. The English-language version of the Treaty of Rome singles out "national treasures" for special protection, as does the French, which names *"trésors nationaux."* The German translation features the more general *"nationales Kulturgut,"* which inclines more toward the Spanish and Italian rendition: *"patrimonio artistico."* Georg Rees, *Kultur und Europäischer Binnenmarkt*, Schriftenreihe des Bundesministeriums des Innern, vol. 22 (Stuttgart: Kohlhammer, 1991), p. 25.

58. Quoted in Steve Austen and Hajo Cornel, "Vorwort: Kultur-Markt Europa," in Internationale kulturelle Stiftung, Kulturpolitische Gesellschaft, ed., *Kultur-Markt Europa: Jahrbuch für europäische Kulturpolitik* (Cologne: Volksblatt Verlag, 1989), p. 12.

59. European Commission, *Eurobarometer* no. 41, pp. 36–37.

60. See "Kohl Backs Language Drive," *International Herald Tribune*, 14 June 1996.

61. The initial literature on ERASMUS, for instance, appears almost solely in scientific education journals, in part because the program built on earlier joint study programs between universities. See, for instance, Ray Hudson, "Sociable Production: A Personal View of One ERASMUS Inter-University Cooperation Programme," *Journal of Geography in Higher Education*, 16 (1992), pp. 84–88; Luigi F. Dona dalle Rose, "The Fruits of

ERASMUS," in *Physics World*, 5 (October 1992), pp. 30–32; and R. V. Parish, "The ERAS-MUS Scheme," *Interdisciplinary Science Reviews*, 18 (December 1993), pp. 327–330.

62. See the inaugural editorial in *Le Magazine*, no. 1 (Spring 1994), inside front cover. The magazine, published by the Commission of the European Communities Task Force Human Resources, Education, Training and Youth, serves as a glossy newsletter for the newly streamlined programs.

63. "Bridges of Learning," in *Le Magazine*, no. 1, p. 2.

64. On 1987–88 see Russell Cousins, Ron Hallmark, and Ian Pickup, "Inter-University Cooperation and ERASMUS," *Higher Education Quarterly* 44 (Winter 1990), p. 85. On 1994–95, "ERASMUS and LINGUA (Action II)," in *Le Magazine*, no. 1, p. 26.

65. Cf. Dona, "Fruits of ERASMUS," p. 31, with Table 5, "ERASMUS and LINGUA (Action II)—Estimated Student Numbers in Approved Applications in 1993/94," in the supplement to the ERASMUS Newsletter, no. 16 (1993?), p. v.

66. "ERASMUS Students Three Years On," *Erasmus Newsletter*, no. 18 (1993), p. 2.

67. Dieter Stollte, director of the Second German Television (ZDF), quoted in "Kanal für Blinde," *Der Spiegel*, 6 May 1991, p. 258.

68. Metz, "Dem Kind muß endlich mehr Freiheit gelassen warden!" *Süddeutsche Zeitung*, 29 December 1994, p. 17.

69. See Table 31, "Kulturabkommen," *40 Jahre Außenpolitik*, pp. 771–773.

70. Barthold C. Witte, "Alte Bindungen und neue Wege nach Mittel- und Osteuropa," *Europa Archiv* 46 (April 1991), p. 201.

71. Deutscher Bundestag (12. Wahlperiode), "Das Interesse an der deutschen Sprache in den Staaten Mittel-, Südost- und Osteuropas," Drucksache 12/2780 (10 June 1992), p. 4.

72. The phrase comes from Deutscher Bundestag (12. Wahlperiode), "Bericht der Bundesregierung zur Verbesserung der kulturellen Lage der Deutschen in Mittel- und Osteuropa," Drucksache 12/2310 (20 March 1991), p. 1.

73. Heinz Ischreyt, "Deutsche Kulturpolitik," in Braun, *Deutsche Kulturpolitik*, p. 22.

74. *Almanach der Bundesregierung*, p. 150. See "Durch Vermittlung deutscher Lehrer geförderte Schulen im Ausland," (Table no. 30) in *40 Jahre Außenpolitik*, pp. 765–770, and Witte, *Dialog über Grenzen*, pp. 238–249. The sovereignty issue, particularly vis-à-vis Third World countries, seems to foretell the gradual exhaustion of a century of interest in German schools abroad. Of course, it coincides with a steady decline in distinctly German populations in many of these foreign centers.

75. German Foreign Ministry, "Die deutsche Sprache in Mittel- und Osteuropa," 1991.

76. "Deutsch im Aufschwung," in *Frankfurter Allgemeine Zeitung*, 29 September 1995.

77. "Das Interesse an der deutschen Sprache," p. 10. In 1990–91, 234,436 Bulgarian pupils and students (38.94 percent of students of languages) studied French, 233,481 (38.8 percent) studied English. Learners of German accounted for 22.22 percent of language studies. See Foreign Ministry, "Verbreitung und Bedeutung der deutschen Sprache in Osteuropa," unpublished manuscript, 1988, and Foreign Ministry, "Deutsche Sprache und deutsche Minderheit," unpublished manuscript, 1990.

78. "Das Interesse an der deutschen Sprache," p. 10.

79. "Das Interesse an der deutschen Sprache," p. 10, and "Verbesserung der kulturellen Lage der Deutschen," p. 5.

80. "Verbesserung der kulturellen Lage der Deutschen," p. 6.

81. Joachim Born and Sylvia Dickgiesser, *Deutschsprachige Minderheiten: Ein Überblick über den Stand der Forschung für 27 Länder* (Mannheim: Institut für deutsche Sprache, 1989), p. 186. After the Tatars, the Germans were the former Soviet Union's largest ethnic group not to have had its own republic. In fact, the Germans were more numerous than Latvians, Estonians, and Kirghiz, all of whom had their own republics and are now indendent states.

82. For a good summary of the debate, see "Sollen sie Krieg führen," *Der Spiegel*, 13 December 1993, pp. 166–169. See also "Kisten im Kloster," *Der Spiegel*, 18 April 1994, pp. 63–65.

83. Witte, "Alte Bindungen und neue Wege," p. 203.

84. Quoted in Jäger and Link, *Republik im Wandel*, p. 414.

85. For elaboration see Andrei S. Markovits and Simon Reich, "Should Europe Fear the Germans?" *German Politics and Society*, no. 23 (Summer 1991), pp. 1–20; Kazimierz Krzysztofek, "European, National and Regional Dimensions of Polish-German Cultural Relations," *Polish Review* 37 (1992), pp. 521–530.

86. "Ein wenig Goethe und ganz viel Loreley," *Der Spiegel*, 24 June 1991, pp. 208–210.

87. From the Polish satire magazine *Nie*, quoted in "Deutsch für die Welt," p. 201.

88. Comment made by Peter Rona, chief executive of the First Hungary Investment Fund, about George F. Hemingway, in Roger Cohen, "Pizza and Persistence Win in Hungary," *New York Times*, 5 May 1992.

89. See "Kohl ante portas," *Süddeutsche Zeitung*, 5/6 August 1995, p. 13.

90. Ischreyt, "Deutsche Kulturpolitik," p. 18, and Peisert, *Die auswärtige Kulturpolitik*, p. 140.

91. David Stewart Hull, *Film in the Third Reich* (Berkeley: University of California Press, 1996), p. 191. One account of these developments, by Gründgens's friend and former brother-in-law Klaus Mann, is the novel *Mephisto* (later filmed by István Szabó).

92. For an assessment of the role of the German political foundations, see Ann L. Phillips, "German Political Foundations in East-Central Europe," paper presented at the American Institute for Contemporary German Studies, 28 April 1995.

Conclusion: The Predicament of the Berlin Republic

1. "SPD droht mit Ablehnung des EU-Vertrags," *Süddeutsche Zeitung*, 16/17 March 1996.

2. "Nur eine Minderheit setzt auf Brüssel," *Süddeutsche Zeitung*, 16/17 March 1996.

3. An example of this normalizing presentation of the Holocaust can be found in Karlheinz Weissmann's new volume on national socialism. He presents the Holocaust in a few dispassionate and matter-of-fact pages, virtually indistinguishable in style from his discussion of sports under National Socialist rule. See Weissmann, *Der Weg in den Abgrund: Deutschland unter Hitler, 1933–1945* (Berlin: Propyläen Verlag, 1995).

4. For a powerful presentation of German memory and victimhood in the contemporary debate of the Federal Republic, see Jane Kramer, *The Politics of Memory: Looking for Germany in the New Germany* (New York: Random House, 1996).

INDEX

241